THE HIGH CALLING

The

HIGH
CALLING

A Christian physician's journey through the career of medicine

ALESSIO C. SALSANO

The High Calling
© 2011 Alessio C. Salsano, M.D.

Bible quotes from the authorized *King James* version rendered into modern English by the author.

Published by
Deep River Books
Sisters, Oregon
http://www.deepriverbooks.com

ISBN 978-1-935265-64-1
ISBN-10 1-935265-64-4

Library of Congress: 2011941535

Printed in the USA

DEDICATION

I dedicate this book to all my colleagues who through self-sacrifice and long hours of hard work have, in their own small way, helped to alleviate some of the suffering in the world; to my wife, who has endured with me through many trials; and to the Most High God, who has always been with me through all my trials and triumphs.

*"...forgetting those things which are behind, and reaching forth
unto those things which are before,
I press toward the mark for the prize of the High Calling of God..."*

SAINT PAUL TO THE PHILIPPIANS

TABLE OF CONTENTS

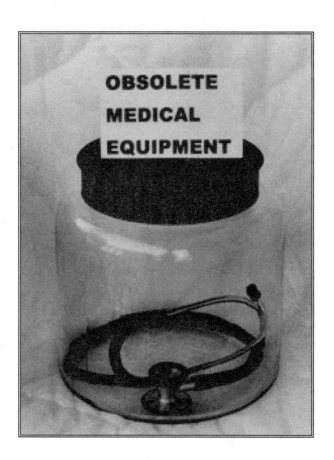

*Dr. Reitman noticed on the desk a stethoscope inside a jar with
a sign over it, "Obsolete Medical Equipment."*

PAGE 102

INTRODUCTION

"My mouth shall speak of wisdom…"

PSALMS 49:3

I am a doctor, a medical doctor, or as some prefer to call me, a physician, a practitioner of the medical arts. In fact, I am an internist, who specializes in the treatment of the internal diseases and afflictions of the adult patient. I have been devoted to my profession for over 30 years. I have endured long hours of work, too little sleep, constant sacrifice, and the neglect of my own family's needs.

Although medical doctors have always made good incomes (I've never seen a medical doctor yet applying for welfare), the financial rewards have eroded considerably in the past quarter century, but the true rewards for a doctor, perhaps, have always been the saving of life, the satisfaction of making the correct diagnosis, and the unsolicited thankfulness of the grateful patient.

So, like many of my colleagues, my world has been one of rising early, caring for the hospitalized, attending an office full of patients, answering emergencies, calling orders to nurses, struggling with insurance companies, running a business, defending my medical decisions before peer review panels, and fending off the hostile actions of litigation attorneys. I have seen the sick healed, prayed with many patients, cried over some, and I've wept in my wife's arms over those who didn't recover. With some I've had words of anger, with others words of comfort and assurance. I have excoriated employees and nurses only to later apologize, and then to be excoriated in return.

In a world swirling with insecurity and strife, with new diseases, especially infectious diseases, often racing ahead of our technical expertise to deal with them, the doctor, practitioner of his ancient profession, standing in his white coat, stethoscope in hand offering calm words of reassurance and dispensing cures to life's numberless maladies, is often the final defense before the onslaught of the unknown, pain and extinction.

This is my story and in it I hope all who read it will see something of themselves, for I long ago realized that in this life we are all together. As Paul the Apostle said long ago, "None of us lives to ourselves and none of us dies to ourselves..." (Romans 14:7).

Chapter One

BEGINNINGS

"Before I formed you in the womb, I knew you..."

JEREMIAH 1:5

Since early childhood my father, Frank Salsano, recited to me a story about my birth. When I was newly born he had a "man-to-man" talk with my grandfather, Alessio (after whom I was named following an age old Italian tradition), well into the night about what I would be when I grew up. My father held to a conviction that he would not interfere in my career choice, but my grandfather stubbornly insisted that I would become a doctor. They had had a strained relationship throughout Dad's youth, but my birth had brought them together in a reconciliation and my father savored it. So when Alessio died three weeks later of a massive stroke, Dad's loss was the more poignantly felt. It was in his loss that he made a vow to fulfill his father's wish and so was planted the seed of a medical career.

Frank passed away quietly in his sleep on Christmas day, 2003. From early childhood he had always had an impetuous spirit which often brought him into conflict with people, in the family and out. When in the Navy, during World War II, he went AWOL in Newark, N.J. (where he grew up) to visit family in direct defiance of orders and was promptly jailed and busted two grades in rank, but in spite of this misadventure Dad owed much to the Navy.

He enlisted in 1945 because he knew he'd be drafted and in the Navy he would at least "see the world." Frank saw action in the Eastern Mediterranean where the U.S. military was engaged in suppressing communist insurgencies at war's end, and a grateful nation awarded him a flag at his death, now neatly folded into a flag box I have proudly displayed in my office.

It was, however, the attitude of a junior officer that impacted my father's life the most during his naval career for, until then, his pugnacious nature seemed to have destined him, as many who knew him believed, to a lifetime of prison sentences. This officer, nameless to me and forgotten by all except He who sees all and divinely directs the affairs of men, saw a spark of intelligence and potential in the wiry, thin Italian youth under his watch and constantly urged him to get a college education once he left the military.

Dad never told me anything else about his Navy mentor, but he took his advice and once back in civilian life entered college under the GI bill.

Of course his blue collar family members protested. My grandfather minced no words. "Why don't you get a real job in the port and start making some money? Dad, however, persevered and entered junior college, and when his first semester grades came back as straight A's, all protests vanished into thin air. Montclair State College followed, and a short time in graduate school, and by the time I was born, my father's faith in higher education as the chosen way of life was unshakable. It was this steadfast confidence that he instilled in me, propelling me ultimately into my chosen profession.

Yorkie, (that was the nickname given to Frank by all his intimate friends because he spoke with a New York accent) had a lifelong career in social work, but a love of science never left him. I know he once contemplated a career in biology, perhaps medicine, but for reasons unknown to me, he never pursued it, except through me. From the moment I was old enough to flip a page, he inundated me with illustrated science books. I can still visualize in my mind the vividly colored pictures of nuclear chain reactions, heroic white corpuscles attacking evil germ cells, electric and magnetic fields interacting in space, and of course, rockets.

His passion for science dovetailed with America's obsession to win the space race with Russia in the late 1950s and 1960s.

For better or for worse, I owe the initial push into a medical career to my father, but my story really began at the dawn of the twentieth century, in the great migration of European immigrants to the fertile shores of America. My Italian ancestors, back then, were poor tenant farmers in Southern Italy, and they saw in America a chance to make enough money to better their lives when they returned home. Of course, once in America, they were absorbed into the melting pot culture and like so many others such as Jews escaping persecution in Russia and Slavs fleeing overcrowding in Eastern Europe, they embraced America, which became their new home.

It is difficult for us today, descendants of those hardy pioneers, to appreciate the awe in which they held the educated, professional man, and especially the medical doctor. To become a physician was to reach the pinnacle of success, to achieve the unattainable goal. The respect extended to the local physician practically reached the level of reverence. It was every mother's dream to be able to say,

"My son, the doctor." I remember one time discussing this with a surgeon colleague who recalled growing up in the Jewish enclave of Brooklyn, New York. As he reminisced, when the medical doctor arrived in his black sedan to make a house call, people and cars instinctively moved aside. It was as if Moses himself had returned to part the waters of the Red Sea!

It was this reverential awe of the medical doctor that inspired my grandfather and in turn my father, which then was passed on to me, and when an older cousin, Steve Vanna, or as we all affectionately knew him, Junior, actually did become the first M.D. in the family, the ultimate achievement of life became attainable.

So with this background, life for me began. I must confess that growing up I really did enjoy science, although biology was not my strong point. In fact, the thing that seemed to impress people the most about me was that I loved to talk, but this was often more a liability than an asset.

One hot summer night in the New Jersey suburb of Edison, my family and I were sitting on our neighbor old Mr. Deltoro's porch, and I was talking up a storm. The Deltoros were a nice family, first generation immigrants from Puerto Rico, and Mr. Deltoro was a hard working patriarch and a no nonsense kind of guy you didn't trifle with. So after some time of enduring my exercising my First Amendment rights of free speech he said pithily in his Hispanic accent, "Alessio, you should be a lawyer when you grow up, you love to talk!"

Not knowing quite how to take his comment, I simply smiled sheepishly. When you're ten years old, you're just satisfied that you got someone's attention. Some years later in junior high school, Frank Dominguez, my Ancient and Medieval History teacher, with a bit more candor, after I gave a rousing oral report on Socrates, predicted that I would one day make speaking my profession. How prescient he was, for as I have learned over my thirty years of practicing medicine, one of the traits that marks an exceptional physician is his ability and willingness to communicate to his patients. Please excuse my presumption, but I must say of myself, if nothing else, I was at least a good communicator.

High school for me was something of a disappointment as far as education went. I was more interested in bicycling the New Jersey countryside with my best friend, Mark, than making top grades. Yet, though mentally shelving my aspirations, I never gave them up. I owe it to Dad, I thought, and besides, if Junior could do it so could I. Of course, everyone knew back then (everyone being the baby boomers then coming of age) that the competition for medical school was fierce and top grades an imperative. I knew it, too, but at the time I just wanted to have fun. (I even flunked French class in my junior year.) I was no Richard Stark. Richard Stark had virtually straight A's, S.A.T. scores close to 1,400. He was studious, focused, and the teachers loved him. He also aspired to being a doctor. We fortuitously were thrust together in senior year advanced placement biology as lab partners. A.P. Biology was also a disappointment for me, and in the end I didn't even get the credits for it. The entire year was one big lesson in humility. For some reason, Mrs. Bodnar, the teacher, singled me out for ridicule while Richard was her pet. In everything: lab work, exams, Q and A sessions, he was perfect and I always fumbled. One day before class began, we were all sharing our career goals. When I mentioned that I wanted to be a doctor, the laughter began with Richard and extended to the entire class. "You, a doctor?" It reached such an uproarious din that the teacher came in with a look on her face as if she had just entered an insane asylum.

From then on I kept my ambitions to myself, and although I continued to be Richard Stark's comedy relief, I resolved that in spite of my classmates' ridicule I would not lose confidence in myself. "Lord, by your favor you have made my mountain to stand strong" (Psalms 30:7). Well, as I said, I missed getting college credit for A.P. Biology, but I managed to graduate in the top twenty percent of my class, and my S.A.T. scores were good enough for me to easily gain admission to Rutgers University, in the core College of Arts and Sciences.

Chapter Two

COLLEGE AND FINDING GOD

"No one can come to Me unless the Father who sent Me draws him... "

JOHN 6:44

College for me was just as fulfilling as high school was disappointing. Rutgers is the state university of New Jersey. It was then, and still is, an excellent institution of higher learning, but unlike the Ivy League schools it became a state funded school and lost something of its original elite status. "If you can't go to college go to Rutgers!" was my best friend Mark's continual taunt (he was on his way to Georgetown University).

Actually, I was thrilled to be going to Rutgers. First, I lived only eight miles off campus and could easily commute. Second, being state funded, the tuition was low, and since I didn't live in school housing it saved me, and by extension, my father, a bundle. Third, I would not have to make new friends in a faraway place. As things turned out, my college years were the most important years of my life, since it was during that time I committed myself to a medical career and at the same time found God.

Several friends from high school started Rutgers with me and I hoped to see a lot of them, but orientation week put that thought to rest. There were so many thousands of students in my freshman class alone the only way I was going to see anyone I knew was with a pair of binoculars. As far as tuition went, the base tuition for my first semester at Rutgers in 1971 was, hold on to your hat, 190 dollars! In fact, by 1975, the year I graduated, it was still less than $400. I literally was able to pay for my college education working part time at the Foodtown deli in Metuchen, New Jersey, where, I must proudly say, I learned to perfectly wrap everything from leftovers to impossibly shaped Christmas gifts.

Orientation was fun, but I had resolved in my heart that college was going to be serious business. I may have been the stooge in Mrs. Bodnar's biology class, but I was determined to excel in college and rise above the contempt of my former peers. There was one thing, however, I swore I would never do, and that was take another French class, no matter what it cost me. (It did ultimately cost me membership in the prestigious Phi Beta Kappa Society.) Having already flunked it in high school, I had developed a major phobia over it, and besides, I reasoned, one bad grade in French would ruin my GPA and my chances for ever making it to medical school. My whole self-esteem was on the line here, so when in orientation, all students were recommended to take a short proficiency and placement exam for foreign languages, I was so confident in my lack of competency I proudly took the test, knowing I wouldn't be placed. Wrong! Somehow, don't ask me how, the graders said I qualified for an advanced curriculum. I made a quick trip to the registrar, however, and dropped foreign languages permanently. There's no question it preserved my grade point average, but at the price I mentioned above. But, I had no regrets. Medical school was my goal and to that end I threw myself manfully into the college experience.

My very first class, ironically, early on a Thursday morning was freshman chemistry recitation. Unfortunately, there was nothing to "recitate." My time block had not yet attended a regular lecture, but we did get to introduce ourselves to each other and to learn what was expected of us in the course. It was a deceptively undemanding start to my first semester at Rutgers. Later that day, my first biology lecture made a totally opposite impression. There, we were handed a course outline book by the taciturn preceptor, but where, I thought, was the professor? Answer, on closed circuit television. Two TV's were situated above the chalkboard and when they snapped on, the biology professor, who looked like a cross between Mr. Rogers and Alexander Kerensky, began speaking a mile a minute. After five minutes of staring, mouth agape, at this novelty, it suddenly dawned on me that I was supposed to be taking notes. I began feverishly writing, trying to also jot down between his pauses (there weren't many) what I remembered from the first five minutes. Holy smokes! How could anybody talk so fast? As the lecture wound down, he sort of loosened up a bit and began discussing the origin of life.

Now, I thought, this could be interesting. After reviewing the then current scientific theories, in deference to the antiquity of religion and philosophy, he ran down man's earlier attempts to explain it all. We heard about the Hindu world elephant, and various tribal, animistic legends, but ironically, nothing about the biblical account of creation. How curious, I thought, at least in America, which in 1971 was still overwhelmingly Christian with a sprinkling of Judaism, that the story of Genesis which all of us, Jew and gentile, had grown up with would be

16

overlooked. Perhaps he didn't want to offend us by grouping it with obviously mythological accounts. By class end, everyone looked bored and exhausted as we shuffled out of the building, but I continued to ponder the matter. Although I had grown up Roman Catholic, adhering to the basic observances of my religion, I never really considered the issue of life's origin. For me, the first day of college introduced me to the clash of science and Christian faith, an issue I would grapple with over and over again for my entire adult life.

Rutgers was not a party school. I was one of a large population of commuting students, and for me anyway, as soon as my last class of the day ended, I headed home to study. I had made my decision to forego any socializing and to concentrate on academics. Some friendly contact though, was inevitable, especially in the system of scheduling blocks where students who took the standard premed courses typically took them in the same time slots, so I ended up seeing the same faces day after day.

Now having a car on campus offered great freedom of movement, and dorm students without cars were constantly hitchhiking. One day I gave a lift to a student with whom I had many classes in common. He was a very pleasant young man, who like me, was aspiring to become a medical doctor. Our conversations revealed to me that I was a little insecure in my ambitions while he exuded supreme confidence. I admired him for that, but it did leave me a bit downcast. "Oh well," I said to myself, "one day at a time. I've just got to take one day at a time." I decided to focus on my immediate challenges.

Only a few weeks later, that supremely confident student was taking remedial chemistry and not long afterwards had dropped from premed completely. "Sic transit Gloria Mundi!" Needless to say, this reinforced my one day at a time philosophy.

Rutgers University is truly a mega college. There are campuses all over the state of New Jersey, but the core college, including the original 1766 campus where I attended, sits on the banks of the Raritan River in the city of New Brunswick. In my day, you could still see the rowing teams practicing under the shadow of the large riverfront dorms. Across the river situated atop a steep bluff was the science campus, including Rutgers Medical School, whose rooftop would one day become my "special place."

After the initial flurry of activity faded, freshman year settled into the tedium of lectures, recitation class, homework, exams and science lab. English Literature 101 was included in this mix and, in all honesty, for a biology major, I thoroughly enjoyed it. The reading assignments were lengthy, but worth the effort. Second semester was devoted to Utopian Literature, including Thomas Moore's classic "Utopia," "The Time Machine" by H.G. Wells, and Arthur Clarke's "Childhood's End," among others. One segment of the course addressed the theme of popular rebellion which introduced me to the likes of Robert Heller's "Catch 22" and Fyodor Dostoevsky's massive tome "The Brothers Karamazov."

Now, unlike English Lit., there was no illusion of enjoyment in freshman calculus. It was the bane of all first year premed students. In my class it was doubly difficult because of the humorless professor who was so absent-minded he walked up and down in the front of the classroom completely oblivious that one pant leg was rolled up in his sock. His assistant was even more eccentric. At times he looked and walked like Igor the Hunchback, but was a worse dresser.

Fridays began early in that first year, with General Chemistry lecture at 8:00 A.M. The next hour I was free, but had to travel back from University Heights to New Brunswick for calculus recitation with Igor, then it was back to University Heights for biology lab.

The Nelson Biology Lab building was a sprawling complex that would be, over the next four years, my second home. The graduate students who led the lab sessions were not so far removed from the grind of college. The result was that we often finished early and were released for an early and well-earned weekend off. On one of those early dismissals I decided to do a little exploring. I had no love interest at the time, and was going to go home and study anyway.

The Nelson lab building zigzagged at right angles and I was compelled by my curiosity to walk the corridors till I found the end of the building. When I did find it, I was a little disappointed, as no pot of gold awaited me at the end of this rainbow, just a simple fire exit with a small reinforced window. Yet, peering through that window, I could see the large frowning façade of the medical school tower only a short walk across the field. Just what would it feel like to be inside a medical school, I wondered. I decided I would find out. When I entered through the glass doors, it was as if I had entered a religious shrine or a medieval cathedral. The quietness that attended a late Friday afternoon only amplified the sereneness and awe I felt. The school had a wide open foyer two stories high and very capacious, with a cantilever stairway suspended from the ceiling at one end. Decorating the walls above and around me was a series of sixteenth century anatomical engravings by Vesalius. All the awe and wonderment of my Italian ancestors welled up in me as I reverently entered that foyer, like a pilgrim entering a Holy site. As I stood there, the silence was broken by two medical students who entered from a side door conversing, ascended the stairway and disappeared from view. It was then I noticed doors everywhere. I was standing in some central location which accessed the entire building. I walked over to one door and peeped in. There I saw rows of incubators and refrigerators humming. What cell cultures and microbial soups were being nurtured within I could only guess. This place, I thought, truly was a shrine, dedicated to man's ingenuity and progress, and deep in me I felt I belonged there, too. I looked at my watch and saw it was getting late and I had to go, but I would return often.

As freshman year drew on I began to unwind a little. My two closest friends since Mark left for Georgetown were Ron and Walter (who we always called Herb). All week long I studied, and beyond that my social life was very simple. On Saturdays I would hang out with Ron and Herb at the local malls, and on Sunday I played football behind Saint Joseph's High School early in the day, then back to studying Sunday night. One Saturday I was browsing with Ron in the Bamberger's book section when I found a little paperback entitled "The Universe and Dr. Einstein" by Lincoln Barnett. Physics was coming up in sophomore year and I wanted to learn more about the genius of Albert Einstein so I bought the book. What a fantastic read! It gave me a new outlook on the world. What incredible mysteries lie in the farthest reaches of space and time. And to the author's credit, he willingly admitted that more and more scientists were realizing the impossibility of explaining existence without recourse to God. Now this was a reflection worth pondering. The longing of my heart to be reassured of God's existence was becoming stronger as I progressed in my learning.

It took a while, but by the end of freshman year I had perfected my ability to take notes. Textbooks were great for reference and to round out your knowledge, but good lecture notes were indispensable. I found myself actually going to the textbook after the course was over more often than while I was taking it. This technique served me well, and when my first year of college ended I had registered straight A's like my father before me, and of this I was justly proud.

Sophomore year began and it soon became apparent there were some science courses which good note-taking, book reading and even straight memorization couldn't help. You either knew it or you didn't. Chief of these was

Organic Chemistry. Typically taken in sophomore year, Organic Chemistry was the maker or breaker of the med school hopeful. I now understand that while taking it you actually have to think like a scientist. It was impossible to memorize organic molecules. You had to visualize them interacting in three dimensions! This was an ability that simply could not be faked.

Dr. Denny was the chairman of the department who ran the course and what a foreboding patriarch he was. There was a rumor about a young student he had in tears, who had petitioned him for a better grade, otherwise, her medical school hopes were ruined. He simply sat back in his chair and said casually that she should get out of science since she didn't have what it takes to make it. This was foreboding.

When I started Organic Chemistry, all this uncertainty was plaguing me, but in the final analysis it turned out to be one of my best performances. I was able to master the three-dimensional thinking it required and aced both semesters. In the second semester midterm, I scored the highest grade in the two combined classes.

I breezed through Organic Chemistry, but not so Mr. Godwin's speech class. How ironic that an elective I only picked to fill my schedule turned out to almost be my undoing. Grading was based on three speeches we would give before our classmates on self-chosen topics.

My first topic was Albert Einstein's Theory of Relativity. I wanted to pass my enthusiasm for this topic on to my fellow students. It was at the time my Sina Qua Non and I was excited about it. My speech was impeccable, my audience spellbound, and when I finished the students rated me excellent. I knew I had it in the bag, but then Mr. Godwin handed me my grade, a D! He decided it was too technical. I could see my medical school career sinking into quicksand fast, but all I could do was try harder.

The next topic I would choose carefully. I'd give him what he wanted to hear plain and simple. My talk was on ecology, but I did everything he wanted, and the result was a B minus. I had had it with this solipsist! Nothing would please this guy. He was every student's worst nightmare.

After the second oral presentation, my overall course grade was barely a C. Not bad for such a hard marker. My final presentation was coming up and it was my last chance. I decided to stake everything by confronting Mr. Godwin at his strongest point. I gave a speech on the act of speaking, and Mr. Deltoro would have been proud of me. As I proceeded I could see that I was connecting with my classmates and out of the corner of my eye I could also see Mr. Godwin's approving nods. I got an A minus, bringing my final grade up to a B, which was more than I expected.

Sophomore year, however, with the exception of Mr. Godwin's speech class, was actually enjoyable. Organic Chemistry was no problem and my other core science requirement, physics, was equally satisfying.

My earlier dalliance with Lincoln Barnett's book gave me an interest in physics beyond getting a good grade, but I got As in both semesters just the same.

It was in sophomore year that I discovered another lifelong interest of mine, ancient history. The History of Rome was a two-semester course that required a large amount of reading, but what classics of literature; the speeches of Cicero, Caesar's commentaries, Polybius, Livy, Tacitus, and of course, The New Testament. Christianity is an integral part of Ancient Roman History, in fact, The New Testament is by far the single most documentable ancient writing. Being raised Roman Catholic I resonated with all this. I had always been drawn to issues of religion and science, but the Christian faith was still for me an intellectual affirmation and a matter of my Catholic tradition. I still felt like an outsider looking in, as it wasn't yet in my heart. Despite this, I couldn't restrain my excitement when I read in the core textbook of the course, H.H. Scullard's "A History of Rome," the bold statement that the only reasonable explanation for the dramatic energy and conviction of early Christianity in the face of strong institutional opposition was the factual event of the resurrection of Jesus Christ.

The world in 1972 was getting cynical and jaded, with Vietnam, The Cold War, and The Civil Rights Crisis. America was moving away from religious faith into a secular, materialistic world view. So to find a kernel of hope in such an unlikely place was like finding an oasis of water in a trackless desert. I loved that course.

Springtime on Rutgers campus was especially nice. There seemed to be just the right balance between ivy covered brownstone and modern urban quaintness. I often enjoyed visiting the original eighteenth century campus with its colonial structures and centuries old ambiance. It happened on one of those balmy spring mornings as I walked to class, the walkways and commons were littered everywhere with small paper leaflets. I was contemplating who was the cause of all this mess when I encountered him, an unassuming, portly, elderly man who was handing out pamphlets from a large cardboard box. He gave me one rather perfunctorily, and I walked on, reading as I went. Little did I realize at the time that I was about to begin the greatest adventure in my life, the adventure of finding God. In fact, I had been given a gospel tract, one of several that year, as various groups gained permission to make campus distributions. This was before political correctness had choked off all such non-militant evangelism, but I wasn't born yesterday and I believed I had enough intellectual integrity to read the thing without becoming seduced.

As I read, however, I couldn't deny the power of those biblical promises of hope and redemption it offered. God's word springing to life from those pages touched my heart deeper than anything else ever had, and a faint voice inside of me that grew stronger each day was saying, "Alessio, there is something more to life than personal achievement." Well, class was starting so I shrugged all this off, but unlike the vast majority of students that day my tract did not end up in a litter receptacle.

Sophomore year ended. Halfway through college I had managed to make all A's except for my hard won B in Mr. Godwin's class. Junior year for me was an opportunity to enjoy more electives. I managed to put together a very eclectic schedule. Classical Mythology, Written and Oral Exposition (I made sure this wouldn't be another Mr. Godwin fiasco), and Art History. Art History of course meant Western Art, so again, paraded before my eyes as in Roman history was the whole panorama of the Christian experience. But what did these stark medieval images, rich in symbolism, have to do with a heartfelt belief in God? I still felt like I was on the outside looking in, but my encounter with the gospel that spring kept haunting me. If God was real, it seemed only logical that he could be found, understood, and embraced, but was it necessary to go through endless trial and error before finding him?

Religion was rarely the central topic in my family when I was growing up, but at one Christmas dinner I vividly remember the adults discussing religion openly, and my uncle Al saying, "God must exist if all the religions preach it." Well, that seemed to make sense, but in detail it's hard to reconcile the inchoate impersonal force of Buddhism with the emotional, articulate God of the Old Testament. It seemed to me that the world religions were so vastly different that it was more likely that they were all wrong than all right. As sincerely as they were practiced and believed, they were merely man's attempt to explain existence. There had to be a better way. I repeatedly shelved these ponderings, otherwise I would never get my studies, which were considerable, done.

In junior year I took Comparative Vertebrate Anatomy which required a marathon of memorization. Many people told me to avoid it because a bad grade in it would be fatal, and an A was almost impossible to achieve. On the other hand, an A if attained would look great on my transcript. It was tough, slogging work, but I did pull down an A with abundant self- congratulations. In Art History, however, I only managed a B. Maybe I was too over-confident. Students in high profile majors like biology and political science tended to look down on art majors as air-heads, so perhaps I didn't apply the time to it I should have. Despite that, I did enjoy one element of the art course, art lab.

One day I brought my friend Ron to campus and we were looking at art pictures when he made a sound of disgust. It turned out that he came upon a copy of a Grunewald Tryptict which depicted Christ's Crucifixion. The painter obviously made his subject appear as gruesome as possible to drive home to the observer the great suffering endured by the Son of God. To Ron, however, who was not particularly religious, it bordered on blasphemy. "Anyone who painted Jesus like that should be shot," he said. (I never knew he had such feelings!) My explanation for it, as stated above, didn't placate him, but it was one more experience that got me thinking. If the event pictured really did happen it must have been gruesome, but why would God allow it? What did the Passion of Christ have to do with belief in God? No answer to these questions was immediately forthcoming.

The college experience for me was virtually a self-contained world. The daily routine of classes, studying and test taking went on as if the end would never come. I began taking regular walks over to Rutgers Medical School. Strolling those hallowed corridors kept me in focus, because I was beginning to ask myself fundamental questions about my life goals, such as what they really were, and what was the meaning of it all, anyway?

Junior year was the year premed students took the MCAT, the medical college admissions test. It was the SAT exam for medical school. In my day, the test had four parts: science, math, vocabulary and general knowledge. Only vocabulary was something I needed to work on. I tackled it in two ways: one, by memorizing in detail a 500 word list published specifically for the MCAT, and two, by doing crossword puzzles. The latter activity became another lifelong pursuit, and even now in my 50s I can often complete the New York Times Sunday puzzle in one sitting.

My MCAT scores ultimately were excellent and junior year ended with almost straight A's, except for the B I got in Art History. Dr. Passmore, my counselor, told me I was a shoo-in for medical school acceptance, yet something still was missing. My college experience had done what college is supposed to do, it made me think. So in thinking I asked myself, "Why am I here? Is there a God? Did man just evolve mindlessly from inanimate matter or was he created by a supreme being? Which religion, if any, was true?"

I read the different tracts and bibles I received. The tracts were compelling, but I wanted more than some man's word on it, so I read the Bible myself, but it was like reading a foreign language. I decided that I needed help.

Rutgers' main library, the Alexander Library, had a large religion section. I would start there. As I perused the shelves, I quickly learned that religion was man's great passion through the ages. In that sense, Uncle Al was right. It was amazing to me all the incredible theories about God that were put into print, but judging by the great number of variations it presented, Christianity appeared to be the most divided and confused religion of all. Yet Christ himself even said, "Do you suppose that I came to give peace on earth? I tell you, not at all, but rather division" (Luke 12:51).

So every day when I had a break I would spend time in the religion section of the university library, leafing through dusty books which probably hadn't been opened in a generation. Medical school for me was all but assured, yet my uncertainty about life was showing. This was in contrast to the popular notion of the confident, in-charge doctor I was planning on becoming.

In any event, I did apply to Rutgers Medical School and was accepted. I didn't apply to Harvard. I knew my place. I did, however, apply to Johns Hopkins and at least got a rejection letter. Tufts University didn't even do that. With med school acceptance behind me, senior year was much more relaxed, and I got a chance to indulge some electives I had always wanted to take. I took two astronomy courses. Descriptive Astronomy, mainly focused on the then fledgling science of planetary exploration, and Physical Astronomy, which dealt with the universe itself, questions of ultimate origin and issues on the forefront of modern physics: Quasars, Pulsars, The Big Bang and Black Holes. My most enjoyable course that year, however, was titled "Religion and Science." The professor, an ordained Episcopal priest, led a challenging and at times controversial excursion into the very issues I was wrestling with. My classmates and I represented a true cross-section of backgrounds, all united by a common desire to find answers to the modern science versus religion dilemma. One student, Al Kelsey, was, like me, on his way to Rutgers Medical School, and we would soon become good friends.

Of course it was inevitable that evolution would come up as the major topic of discussion despite the professor's strident wishes to avoid it.

Now I grew up, like most people in the twentieth century, accepting the theory of evolution as an accomplished fact, but not giving it any serious thought in my day-to-day life. The ultimate implication of evolution, however, is that the world, all life, and human thought were simply accidents of random, mindless physical processes. This really amounted to a philosophy known as materialism, where all that exists is physical entity; matter, energy, space, period. God and spirit are not only non-existent, but irrelevant. Death is not merely the end of life, it is the extinction of thought, utter non-existence. Even as a child I rebelled against this. Anyone who truly ponders the reality of this can only fall into deep despair. My friend Mark, attending Georgetown University, ironically founded by the Jesuit religious order, became exposed to this belief system, embraced it, and his mind snapped.

Charles Darwin confessed his deepest wish that it not be true, and Thomas Huxley, Darwin's great apologist, once said, "He'd rather be alive in hell, than non-existent." But the truth is that, as I learned over the years, objective science and many scientists themselves are coming to accept creation over evolution as a better explanation of origins. Against this, the atheist's main argument is the silence of God. If he is really there, why does he not make himself known? But God doesn't need to prove himself to anyone. We need him, but he doesn't need us. So Paul said to the Athenian philosophers, "He is not far from us... For in him we move and live and have our being" (Acts 17:27-28). God reveals himself to those who seek him with all their heart. So evolution became the key topic, and I fell squarely into the creationist camp, but I still hadn't found my peace with God.

Senior year came and went quickly. I graduated Magna Cum Laude (I missed highest honors by one grade), but I had achieved all the goals I set for myself when I started college. Linus Pauling, the great chemist and humanitarian, was our commencement speaker. He must have been ninety years old, and of all things was himself a confirmed atheist. How it would have been to sit and talk with him one on one about the momentous issues of life I can only guess. My father and mother were very proud of me, as was my paternal grandmother, but one person who helped raise me was not there. That was my mother's mother, who had died of breast cancer two years before.

She was a very doting grandmother, high strung also; the quintessential Italian matriarch, who never lost her heavy Italian accent despite being in America almost sixty years. One night in the hospital, I sat at her bedside when she was dying. She laid there quiet, eyes open, blankly, staring. When I got up to leave, I bent over to kiss her good-bye when she suddenly thrust her arms around me and called out my name over and over, "Lessie, Lessie!"

When she settled back down I said with a startled voice, "It's all right Nana, everything will be all right!" Even as I knew and she knew it wouldn't. When I left her room and made my way to the elevator I cried all the way down to the ground floor. Deep in my heart I yearned for the reassurance of God's presence, but it escaped me. All of medical science was helpless to save her in this, her time of greatest need. As I look back 35 years later, I admit medicine has made great advances in treating disease, but to all of us the end must, some day, come. As a physician, I have many times sat at the bedside of the terminally ill patient, and when all of science and man's ingenuity has been expended, there is still prayer, and God, who does exist, hears our prayers and reaches up his everlasting arms to embrace us. "O death, where is your sting? O grave, where is your victory?" asked Paul of the Corinthians.

It was summer vacation and I finally resolved to settle the religion question once and for all. Each Sunday I would attend a different church and I wouldn't stop until I found the truth. Taking a quick ride through Metuchen, New Jersey, I looked for churches to attend. A small Episcopal church looked promising, but on a hill overlooking Middlesex Avenue was First Baptist Church with a big sign out front: Vacation Bible School. At the time, I had no idea it meant for children, but if someone was going to teach the Bible I wanted to hear it. I would start my quest there.

Sunday, June 29, 1975 was a pleasant, sunny day and in the service, Pastor Lytle gave an impassioned sermon on the Epistle of Saint Jude which touched my heart, and I knew then I was in the right place. The next day at my summer job on break, I took the youth pastor's advice and prayed the prayer of salvation, thus entering into an eternal covenant with the risen Son of God. True prayer, however, is not a magical incantation that summons up God like a genie. Anyone can recite a prayer, but when it springs from your innermost heart and is the final outward expression of your deepest longing, God hears and answers.

I was so excited. The Bible, which until then was incomprehensible to me, suddenly became easy to understand, and where I formerly had attended church out of a sense of obligation, it was now the highlight of my week. My old friends did not quite understand what happened to me and eventually fell away, but new friends from church came in to replace them.

There was one dilemma, however, that faced me that I did not relish addressing. Attaining medical school was a dream come true, but it also was for me a self-affirmation, an esteem boost. Now that I had found my confidence in the Christian faith, medical school and the whole doctor thing seemed unimportant, but I was all ready to start my medical career that fall. I debated what, if anything, I should do, and how I could possibly express my second thoughts to Dad. Events would soon make my pathway clear.

No great victory in life is ever won easily, as I learned one morning soon after my epiphany. It was probably five o'clock in the morning when I awoke to hear the shower running. I knocked on the door. "Dad, are you all right?" When I entered, I found him holding his arms across his chest, sitting in the bathtub with the shower on. "We're going to the Emergency Room," I said. So I took him to John F. Kennedy Memorial Hospital where he was diagnosed with an acute myocardial infarction, a heart attack. Now medical science and religion would have to work together to pull Dad through, so while the doctors worked, I prayed.

Today when a patient with a heart attack gets to the E.R., if it's within twelve hours of onset, he is immediately taken to the cath lab by the on call cardiologist. Under catheterization, his blocked artery is opened with clot dissolvers (thrombolytic medication). A stent, or artificial tube is slid into place and he can be home in a couple of days with minimal damage. In 1975, my father was put in ICU, loaded with Valium, placed on blood thinners to prevent a stroke (a dreaded complication in those days) and watched closely for signs of arrhythmia or heart failure.

He was hospitalized for three weeks and went home with 20 percent of his heart muscle gone. Such has been the advance of medicine at least in treating this dread disease over the brief time span of my career.

Frank Salsano was a stoic man, but even he knew the seriousness of his condition and it inclined him towards impatience and emotional outbursts. One day while visiting, I casually mentioned my religious awakening and my second thoughts about a medical career. Bad idea! To say he hit the ceiling was not to indulge in too strong a hyperbole. He began petulantly ringing the nurse for a Valium. Well, that settled it for me. No more second thoughts about medical school. I was in it for the duration. After all, I told myself, the Bible does say to honor your mother and your father.

As orientation day approached, I accepted the inevitable fixation of my course. I would honor God by my devotion and fulfill my destiny by becoming a doctor. Science and religion for

me would become permanently intertwined. I wouldn't fret over the details since God, I concluded, was big enough to handle them without my help.

Chapter Three

MEDICAL SCHOOL AND FIRST LOVE

"And they seemed unto him but a few days, for the love he had to her…"

GENESIS 29:20

So Dad recovered from his heart attack and I started medical school. Walking through the glass doors of Rutgers into that familiar foyer for the first time as a real medical student was, in a word, awesome, and also a vindication of my high school classmate's poor opinion of me.

During orientation week we met many of the basic science professors and of course were introduced to each other. How different it was to orient here in a class of 100 students in contrast to college which numbered in the thousands. The ratio of those two numbers, by the way, approximated the acceptance rate for medical school in New Jersey, which was one out of twenty-five highly qualified applicants. We all realized that we were a privileged minority, a fact which alternately bred pride and humility. We also got to meet some of the upper classmen who were assisting with orientation.

My summer vacation, apart from preparing for freshman year at the medical school, was happily spent learning more about my new found faith. It was a joy to go to church and to plunk down twenty dollars (more than twenty percent of my weekly pay at my summer job) into the collection plate each Sunday. I also regularly attended the Wednesday night Bible study and the Sunday night fellowship. It was at First Baptist, Metuchen, where I found a new circle of friends, and the woman I eventually married.

It was a time of getting to know the God of the Bible more and more. It was amazing to me that the omnipotent being who thundered on Mount Sinai and gave the world the sublime moral code of the Ten Commandments really loved me, an insignificant blip on the time line of eternity, but if the Bible said it, I believed it. Ancient Israel rightly stood in awe of this creator, who loved mankind so much that he deigned to become one of us that we might know him personally, like a friend. It is hard to convey the feelings I had as a new Christian believer to those who have never experienced it. There was a certain wide-eyed innocence like a little child, but also a grim determination to live right for God. You want everyone to be your friend, yet, at the same time, you're prepared to be disappointed when the strength of your convictions drives people away. And it was this interplay of conviction and conviviality that dominated my entire medical school experience. So as I stood in my small group at orientation listening to Eric Jackson's introduction, I determined that I would boldly identify myself for what I believed by saying something profound, but which in reality turned out to be just plain weird. "You know Saint Luke was a physician," I shot out to Eric, who stood there momentarily stunned by my totally unexpected comment. But true to form he quickly retorted, "No, he went to the med school down the street!" That snappy repartee got a few laughs and after giving me a quick glower he continued with his presentation. Needless to say I got the hint, no more off the wall comments, at least not that day. Years later as an intern-resident team at Middlesex General Hospital, Eric and I would recollect our first meeting, as I will come to relate.

The high point of orientation, or perhaps the low point, depending on your perspective, was the tuition review. Medical school education is very expensive. Even in 1975 the cost of one year at a first rate private school like Harvard or Tufts was over ten thousand dollars a year (Today a Harvard education costs more than forty thousand dollars a year!). My first year's tuition at Rutgers was about $2,500, which was a pile of money for a third generation immigrant son of a social worker. I didn't qualify for state support, but because of Dad's heart attack and the subsequent loss of his second job, I did qualify for an interest-free loan from the federal government, which helped.

The four years of medical school divide sharply in half. The first two years are devoted to basic science, consisting almost exclusively of lecture and lab courses, while the second two-year interval is predominantly clinical with time spent almost exclusively in hospital and doctor's office settings. The common thread, however, in all this was progressively more patient-based education.

During the first year, volunteers were invited into the lecture hall to discuss their illnesses and to allow us fledgling doctors to begin associating the written word with living reality. The second year was more intensive yet, with regular sessions as observers in real doctor's offices and at the hospital. It was, however, in the third year that we actually began participating in the care of the patient. Finally, during the fourth and final year we took on more direct responsibility for patients, answering to the attending physician who served as mentor.

Basic science was for me largely a recitation of my college experience, at least in the first year. The difference was in the frequent correlations with actual medical illness. The one course, however, that was completely new was Human Anatomy, where we dissected for the first time an actual human body. The course was divided into lectures and into anatomy lab, where dissection took place. The cadavers were obviously donated, and their identities were kept strictly anonymous. We were grouped, four students to a body, and took turns dissecting and observing while watchful professors strolled among us offering help and provoking thoughtful intercourse.

The first day of anatomy lab was memorable. The lab was a huge auditorium, well lit. Lined up in neat rows, regularly spaced, were dozens of stark metal gurneys, and lying on each gurney draped in canvas and plastic was the human subject, our new assignment. We shuffled into the room, paired off, and awaited further directions. As one student slowly pulled back the drape, I gazed upon the embalmed body of an elderly man whose face was frozen in the rictus of death. It became too easy once we got underway to forget that this body we were dissecting was once a living, breathing person like us, and like us had hopes and dreams. I could imagine him as a child crying in his mother's arms and as a father consoling his own children. And what of his eternal soul? Where did he stand with God? I was reminded of Yosarian's statement in Robert Heller's sweeping novel, "Catch 22," "The spirit gone, man is matter"; and Jesus' own words, "The spirit gives life, the flesh profits nothing" (John 6:63). Surely, the physical shell we were about to probe into was no longer of any profit to the individual who once inhabited it, whatever his benefit would be to medical science.

So medical school began and any euphoria it kindled quickly evaporated into the monotony of hard work and study. Not that there weren't some light moments. No one can continually toil away without an occasional break, and laughter has always been a great diversion. In high school and college, my friend Ron was something of an expert at mimicking people; celebrities and even our everyday acquaintances. I was no match for Ron, but did some passable imitations. One day in anatomy lab we were discussing our latest lecturer, Dr. Reisner, when I repeated something he said in Dr. Reisner's own voice. I did it spontaneously, off the cuff, but in no time every student around me wanted to hear me imitate the professor's voice. One day during anatomy lab, Steve Lapoff, my dissection partner, even called over one of Dr. Reisner's colleagues to hear my rendition, What a mistake! He gave me such a glare that I found myself envying the half-dissected cadaver lying before me. Obviously, not everyone appreciated such flattery.

Despite that embarrassing experience, throughout medical school and residency I continued, by popular demand, to do random imitations, and it was heartening to see my hardworking colleagues and friends laugh. Although my longing was to share the deeper joys of my faith in God, it was a ministry of sorts to instill a little lightheartedness into those who toiled daily with life and death situations, sleep deprivation, critical decision making and disappointing outcomes, so I kept at it. After all, "A merry heart doeth the body well, like a medicine," said Solomon in Proverbs 17:22.

Not everything I did, however, provoked amusement. It was soon after I entered medical school that a contentious and serious issue confronted me; the issue of abortion. By 1975, Roe versus Wade was only two years old, and it was only countenanced with great care, but was clearly there to stay. During that first year I was very burdened to share my faith with my classmates and struggled with how to do it in a non-confrontational way (except for the Bahai student who when confronted with the Book of Revelation said, "I'll die before I believe that!"). It then struck me, why not put some tracts in the lab areas where we all had our own desks, eight to a room, and if anyone was curious they could read them at their leisure? What a great idea! I immediately ordered what I thought to be the topic of most interest, evolution, but to my surprise, when the tracts came in the mail they were on abortion. Somebody goofed, or did he? Was God trying to tell me something? I decided I had received a divine directive to distribute these tracts instead of the ones I ordered, but I was a bit apprehensive that I might stir up a hornet's nest, and I was right. A couple of days afterwards, a delegation of upper classmen approached and chided me for indulging in such a controversial and divisive subject (I must admit the pictures in the tracts were pretty graphic). My response was conciliatory but firm. I understood their protest, but wanted them to understand I was following the deepest convictions of my heart. We were in a proverbial Mexican stand-off. On my part, I thereafter refrained from solicitations on controversial social topics, and on their part, at least they did not cause trouble for me with the administration.

One good thing did come out of my notoriety when I met a fellow student, Melissa Miller. Melissa was a delightful black woman. She had an outgoing and bubbly personality and like me she was a born again Christian. Unlike me, however, Melissa grew up in an evangelical church, but by the time she attended medical school she was having a crisis of faith. Her crisis ended when she received what John Wesley called the second blessing and what is called, in the modern church, the baptism of the Holy Spirit. Well, whatever happened to her, she had overnight rekindled her enthusiasm about God. So there we were, two wide-eyed enthusiastic co-religionists in a pedantic sea of secularism.

Freshman year ended without fanfare. Since everyone was headed for the same goal, the fierce competition for grades, so prevalent in college, was gone. Grades were simply pass, fail or honors. Anyone who failed a course simply took it over again. Honors were nice, but not essential. I believe it mainly served as an outlet for the more obsessive-compulsive types (of which there were many) in our ranks.

One Sunday night, that summer after freshman year, First Baptist Church held a farewell party for the pastor who was retiring to Bermuda. I was conversing with some people when Henning, a friend from Denmark who was attending the church while completing a tour of duty with the American branch of his Danish employer, said to me, "Les, you should go see that little girl Doreen has with her. She is something else!"

Doreen Roberts was "babysitting" a preteen named Beth whose mother was living a kind of Bohemian existence, and was trying to get her out to some positive experiences, including church. We talked that night and participated in some church ministries over the next few weeks, then began dating. I was very naïve about dating, having been cloistered in academia for so many years, and was very shy around girls. I had had exactly one very brief dating experience that maybe lasted three days, but with Doreen I was smitten. She was to me then, and still is now, the most beautiful creature I ever laid my eyes on. She was a Christian, who seriously desired to serve God and had even prepared at one time for the mission field. She also, like me, was 100 percent Italian, Roberts being a legal name change her father made to avoid a perceived ethnic bias when he attended college in the South back in the 1940s. Now if there be any truth to the sanguinary Italian temperament, one need look no further than our relationship for the proof of it. For three and one-half years (the length of the great tribulation to those who are biblically inclined) we had a rocky and tempestuous courtship. We alternately prayed and squabbled. When we finally got engaged my future father-in-law asserted that it would be a miracle if our marriage lasted a year. I admit this was due in part to the demands of medical school, just as the demands of private practice would be in the future.

So the second year began and the curriculum became definitely more clinical and patient based. Pathology was a very interesting course led by Dr. Morrison, a commanding old Irishman who spoke with a delightful brogue. His lectures would often lapse into nostalgic recollections of the past. One that always intrigued me was a story from his internship in the early twentieth century in Ireland when practitioners often succumbed to the deadly diseases they struggled to cure.

Self-preservation is a powerful instinct, but it is the selfless desire to do good at one's own peril that is a reflection of the divine nature, which God implants in all men and women who exhibit it. "Lord, grant that I would be a reflection of your goodness and mercy to those I am called on to serve."

Neurology was another interesting course, and neuroanatomy, the practical part of it, involved studying various diseased brain specimens preserved in formaldehyde. One night to impress Doreen and her sister, I brought them to the neuroanatomy lab to show them the brains. She later told me she couldn't sleep for three nights. Okay, so there were no more trips to see body parts!

By the second year, all the students were getting to know each other well enough to be on a first name basis. There was Al Kelsey whom I met as an undergraduate. Larry Swayne, who stuck close to Al and was the son of a physician, also was a frequent study partner. Steve LaPoff was my lab partner. He was a good-natured fellow, but had a pathologic fear of needles and actually sought counseling to overcome it. He definitely did, because the last I heard of him he was performing tracheotomies in the emergency room. Everybody liked Steve because of his amicable disposition. By our proximity in lab, I was constantly evangelizing Steve, who always acknowledged my enthusiasm for God. Seth Silverman, on the other hand, whom I had known since fifth grade, gave to me as good as he got. His questions and criticisms, I must admit, got to the heart of the issues of religion, and I am grateful for him and for all the Seth Silverman's of the world who ask the tough questions that shake us out of our complacency.

Bob Stiller, who usually paired up with Steve and Seth for school work, became a friend on a slightly different plane. Bob was an incredible guy. He was raised in a Jewish home and, though never repudiating his tradition, he sincerely sought for truth and meaning in life beyond the pale of his childhood roots. Furthermore, he was engaged to a young woman who had been raised in the fundamentalist Christian faith, so he was very familiar with the tenets of Christianity. As you can imagine, I deeply resonated with Bob, and we had many searching talks as study and class work allowed. It was through my discussions with Bob and a warm friendship with a young Jewish believer in Jesus I met at church named Gary that I began what was to become a lifelong passion for the Jewish people.

I grew up in Newark, New Jersey, in a solidly Italian section of the city called Ironbound, because its area was ringed by railroad tracks, highways and trestles. It was so Italian that the only adult I knew growing up who wasn't Italian was a friend of my father's we all knew as "Porky," who was Portuguese, which is about as close to Italian culturally as you're going to get. Dad was a career social worker for Essex County, New Jersey, and often served in the court system on various welfare cases. Through that work he met a retired Jewish businessman named Herman Cohen. Mr. Cohen was a distinguished elderly volunteer, and he and my father often worked as a team, uncovering welfare fraud as well as vindicating those truly in need. But more than that, Herman became like a second father to Dad, and when he passed away, unexpectedly, my father felt the loss personally. Dad, because of this, and partly because it was in his own egalitarian nature, instilled in me from a young age a strong conviction against prejudice. Anti-Semitism just didn't exist in my upbringing. But neither did racism of any kind, and when I became a Christian, one day it struck me like a fire bell in the night. If Jesus Christ really sacrificed his life to redeem every individual, then for me to hate anyone was more than wrong, it was blasphemy, as if I were setting myself higher than God. John the Apostle said, "Whoever hates his brother abides in death" (1 John 3:14). To be true to my faith, hatred and prejudice had to go, but they still rear their ugly heads at times, and must continually be re-conquered.

Bob did occasionally come with me to church or to Bible study and I've always considered it a high point of our friendship when I introduced him to Gary, who was able to relate on a far more personal level than I ever could. Bob came to faith eventually and ultimately fulfilled his goal of becoming a gynecologist, and wherever he is now I'm sure he is a very good one.

Throughout college I got used to sitting in on science lectures heavily laced with references to evolution. Despite my strong personal conviction about it, I had to admit then that the theory of evolution seemed to fit the known facts. But I later learned that the facts of science can be interpreted just as easily, often better, in a creationist framework, but as a young student I was often intimidated by the evolutionary juggernaut. Medical school lectures were, if anything, even more evolutionary, and the high point of all this speculation came in microbiology and biochemistry.

These fields of science were in the forefront of DNA analysis at the time, which had only recently achieved the remarkable accomplishment of cracking the human genetic code. As I absorbed all this evolutionary commentary, I found that most of the information could easily be re-interpreted in a creationist model. There was, however, one piece of information that greatly troubled me. This involved what we know as the slow viruses, of which mad cow disease is the most familiar. Viruses closely related to human DNA enter and literally embed in it. Some cause disease, but others amazingly become part of our genetic code and are passed on to future generations. In the 1970s as DNA was beginning to be "decoded," scientists found that these "virus genes" were present in other animal DNA, not just human. In fact, the same viral DNA in humans could be found in apes, earthworms, etc. The interpretation of all this was that the viruses existed in our pre-human ancestors and could be traced up the evolutionary tree to human beings, thus proving our evolutionary origins. Q.E.D.! I could not accept this, but didn't know how to refute it, until the lecture on tuberculosis.

That scourge of the early twentieth century was largely contained by the discovery of the antibiotic Streptomycin in the 1940s by the great Rutgers microbiologist Selman Waksman. It then dawned on me that the Selman Waksman Institute for Microbiology Research was on the Rutgers campus not far from the medical school. Surely they had a library, I thought. I would start there. My research turned out to be very fruitful.

The truth was that there were literally thousands of viral DNA's interchanging between all types of species, not just humans and apes, as if all our DNA's were somehow joined in some unbelievably complex web of life, yet all being distinct and unique entities. To me it seemed to point more to the marvelous complexity and fluidity of life rather than to its evolution.

This entire subject, in fact, dovetails into the bigger issue of the human genetic code itself. Researchers in recent years have mapped both human and chimpanzee DNA and have found them to have 97 percent concordance, which would seem to imply a common evolutionary ancestry. But the amazing truth is that men and women actually have less DNA concordance with each other, about 95 percent (this is in DNA sequencing, not sex chromosome content), which would tend to buttress many women's claims that men really are a bunch of apes.

The truth we now know is that most of our DNA seems to be "empty space," genetically speaking, like scaffolding upon which, here and there, a gene is located. It is truly amazing how little of our DNA actually is involved in genetic expression. The 3 percent concordance between human and chimpanzee DNA probably represents a critical and unbridgeable difference.

So much is true, but I could see then as now that there was more at stake in this than just an intellectual exercise. After all, why dedicate yourself to saving lives and to relieving suffering if human life has no more value than the inanimate matter from which it evolved, or than the "beasts that perish." Why honor life as sacred if our destiny is ultimately eternal extinction. In the ancient pagan world, human life was considered cheap and expendable. When a child was born and was unwanted, for instance, the parents would sell it into slavery, or even nail its feet together and toss it into the woods, hoping for a quick end at the mercy of wild animals. Christianity, building on the solid foundation of Jewish moral principles, changed all that. Most of the great patriarchs of modern science held to this Judeo-Christian foundation, but their offspring, the scientists of today (though not all) have departed from it, and echo the sentiment of the late Stephan Jay Gould of Harvard when he referred to human life as having no more significance than a twig lying on the ground. Are we sliding back into pagan darkness? I resolved to myself that I was not going to be a part of it.

As if oblivious to these deep theological rumblings of mine, the routine of medical school rolled on. Some topics were unanimously agreed upon to be harder than others. The physiology of respiration (breathing and oxygen exchange) was one, kidney physiology was another. One of my classmates once said the kidney depressed him, but depression or not we ultimately learned what we needed to know.

Christmas break was a welcomed rest in the second year, but a new assault on my Christian sensibilities soon presented itself. Sex week. For five days between the semesters we were required to attend a series of lectures and discussion groups on the various forms of sexual deviancy (or to be politically correct, alternate sexual lifestyles) in America. I was offended by the mandatory attendance rule, but looking back I can see that it was necessary for me as a doctor to at least be aware of this area of human activity. So as we sat in the auditorium, paraded before us with evangelical zeal and no apologies for the obvious attempt to promote their causes were: sadomasochists, pedophiles, transvestites, homosexuals, bisexuals, hedonists and more. In the discussion groups I had a chance to voice my concern over accepting all this as normal, but about all the preceptor could say was, "Well, you can find just about anything in New York!"

By the end of the week I was determined to have a say in all this. So on the final day, after the concluding statements, I stood up and called out from my seat in the auditorium, and asked the professor if I might take the stand to say a few words. Steve LaPoff, sitting next to me, groaned and shook his head as I walked down to the podium. In short, I acknowledged all the advocates of alternate lifestyles, but affirmed that sex between a man and a woman in the bond of marriage and the Judeo-Christian ethic was still the better way, which God intended for humanity. I wasn't sure how my bold maneuver would go over, but after I made my speech I received a standing ovation. Apparently I wasn't the only one who felt that way.

I started the second semester with a strong sense of pride that I had stood up for my beliefs, but couldn't help but feel a degree of animosity from the course leadership all the rest of that year. Second semester of the second year of medical school marked the end of classroom work for the up and coming doctor. Though lecture and book study continued, we were heading out of the classroom for good. Most of the training from then on was clinically based and outside of the lecture hall. We spent much of our time observing actual doctors in the office and the hospital. The students all formed into small groups to make these outings, but no one wanted me in their group, which was probably a consequence of my religious stridency. As all the cars pulled out for the first assignments, I stood alone on the medical school landing, but Seth, Steve, Bob, Al Kelsey and Larry Swayne came to my rescue. "Come on with us," they said. As I hopped in the car I thought, *I knew I liked these guys for a reason.*

Those out of class sessions were tailored to expose us to a wide array of medical specialties and clinical settings, obviously to give us some idea of what area of medicine we were most attracted to. Morristown Memorial Hospital was a popular destination for many students.

Morristown is a colonial town nestled in the quaint upland suburban area of northern New Jersey. A whole group of us would meet at lunch and swap stories of our experiences from earlier in the day. One student named Joe, who was well known as a philosophical type, shared a very tragic story. It turned out that a young girl not quite twenty years old was swimming with friends at a local pond and dove into unexpectedly shallow water and hit the bottom head first, snapping her neck. The injury to her spinal cord knocked out her breathing muscles, causing an immediate respiratory arrest, but one of those present knew CPR and kept her alive until a tracheotomy was done and she was put on artificial life support. Her life was saved, but she was permanently quadriplegic, paralyzed from the neck down. Our lunch time discussion now turned to issues of quality of life and the decision to withhold life saving treatment. Joe was very forthright in his conviction that it would have been better to let her die rather than save her to live permanently paralyzed and bedridden. Her injury and prognosis was exactly the same as actor Christopher Reeve twenty years later. I took up his challenge, however, and contended that I was in favor of saving her life at any cost because as long as she was alive she had hope, and that it was the Christian duty to save life, not to forfeit it. Well, Joe didn't buy it. "I'll die before I believe that!" he said (I had heard that before). There was no point in arguing the matter so I dropped out of the discussion, but the vision of the poor girl haunted me. I felt an overwhelming impulse to go to talk with her and pray with her, and one day after all my work was done that is what I did.

She had her own private room in ICU and when I entered, I introduced myself as one of the medical students who had heard her story. Then I said to her that God loved her and that he had a plan for her life and that her life mattered. "If you put your trust in God he will never leave you no matter what happens. There is no tragedy that can separate you from the love of God through Jesus Christ our Lord," and then we prayed. Her eyes widened and she smiled at me in a way that said, "Thank-you so much for coming." For the first time in my life I felt a tear well up over a fellow human being's spiritual and physical welfare. It would not be the last.

The third year began for me with a bang. The final two years of medical school are devoted to the basic medical specialties and is virtually all hospital based. My third year was divided up as follows; eight weeks of pediatrics, eight weeks of obstetrics/gynecology, eight weeks of psychiatry, twelve weeks of medicine, and finally twelve weeks of surgery. Pediatrics began for me at Muhlenberg Hospital in Plainfield, New Jersey. When we arrived, the unpleasant truth was presented to us; we would begin doing "call," which meant staying overnight, and one of us would start that very night. So like brave men facing uncertain calamity we braced ourselves, and as the schedule was presented to us guess who had the duty first!

I was shown to the room where I would be sleeping, that is, if I wasn't up all night with the intern treating emergencies. The on call rooms at Muhlenberg were in an abandoned ward of the old nursing school that adjoined the hospital. When I entered the room, the dust on the floor was so thick it billowed up as I walked. Rooms like this would be my home away from home for the next six years of my life. Ironically, the night wasn't too bad. I got dinner in the hospital cafeteria for free, and got to tag along with the resident and see some interesting cases. He admitted a couple of patients from the ER and answered a few hospital calls. Then he let me go to bed in the dust bowl.

The next day I proudly related my baptism of fire to my classmates, who ate up every word. And I only embellished it a little. "Did you sleep? How was the room?"

"Not too bad," I said. "I slept about five hours, but it was a little difficult to breathe with all the dust."

"Dust?" Bob Stiller's countenance suddenly dropped. "I'm very allergic to dust."

But we all endured: dust, loss of sleep, grilling and drillings from our superiors. It was all part of a hardening process. A kind of doctor's boot camp.

Psychiatry, my next rotation, was more interesting than grueling. Rutgers Medical School maintained a small psychiatric hospital on the University Heights campus, so in our training we got to see some pretty serious mental illnesses. A significant number of those patients had what a colleague much later told me was the fashionable diagnosis of the day: hysterical psychosis, or in other words, a mental breakdown or temporary insanity. I learned one thing from my time in psychiatry: there are many people functioning precariously close to their mental breaking point, and that everyone has their limit and will mentally disintegrate if life stresses push them beyond it.

The personal stories were as varied as the number of patients admitted. When new admissions arrived we were assigned to them on a rotating basis. It was my turn when a very nice young woman was hospitalized. I don't think she was twenty years old. She came from a well to do family and was raised in the biblical Christian faith, but as a teenager she strayed from her upbringing, dated and then married a high school sweetheart against her parent's wishes.

With little money, they led a simple and non-conformist existence in the post-hippie culture of the late 1970s, and were apparently happy. She was quite devoted to her husband. Then one day her edenic life toppled. The young man she was married to announced that their marriage was getting stale, and to revive the passion he proposed having mixed sex with other couples. Of course he knew a couple that was ready and willing. Because of her commitment to her husband and probably because of reluctance to go to her parents for help, she went along with it. Well, before long, mixed couples turned into one night stands and the poor girl found her life spinning out of control more and more until she finally snapped. You see, her upbringing, which sanctified marriage and taught her right from wrong, was clashing violently with her need to be loved and nurtured by the young man who obviously had no such commitment to her. In the hospital we had some nice talks and prayed together. I happily relate the story because she recovered from her mental breakdown, but sadly this nice girl went back to the dysfunctional relationship that precipitated it in the first place. I never heard what happened to that patient in the end. But since I was seriously dating Doreen at the time it gave me pause to think. Marriage is not something to do on a lark, and if you marry it is critical, for a Christian at least, that you have a spiritual bond holding you together. This young lady didn't and, in her life, it led to a catastrophe. I won't go into detail about the next patient I encountered, but when I first met her she was walking and talking like a robot because aliens, using her bedroom radio had taken over her mind! Before I learned what became of her my rotation ended and I was back at Muhlenberg Hospital for OB-GYN.

The change of rotation came, but not until I learned a serious lesson in the biblical warning, "Be slow to speak...", and in my professor's warning about setting boundaries with patients. This occurred to me during a part of the psychiatry rotation where we saw patients in a community health clinic. There I met a young woman (older than myself, however) who was very anxious and depressed over a recent divorce that left her a single parent with no extended family for support. When I was assigned to her case and heard her story I had a deep yearning to reach out to her and share God's love. I started by meeting her after hours and explaining the gospel to her, even bringing her to a local Bible study I attended, which, besides really upsetting Doreen, was never meant to go beyond spiritual concerns.

Now, at first, she appeared genuinely interested in hearing the gospel, but after awhile I found myself more and more being treated like a boyfriend. "When will I see you again? Why don't you stay longer? I missed you the other day!"

Oh my goodness, what did I get myself into? My naivete, and my carelessness over boundaries, had caused my good intentions to backfire. I began avoiding her calls and indulged in what you would call a communications black out. One day I came home and my mother asked me, "Who's this Anna lady that keeps calling you?" Thank God the rotation ended! How much did I then realize the truth in Paul's exhortation to young Timothy, "No man entangles himself with the affairs of this life; that he may please him who has called him…"(2 Timothy 2:4).

Obstetrics and gynecology was totally different from psychiatry. Our involvement with patient's illnesses was becoming more direct and intensive. Although the course was supposed to be divided equally between the two disciplines, it was far more weighted towards obstetrics for several reasons. First, our check-in station and home base was the residents lounge in the labor and delivery suite, so we were always present when someone was ready to have a baby (which was all the time). Second, the core textbook for the course was William's "Obstetrics," the bible on pregnancy. Third, the abundance of patient activity in labor and delivery offered the greater potential for hands-on learning.

I am proud to say that I virtually read "William's" from cover to cover during that rotation, and still had time to learn a few things in the greater classroom of life. This was more than a theory for me because it was very evident that my medical training was absorbing more and more of my time, leaving less time with Doreen (a bad omen for the future) and less time with God. I did not want to become bitter over it.

One day after being on night call together, the Intern and I met to do morning rounds early. "The private attending always bring a box of Dunkin Donuts to the nurses lounge in Labor and Delivery," he would proudly say. "And if we get done in time, we can go have a donut." The way he accentuated that word, "do-nut," I knew he was set on having one, heart and soul. He must have repeated it to me three more times on the wards: "We can go have a "do-nut." Unfortunately, it had been a busy night, so there were a lot of patients to see, but undeterred, he kept his goal in focus. So we finished our work and rushed down to the labor suite to get… an empty box of donut crumbs. I think the only thing that prevented that Intern from going postal was the fear that a bad recommendation from the department head would ruin his chances for a pathology career. "It's okay," I said, "let's just get something from the cafeteria." He walked away murmuring to himself, "I can't wait to get out of this g_____m place (expletive)! I hate this place!"

I'll never forget the first time I delivered a baby. Well, okay, I actually did forget the details, but it truly was an amazing and wonderful experience. Ninety percent of the time the baby comes out so easily all you need to do was stand there with a catcher's mitt, but it's the ten percent of exceptions that requires six years of intensive post-doctorate training, and that generates the inconceivable malpractice premiums, in some states exceeding $200,000 annually! What impressed me the most was how inanimate a baby is when coming out of the birth canal, yet seconds later it's screaming its head off. The afterbirth or placental membranes was also impressive in a different way. Once out of the mother, following shortly after the baby, this vital marvel of creation that nurtured the unborn child through nine months and ushered it successfully into the light of day had become just a useless mass of tissue to be incinerated. It looked like, quoting the department chairman, Dr. Malatesta, "a pile of ground meat someone set off a hand grenade in." Such are the unfathomable mysteries of life.

Of course babies aren't the only ones screaming in labor and delivery. One day I arrived at the delivery suite and heard a woman yelling uncontrollably. I asked the nurse how far along she was in her labor. It sounded like she'd be delivering any minute. "Oh, her? She's not even in labor. She's having hysterical contractions." It was time for a "do-nut."

Although the obstetrical ward could be explosively busy, there were times of quiescence which explains how I was able to read the entire core textbook. The resident lounge was home base where all the students checked in, got their assignments, and presented cases to the house officers (resident doctors). In between all this activity, we got to chat with each other. That's when I got to know Mark Davis, my fellow student.

Mark was raised in a Jewish home, and like Bob Stiller was exposed to Christianity and was drawn to it, but in Mark's case his search led him into a rising cult of that day, the Jehovah's Witnesses. Now, we really did have a lot in common for, as I related to Mark, I also was drawn to this group, but left them because I could not accept their theology which brazenly denied the diety of Jesus Christ. Ironically, that was the very belief which attracted Mark. I think for him, being Jewish, it seemed a safer form of Christianity. Now in my instance you might conclude my pulling away from the group was due to my being raised Roman Catholic with its strong emphasis on the Doctrine of the Trinity, but such nuances of theology meant nothing to me growing up. My parents weren't Catholic Apologists.

What turned me away from the Jehovah's Witnesses was my reading the Bible for myself, which seemed to me to flatly contradict their doctrine in both Old and New Testaments. Needless to say, Mark and I had some heated talks over this. I inundated Mark with scripture verses to the point he was speechless, but in the end he stuck to his beliefs and I to mine. All the persuasion in the world could not sway him, which taught me a very profound lesson about faith. It comes from the heart, not the mind, and it comes from the heart because God himself puts it there. Jesus said, "No man comes to me unless my Father who sent me draws him" (John 6:44). The Church isn't a debating club, it's a house of faith. People may outwardly conform if coerced at the point of a sword, but their heart will remain un-regenerated. And that, by the way, is not a call to hate someone who rejects your belief. Christians are called to love others. The second greatest commandment is to love your neighbor as you love yourself(Matthew 19:19). The early Christians demonstrated that kind of sacrificial love and the pagan Roman world was converted. So despite our disagreement I loved Mark and I even saw in him a bit of myself. So that, as the saying goes, settled that.

I met some other memorable people at Muhlenberg Hospital that year. There was an Indian house officer who was a Seventh Day Adventist with whom I had many searching discussions. There was Dr. Malatesta, who so graphically described the condition of the afterbirth. His lectures were a favorite among us students, always being laced with ironic wit and double entendres. Every lecture ended with a short promotion of the true love of his life, skiing in Vermont.

There was Dr. Bakshi who was always so nice to work with, and who eventually delivered my first child. I also got to know an R.N. in the nursery, a truly delightful Christian woman. She loved God and loved people, always praying for others and sharing her faith, not for any other reason but that she cared. Her job literally was her ministry, comforting new mothers through both their joy and their sorrow, counseling fellow employees, and I marveled at her mastery and admit that I was a little envious.

I recall a very tragic event when a woman delivered a child with a fatal heart anomaly. Emergency surgery could not save the baby's life and the mother, of course, was devastated. Now many people approached this grieving woman with words of encouragement, but she angrily rebuffed them as she worked through her loss. That nurse, however, knew enough to hold her words and do her job with supreme kindness, while, I'm sure, silently keeping the woman in her prayers. I learned some valuable lessons from this lady, first, that God puts you in a particular place for a reason. Your vocation is his calling on you and you can be a blessing to others wherever you are and whatever you do. Second, that if you want people to take your words seriously, they've got to see that your life matches up to your rhetoric. Nowhere is this truer than in health care where patients suffering pain and tragedy will respond to a caring heart first, and then later be responsive to the words of eternal hope. It has been said that during the fall of the Roman Empire, multitudes of people came to the Christian faith because, in plague and war, the Christians stayed behind to comfort the afflicted and heal the sick when everyone else took off to save their own necks. This was the high standard that would become my goal as a doctor, however fitfully I adhered to it.

I learned one other thing from this unique and gifted individual. A day came when she herself had to endure a great tragedy. I'm not sure what it was, perhaps some trouble in her marriage. One night I dropped by the nursery, having heard about her situation, and thought I could share some words of comfort with her, but she was in no mood and curtly waved me off. My feelings were hurt, but I could see one thing clearly: there are no spiritual giants in this world. We are all vulnerable, fellow travelers in life, and we all have our limit. We should never fester over offensives, we should always forgive, and we should never put another human being on a pedestal to be idolized. In ancient times when an idol was proven false it was cast down and thrown into the fire. Much bitterness results from the idolization of fellow human beings who in some way or other disappoint us simply because they are human. "God grant me the grace to never worship a person and help me to always forgive, and to humbly endure when my day of trial comes."

Obstetrics and gynecology ended, and looming ahead of me was the apotheosis of third year medical school; the medicine and surgery clerkships. Twenty-four weeks, half a year, of the ultimate, grueling excursion into hospital care. Pediatrics, psychiatry and OB-GYN would be like nursery school by comparison, and they in no way prepared you for the experience. For me, the medicine rotation came first, six weeks at Middlesex General Hospital in New Brunswick, and six weeks at Princeton Medical Center. In medicine, the hospital day always started early with morning report, where the night staff presented a summary of all admissions, incidents and exceptional activity to the Chief of Medicine and the entire assembly of interns, residents and students for general discussion.

It was six-thirty Monday morning when my fellow students and I shuffled warily into the Department of Medicine office. To get there we had to walk through the Internal Medicine ward. Nurses were darting in and out of rooms. One or two interns sat at the nurse's station busily recording their findings on the patient's charts. The air was heavily laden with the smell of human excretions and antiseptic solutions, odors so new to us then, but to which we would shortly become immune. I took an inconspicuous seat in one corner of the briefing room. There was a long table, empty but for two or three half-filled Styrofoam coffee cups and the stack of papers the chief resident was working on. You could hear a pin drop as we all quietly awaited the entrance of the Department Chief, Dr. Benson. Unfurled on a wall opposite my chair was a life-sized poster of Darth Vader with light sword in hand ready to jump off the wall and engage us in mortal combat. It was going to be a long twelve weeks.

Gordon Benson was a statuesque martinet of a man, very erudite, who was a well-known specialist in diseases of the liver. He ran a tight ship and expected us to be punctual and to know our stuff. In the five years I trained in his proximity I think I only saw him smile once, when an intern presenting a case report became hopelessly baffled and then broke down. Morning report could last fifteen minutes to an hour, depending on the previous night's activity. Afterwards, we proceeded as a group to see the patients under our care, one by one. In a teaching hospital like Middlesex General, there are private patients with their own personal doctors in attendance. And there are medical service patients who, not having a personal physician, come under the care of the medical school teaching service that was led by Dr. Benson at the time of my rotation. A private doctor may join the medical school staff as an associate professor, whereupon his patients become assigned to an intern and resident, but he continues to supervise the case. Most of the private attending doctors were good teachers, and I am indebted to them for what I learned under their guidance, but some were constant sources of friction and bad feelings, as I will soon elaborate.

As students, we each were assigned a patient to look after, and an intern to whom we were answerable. Now the typical intern was a first year post-doctorate trainee. Interns are not licensed yet, but can write prescriptions and give orders in the hospital, subject to their attending approval (e.g. Dr. Benson). An intern is only two years more advanced than a third year medical student, but his knowledge of disease is exponentially greater by virtue of the intense hospital training he is under. So as students, we stuck close to our interns, following them around like kid brothers, writing down every pearl of wisdom spoken to us.

The very first medical intern I remember was an Indian, Dr. Saberwahl, and my first impression of him was how polite and unflappable he was. "How are you doing, sir?" he would always ask the patient. Then, under Dr. Benson's watchful eyes, his questions became ever more probing and medical, and he proceeded to his exam. I could see that patients responded well to this. What a model doctor he was! Then we came to the patients with D.T.'s (Delirium Tremens or Alcohol Withdrawal Syndrome). Any teaching service in the country has at least a few of these patients: poor, destitute, uninsured and dreadfully ill. There were two patients with this illness in one of the rooms, both awake but totally unresponsive, shaking violently with arms and legs shackled to the bed, foaming at the mouth, with skin as yellow as a banana peel. "How are you doing, sir?" Dr. Saberwahl asked. No response. He then proceeded to a cursory exam. I stood there transfixed at this tragi-comic scene. These two men were dying with a self-inflicted injury, alcoholic liver disease. Even if they were to be medically stabilized, their long-term prognosis was grim, and Dr. Saberwahl spoke to them as if he expected a response, even though he didn't. It all seemed so futile, but futility, I came to learn, was always present in the battle with disease and suffering. I understood then that learning to cope with it is a necessary part of a doctor's training, but one you won't learn by reading text books.

My turn for night call came up and this time I knew it in advance, so I packed my toothbrush, shaving kit and confidently faced it. In medicine, I soon discovered that night call meant exactly that; calls at night. Tooth brushing and shaving would become luxuries often neglected. As a student it wasn't so bad because you were called only if the senior resident felt you could learn from a particular patient's condition, but the poor intern was usually up all night managing every medical admission to the hospital: strokes, heart attacks, pneumonia, dehydration, etc. In fact, everything, with the possible exception of Letterer-Siwi syndrome (which no one saw, if it actually existed!). It was in third year medical school that we experienced the front line in the conflict with disease, the Emergency Room.

Day and night, a flood of sick and injured people came through those doors, like refugees from a war zone. Emergency physicians are often of necessity a little footloose and at times non-conformist. They practice medicine on the edge. An emergency physician once told me if he sat there constantly thinking of what's coming at him next he'd lose his mind. One minute he could be treating a child for a simple sore throat and the next minute be in a life and death struggle with a ruptured aneurysm. The ER is not a place for wimps. Of all the physicians there, the most incredible had to be Dr. Soto, an oriental doctor who, I am serious, couldn't have been over four feet tall. To suture a patient the nurse had to get him a chair to stand on. He looked like a cross between Tom Thumb and Charlie Chan.

So this self-contained world became my universe for the next six weeks. The resident and student quarters were as usual off in some old abandoned ward which gave the discouraging impression that your personal comfort was a very low priority. The rooms were cold, dusty, Spartan and usually empty since most of the occupants were up caring for patients anyway.

Middlesex General Hospital sits in the heart of downtown New Brunswick, New Jersey. Today it is a truly sprawling medical center, the University Hospital of the Robert Wood Johnson Medical School (formerly Rutgers), but back in 1977 it was a fairly modest 300-bed facility surrounded by a quaint urban residential area with lots of Hungarian restaurants and a whole lot of churches.

Because of the heavy snows that winter, plus the fact that parking in front of a church back then was illegal, we were almost always late getting to morning report. Not that Dr. Benson accepted any excuses, but we tried our best. One day an intern named Jaime came in particularly late and was he hot! "You can't find a parking space in this city because of all the g———m (expletive) churches!"

Oh my goodness! I thought. At first I was offended. Why, I walked just as far as he did. But then I reasoned, *Maybe someone in a church had offended him in his past.* I prayed that one day God would enlighten him in that area.

One day followed another. I learned much, but there seemed to be no end to all the knowledge that was ahead of me. I also got to know the many private attendings. There was good-natured Dr. Chinchilla, who was from South America and loved to call me by my full first name, "Alessio." There was Dr. Kerpelman whom no one got along with (although once we rode an elevator together and he was very pleasant, even wishing me luck in my career). Dr. Lifshutz was an old fashioned general internist, admired by all as a doctor who never consulted a specialist, as he did it all. He was also a great teacher and being assigned one of his patients was considered a plum. Then there was the triumvirate, cardiologists: Dr. Reitman, Dr. Keller and Dr. Sicherman. Dr. Barnes Keller was the dynamo of the group, but Dr. Reitman was the senior partner, a kindly old school physician in the Marcus Welby mold. I learned a lot from him beyond the traditional curriculum. Dr. Jasper Van Avery was a soft spoken endocrinologist, who became somewhat of a mentor to me. He also supervised the daily lunch medical education meeting. Topics were chosen for their relevance to our medical training and best of all there was free food. Attendance here was predictably good. Dr. Shiffman, a staff pulmonologist (lung specialist), and a great teacher, gave me some kind words of advice when I needed them.

Dr. Keller was the terror of the interns because his teaching methods were direct and blunt. He usually required active participation by students and residents. Nowhere was this more evident than in his EKG clinic, where he would bring real patient EKG's (heart tracings) and put them on an overhead projector. He would then "choose" a volunteer to come up and interpret them, and God help you if you were wrong, but that's how we learned. Unsurprisingly, his meetings were, unlike Dr. Van Avery's, sparsely attended.

The spectrum of Internal Medicine training invariable included critical care. That is, the care of patients with life-threatening illness, the sickest of the sick: heart attack, stroke, overwhelming infection, kidney failure, internal hemorrhage, etc. Here is where the house officer really cut his teeth. As students in the intensive care unit, we were the perennial "gofers," getting X-ray reports, calling specialists and retrieving lab results.

Medicine in the 1970s was on the verge of a sea change in technology. Anyone who visits a hospital ward today is immediately impressed by the great number of computer terminals. I must admit now, as I look back, I can't imagine practicing medicine without the computer. So much of what I do now depends on this electronic genie, but in 1978, hard as it is to believe, there was one, only one computer terminal in the entire hospital, and it wasn't even a terminal, but rather a free standing printer directly connected to the hospital lab, by which stat results could be quickly sent up in hard copy. When the intern asked us to get the latest blood results we rushed to this printer, pressed enter, and the data came "sputtering out," not spitting but sputtering, "tick…tick…tick…tick…." In the time it took this 1978 technology to print one line, a computer today would have printed out a twelve page comprehensive report, but in 1978 we watched this marvel of technology with unabashed amazement.

X-rays, on the other hand, were still retrieved the old fashioned way. One student was sent down to the radiology department with a list of names to pull, and at the end of the day we would all go down as a group and review the films with the radiologist. Today even this is done on computer. I simply type in a request and "bingo," X-rays appear on screen for my review. It took me a while to get used to this. I was trained to hold the actual X-ray films in my own hands, but in the end, the time saving potential of the computer could not be resisted..

Two forces were constantly colliding in the dating relationship of Doreen and I: my insecurities over the future of our lives together and her insecurities over the demands of my education.

I have always felt inadequate around women, having dated but a trifle in my brief years. On one of our first dates to Fire Island, New York, I actually locked both my ignition key in the ignition and my trunk key in the trunk, much to the hilarity of passersby. That had to be the Olympic gold medal winning bad first impression, but she married me anyway. We met at a church social and our shared faith was the bulwark of our relationship. She wasn't overawed by my doctoring, and I never felt I had to impress her with my accomplishments. One Sunday night after church she introduced me to her mother when I was wearing an old worn out pair of jeans, we chatted very nicely and I was sure I had won her approval. It was some time later that Doreen told me, as I walked away that night her mother whispered, "He'll make a heck of a husband!" I was the prince of bad first impressions. But despite that, we began a courtship with the occasional lover's quarrel. After a particularly protracted one, we met one day by chance in the hospital lobby where Doreen was working with the senior citizens. We made up and after agreeing that we really did care about each other, we made a date to go to dinner later in one of those quaint Hungarian restaurants.

The next day, still savoring our time together, I was walking in a basement corridor by the emergency room with two fellow students when three men rushed up to us. The man in the middle was grimacing while the other two held a firm grip on his bandaged upheld hand. "Where's the ER?" one of them shouted. I pointed. "That way, down the hall to your right." They quickly ran down the corridor and out of view. *What was that all about?* we wondered, when two others rushed upon us. "Hey! Did you see three guys go past here?" they asked.

"Sure, they went to the ER down that way, why?"

"We've got his finger in this plastic bag!"

Yikes! I thought it really was his finger! Poor guy. I supposed that a lover's quarrel didn't seem so bad after all, in perspective. So as the career of medicine even in its incipient stages began impinging on my personal life, it also began constricting my religious devotions. Night call meant not attending church services like I wanted and Bible study by necessity gave way to medical training. The uncertainty of my choice of career at my father's hospital bedside came back to haunt me. Maybe, I thought, I could just finish medical school and get a job as a lab assistant.

It was at times like those when I would make a trip to my "special place" at the medical school tower, and making my way to the eighth floor I would get onto the roof for some time of tranquility and quiet reflection. On a clear day the view was spectacular. You could see a major portion of the central New Jersey tidal plain and upland. The Raritan River would lazily snake off, disappearing into the horizon while the parallel Watchung Mountain chains, like two prongs of a fork, intruded into the sprawling suburban megaplex that lapped at their feet. The tower roof was a great place to rest, to think and to pray. I knew that being a doctor would be a great commitment of time and energy, and I just was not sure I wanted to make that commitment. I thought about my father's expectations of me, and my grandfather's dying request, and also of the long-term regrets of quitting, if I ever did. And what would I do to make a living anyway? Asking others for an opinion didn't help because everyone had their own bias. One older woman at church told me definitely to quit, asserting that it was God's will to do so, but on closer scrutiny I learned that, as a child, her feet were permanently deformed by a botched surgery job for polio and she never trusted doctors again. No, this was a decision I would have to make alone with God's help. "Be strong and of good courage: Be not afraid...For the Lord thy God is with thee whithersoever thou shalt go" (Joshua 1:6).

Life, of course, moved on, like a relentless tide sweeping all before it. Up on the roof all your cares may drift into space, but the next day you report to work just like always. To cover up my insecurities I tended to joke, a little too much I'm afraid, and resorted as in the past to doing impressions. One day the chief resident, who was responsible for my student evaluation, took me off to the side and warned me point blank to stop being a wise guy, as it wasn't appreciated. I took his rebuke seriously, but since I have always believed that a little laughter was necessary in life I minimized, but did not eliminate the joking.

Of course, a quick wit could be a lifesaver at times. One morning near the end of my six weeks at Middlesex, my car, a 1969 Buick hand-me-down, conked out on me. All I could do was use my mother's car. So I drove her to work, then doubled back to the hospital. By then I was hopelessly late and since I hadn't even eaten yet, I stopped at a supermarket and bought a package of Vienna Fingers. I brought them to the hospital with me, perhaps subconsciously considering them a potential peace offering. By the time I made it to ICU it was practically 10 A.M. (rounds started at 8:00). The resident saw me coming as did the entire team. "Well, Dr. Salsano, it's nice of you to join us," he said. "And what's your explanation for being two hours late?"

I paused for a moment then produced the bag of cookies. "It took me two hours to find a store open to buy these!" Everyone was in stitches including the resident. "Vienna Fingers! I love Vienna Fingers!" the intern said as he took the package. So we all had a nice snack and I narrowly avoided an embarrassing write up.

First impressions aren't always true. The six weeks at Middlesex General Hospital went a lot faster than I expected on the first day, but the next six weeks at Princeton Medical Center were the exact opposite. This hospital has arguably gained a reputation because of its shared name with the university town it services. Perhaps its best claim to fame is that it was the hospital where Albert Einstein's brain was preserved and then mysteriously lost. Whatever its reputation, it was insanely busy. Interns on night call here were assured they would not sleep a wink, yet to endure a tour of duty here was to win your spurs, so to speak. Unlike at Middlesex Hospital where we changed house officers often, the whole six weeks at Princeton were spent with the same intern/resident team, so you got to know each other very well.

Princeton was a busy place alright, and Dr. Logothetis, my intern, seemed to muster boundless energy to cope with it. Night call was the nadir of the intern's misfortune with emergency room calls, unstable ICU patients, and nurses constantly paging from the wards. It seemed at times just too much for one person to handle, but in retrospect I came to understand that a doctor, like a good general in battle, must learn to deal with crisis "under fire" and not to give up when problems multiply to the point of being overwhelming. After all, lives are hanging in the balance, depending on his ability to maintain his composure, to reason clearly and to carry out the proper treatment under adversity.

As I watched the interns go from patient to patient and crisis to crisis with barely time to think, let alone sleep, doubts rose up in me again. Did I really want to do this the rest of my life? I began to seriously consider quitting medical school, or at least finishing it and then taking a different career path. I even thought about going into seminary, but by then my school loan indebtedness was substantial and the pay back wasn't far in the future. It was time to get some professional advice, so I made an appointment to meet with the Chief of Medicine at Princeton Hospital.

Princeton, New Jersey, was, and still is, the hub of a very affluent suburban region. As a result, most of the patients in the hospital were private pay with good insurance and under the care of their own personal physician. Conversely, a very few patients came under the care of the medical teaching service, and that particular department was thus relegated to a lesser status. It owed its continued presence at the hospital, if for no other reason, but to benefit medical school education and the Rutger's residency program. It was in this context that I entered the small but well furnished office of Dr. Ream, the medical chief.

Dr. Ream was up in years. He was soft-spoken but always maintained a stern countenance with his glasses riding low on the bridge of his nose. He was the precise image of the pedagogue from long ago. I was invited to take a seat. "So, Alessio, or do you have a nickname...?

"Les...

"Okay. So, Les, I understand you wanted to speak to me about some problems you're having."

I tried to be very honest and upfront with him. I spoke of my religious conversion at the end of college, and my concern that medicine would crowd out the other things that were important in my life. I also shared my concern about disappointing my father and mother if I were actually to quit medicine. He listened very attentively, judging by his expressions. He seemed to be empathetic to my situation. "You know, Les, our Lord has put us all on this earth with certain talents and has a place for all of us to serve him."

Now this was unexpected! In seven years of post high school education, no professor ever referred to "our Lord." He definitely had my ear, but I was still unconvinced. "You see, sir, I just don't know if I want to devote my life to medicine."

He pondered for a moment. "Yes, medicine is a devotion. It's like a priesthood, a high calling." I knew what he was trying to say. The practice of medicine was demanding, no doubt, but if God put you in that place he had a reason for it, and if God is in it, then no matter what you do, you'll glorify him and be a blessing to others. This is what Erasmus meant when he hoped that even the lowly plowman could recite the scriptures and praise God in the most menial chores of life. In Ecclesiastes it says, "There is nothing better for a man...than that he should make his soul enjoy the good in his labor... it is from the hand of God" (Ecclesiastes 2:24). I thanked him for his kind advice and left, pondering the notion of serving God and helping others; the high calling.

Dr. Ream was a great encourager to me, but he was constantly under fire from the hospital medical staff. Private attending physicians wielded enormous political power at Princeton Medical Center, and at times he could do nothing to please them. After all, they brought in the money. Right? I remember he had a cartoon tacked to his office bulletin board showing a man coming home from work in a suit that is ripped to pieces, and as he hangs his hat his wife calls out from the kitchen, "How did the meeting at work go, dear?"

The Princeton Medical staff was indeed an elite caste of doctors. Very independent, they expected a lot of themselves, and consequently from everyone else. Chief of these men of iron was Dr. Harvey Rothberg. He was an oncologist and very active in hospital politics. His word carried a lot of weight in Princeton. He ran the interns ragged, but he was very devoted to his patients. I once was assigned a patient of his who did not want a student bothering him. He had recently been diagnosed with melanoma (a serious skin cancer) and was not happy to be in the hospital. As he was getting back into physical training (he was a PE instructor), he developed a blood clot, phlebitis, in his leg. He knew I was a student and after a short while, he angrily dismissed me, and I was reassigned.

As I think back, it was obvious he was in deep denial of his illness. I'm sure, deep inside, he knew he had incurable cancer. In fact, his phlebitis, in the absence of any precipitating event, was evidence that his body was riddled with cancer. In plain truth, he was terminally ill!

I missed an opportunity to learn about treating phlebitis that day, but I did learn something very important about human nature. People need a cause, a passion, some type of rallying point to keep going. For this tragic gentleman it was his physical fitness that gave him the will to go on. As a doctor you must be sensitive to such things, especially when treating advanced disease. A careless word, an insensitive attitude can knock the last hope out from under your struggling fellow human being. In their final days, patients and family need compassion more than ever. But Dr. Logothetis, taking a more pragmatic viewpoint, consoled me later in the hospital library, "People think doctors are sown like wheat in the spring, and reaped in the fall." In other words, there's little understanding or sympathy for the protracted learning process we, as physicians, must all go through.

Radiology rounds were a riot at Princeton due largely to the constant bantering that went on between one particular radiologist, an ex-military man with a straight face and wry sense of humor, and an eccentric intern named Tom Daniskis, who loved to give him a hard time. There were moments when I thought he was really going to smack Daniskis with his pointer. Dr. Daniskis, who was Greek right down to his accent and his big black moustache, actually had a heart. I suspect his joking, like mine, tended to disguise a more serious and sometimes melancholy temperament. Though we never paired off during residency, he and I had some searching religious talks as we carried out our appointed rounds.

The on call rooms at Princeton were located in an old house adjacent to the hospital power plant, and at first glance they looked more accommodating, but when I checked a vacant room and opened the top drawer of the bureau there must have been a dozen empty pill bottles rolling around inside. On closer examination they were all for tranquilizers; Librium and Valium, the discovery of which did nothing to allay my fears about pursuing a medical career. (Oh, and there also were ants!)

Twelve weeks of medicine rotation ended and now twelve weeks of surgery began. For me this meant six weeks back at Middlesex General and six weeks at the core teaching facility in the Rutgers system, Raritan Valley Hospital. Raritan Valley was a most unlikely teaching hospital. It barely had 100 beds and was located down a one lane side road surrounded by woods, tucked inside a small suburban community. This had to do with the politics behind medical education in New Jersey. Rutgers in the 1970s really had no university hospital. In its place the training program consisted of what was called The Rutgers Affiliated Hospital System. You see, Rutgers in those days was actually a part of the College of Medicine and Dentistry of New Jersey whose main campus was located in Newark, New Jersey. Stanley Bergen, then president of CMDNJ, lavished state funds on building the Newark facility and very little was left for the sister campus at Rutgers. The result was that you had nationally renowned medical experts seeing patients referred from all over the country at a hospital that rightly belonged in Mayberry RFD. Now all this "real politik" raised enormous hackles of discontent at Rutgers, especially in the Department of Surgery where funding shortfalls were most keenly felt. This led one disgruntled professor of surgery, every chance he got, to refer to "that f_____r (expletive) Stanley Bergen."

After being scattered to different locations over the past seven months, it was heartening on the first day at Raritan Valley to see the old gang reunited. Al Kelsey and Larry Swayne were there, and Bob Stiller and Steve LaPoff, too. I had learned an incredible amount of medicine in the past thirty-six weeks and felt sure I could breeze through surgery. However, no impression could have been more wrong. In surgery, practically every day presented the challenge of totally new material to learn. My goodness! Would there ever be an end to a doctor's learning process?

My answer now, thirty years later, is a resounding NO! Even in retirement the process goes on. I knew of an internist once who would bring his old medical journals to a retired bedridden colleague who read them avidly, even in the waning years of old age. It's as if the learning process becomes a permanent part of you, body and soul. No wonder my ancestors revered medical doctors so much.

The rotation itself was roughly divided into two parts: general surgery, namely of the major organs, lungs, heart, abdominal organs, etc.; and specialty surgery: ear, nose and throat, urology and orthopedics. At Raritan Valley Hospital, we all got to meet one of the most colorful academicians at Rutgers University, Dr. Lewis Zemsky. Dr. Zemsky had just finished his residency and was starting up an orthopedic surgery practice at the medical school. The nurses fondly referred to him as little Z (to distinguish him from the big Z, Dr. Zwadski, who was on the senior faculty and a pillar of orthopedic surgery in central New Jersey - but that's another story). Dr. Zemsky was like a computer when it came to orthopedics. His talks were so detailed I imagined he must have memorized word for word an orthopedic textbook. He was also hyper to the point of generating considerable debate over whether he had an actual medical condition.

Al Kelsey and I reported first to his morning ortho clinic. We followed him from exam room to exam room trying to write down everything he said, but it was hopeless, so we just relaxed and settled down to enjoy the ride. One day a very built up young man was in for a painful knee. Dr. Zemsky examined him quickly, then started writing. "You've got chondromalacia. You're going to have to stop the weight lifting and do these exercises (he thrust a handout to him). I'll see you back in four weeks. If you're not improved I may have to do surgery, so you better do what I tell you."

Now that was laying it on the line, but the patient looked tough so we all figured he could take it. But as Al and I stood there and Dr. Zemsky finished his progress note, we heard a faint whimpering. The patient was crying! Dr. Zemsky saw him, and looking incredulous said, "What are you crying about? I told you what to do. I'll see you in four weeks."

Al and I looked at each other, half amused and half amazed. Little Z was obviously not a paragon of sensitivity, but he did, after all, address the pertinent issues.

One day we were following him on rounds (running after him actually) when he went to radiology, demanding that the radiologist review an X-ray he had just sent over. "Look, Lew, I'll get to it when I have time. We're backed up with cases today."

As we walked (that is ran) away, Dr. Zemsky was muttering deep oaths to himself. I always wondered if he would have benefited from some lithium therapy.

Twice a week we all met with him for an orthopedic lecture. As usual, he covered so much information so quickly we couldn't get it all down. Someone needed to install a rewind button on him! One day in lecture he must have caught Bob Stiller daydreaming out of the corner of his eye, so in mid-lecture he asked, "And to what bony prominence does the major extensor of the forearm attach..... Bawb? (Not Bob, Bawb.)"

"I...I don't know," was the answer.

Dr. Zemsky rolled his eyes, "Pathetic! The olecranon process!" Bob nodded his head in agreement.

Oh-oh, I thought. I'd better look like I'm paying attention or I'll be next. The lecture went on and about ten minutes later he stopped again and asked, "And what major extensor of the forearm attaches to the olecranon process, Bawb?"

"I... I don't know," Bob sheepishly replied.

Dr. Zemsky rolled his eyes again. "Pathetic! The triceps!" He then looked at his watch and snapped, "Okay, we're done for today. (I was saved!) But be back here Friday and don't be late!" He then looked straight at me and said, "You too, weasel!" Steve LaPoff busted out laughing. No one was safe under the watchful eyes of little Z.

Hanging out with Dr. Zemsky was a trip, but more serious experiences lay ahead. One that still haunts me happened on a night call, and it involved a motorcycle accident. Anyone who has visited New Jersey knows that the state is crisscrossed with many highways. Raritan Valley Hospital happened to be located where several of these converged and consequently received a large number of motor vehicle accident trauma cases. One night the emergency room paged the surgery team that a motorcycle accident victim was coming in by ambulance. When he arrived, he was pretty beat up and his blood pressure was very low. This happened at a time when CAT scans were not widely available, so we had to diagnose by plain X-rays. All the while, the patient just kept repeating semicoherently, "please get it off my chest, will someone please get it off my chest?"

The X-ray showed a large mass next to the heart. The diagnosis was a traumatic aneurysm of the aorta, a life threatening injury, so emergency surgery was indicated. As a medical student, my job in the operating room was to simply hold the retractor, a device that kept the body cavity open for the surgeon to operate.

It was very difficult to stand motionless keeping constant tension on the handle of that instrument, but the trade-off was an intimate look into the internal structures of the human body. The last words of the patient before becoming unconscious under anesthesia was, "Please get it off my chest." When the surgeon opened his chest cavity there was an enormous pulsating mass encasing his heart and major blood vessels. It had to be penetrated to reach the structures that needed repairing, but when the surgeon cut into it, blood exploded everywhere. It was a false aneurysm. This unfortunate young man's aorta had literally ripped apart in the accident, but the tough surrounding tissues contained the hemorrhage under great pressure, like a water balloon filled just to the point of bursting. He didn't have a chance. He died on that operating room table. We all took off our surgical masks as the nurses began cleaning up. I could see the look of grim resignation on the surgical attending's face. No one enjoys losing a patient under any circumstances. As I glanced back at the shattered remains of this tragic victim, Joseph Heller's declaration in the novel "Catch 22" came back to me, "The spirit gone, man is matter." The patient's chest was flayed open like a side of beef in a butcher shop, ribs protruding and all. And then Saint Paul's warning also echoed in my ears, "it is appointed unto man once to die and then the judgment" (Hebrews 9:27).

The surgery rotation at Raritan Valley Hospital was weighted more heavily with lecturing than actual hands-on involvement, as you would expect, since most of the full time faculty were located there. The six weeks at Middlesex General Hospital, however, was the reverse. As before, we broadly split into two sessions, general surgery and specialty surgery. The surgery residents always seemed to be more uptight than the medical residents. All, that is, except Dr. Butts, a short, unassuming Indian doctor whose colleagues were always trying to set up with a date to help him overcome his shyness. I was assigned to Dr. Butts, who could often be quite bold and outspoken, at least with us students.

One night on call, an elderly man came in with a leaking abdominal aneurysm graft, a serious malady that required urgent surgery to fix. The attending surgeon in this case was Dr. Finklestein. Dr. Finklestein was a man with boundless energy, who boasted he only needed three hours of sleep a night and spoke faster than anyone I knew, with the possible exception of Dr. Zemsky. It made me wonder if hyperactivity was a prerequisite for a successful career in surgery.

It must have been two o'clock in the morning when we started the operation.

My job, as usual, was to hold the retractor. After being cleaned and draped, Dr. Finklestein put his scalpel to the abdomen. As the skin parted under the razor sharp knife, each subsequent layer of the abdominal wall was exposed, the sub-cutaneous fat, abdominal wall muscles which were carefully parted and finally, the peritoneal sac, which like a giant cellophane bag, enclosed the intestinal organs. When this last barrier was opened, the living entrails of the human body were exposed. Even now, decades later, I think back in wonder at the sight of the inter-nal organs. If I were a surgeon and saw them every day of my life, I might not feel the same way, but seeing them, back then, alive, replete with color, pulsating with blood and rhythmic movement gave me a distinct sense, a mindfulness of the nearness of God.

Now, for the surgeon performing such an operation, there were two very strong and competing concerns. One was to move as quickly as possible to resolve the problem and minimize the exposure, and two, to move carefully and method-ically so as to minimize complications. Dr. Finklestein had to move very quickly, because this patient was already in an advanced state when diagnosed.

The surgery was protracted by some complications and it was almost 7:00 A.M. when they were all resolved and Dr. Finklestein, with Dr. Butts' help, was beginning to repair the damaged graft. "Nurse, can you please call my office and have my morning appointments canceled?" Even Dr. Finklestein had his lim-its. As for me, I had been standing there in one place holding that retractor for over four hours without moving. That, coupled with having been up all night, was causing a sick feeling to well up inside me. It started in the pit of my stom-ach like a butterfly growing steadily into a queasy faint feeling, and I began to break out in a sweat. "Doctor, I feel lightheaded. Can I sit down for a few min-utes?"

"No," he said. "You can go ahead and leave."

I made it to the doctor's lounge and laid down. After a while I felt better, got dressed, and prepared to start the day.

Emergencies were dramatic, but much of what a surgeon does is elective, meaning routine and planned, such as a cholecystectomy for gallstones, joint replacement, cancer surgery, etc. One night on call I was assigned to a woman who had been admitted with a breast mass for biopsy and probable mastec-tomy. The surgeon had discovered the mass on exam, and she also had enlarged lymph nodes in her armpit. The mammogram confirmed the mass which had all the findings consistent with breast cancer. When I introduced myself, I could see she was a refined and well-bred woman, about fifty years of age, very polite and considerate, and also very scared. I performed my history and physical, and definitely felt the mass. Deep inside, I knew this very sweet lady could use something more than a good medical exam. "I know this is a scary time for you, but God knows your situation and is there to help you."

Upon hearing this she smiled broadly. "I know. I'm a new Christian. I just recently gave my life to the Lord, and had just gotten baptized, when my doctor found the lump in my breast."

We agreed that in the spiritual dimension this was a trial to test her faith and we held hands and prayed. "Oh Lord, you know our need and we commit it unto you. Please, Lord, in Jesus' name we ask for healing of this breast condition. Deliver your child from this evil and glorify your name, amen." She was very thankful for the word of prayer and we parted.

The next day we prepped for the surgery. After Dr. Cunderman reviewed the mammogram to determine the precise location of the mass, he began the operation. Carefully dissecting down to the exact spot, a strange look came over him. "That's funny. I can't find it. The mass was definitely here, but all I see is normal breast tissue. Nurse, let me see that X-ray again!" He studied the mammogram very carefully. "This is most unusual," he said, and extended his dissection to make sure he was not in the wrong location. Finally he biopsied the breast exactly where the mass was previously sited. The frozen section came down from pathology after several minutes; involuted breast tissue and subcutaneous fat, benign. The surgeon said with a twinge of frustration, "Well, let's close her up."

"But what about the lymph nodes?" I asked.

"I'm not worried about them. There's no cancer in this breast."

The next day I shared the whole story with the patient, who was obviously overjoyed beyond all belief at the news. We both thanked God for what seemed to be a miracle of his healing touch and bid our good-byes. If we never met again, I knew we would see each other someday in glory.

The rotation through specialty surgery at Middlesex General Hospital could be summed up in two words: The Prostate. Prostate enlargement is the most common urologic problem afflicting older men (including myself since I hit my 50s). Probably Dr. Brady, a no nonsense, gung-ho type of guy with little humor, did four out of five prostate operations. He always reminded me of a marine officer from "The Sands of Iwo Jima". One morning I was scheduled to work with Dr. Brady and was hurrying to the operating room (he also was a stickler for punctuality) when I passed Al Kelsey, who was sitting with the newspaper. "Hey, Les, help me with this crossword puzzle."

"Gosh Al, I'd like to, but Dr. Brady is expecting me in the OR."

"Naw," he said. "It takes time to set up the case, he'll just get annoyed if you're standing there getting in his way, you've got time."

"Well," I said, "I don't know…," but I loved crossword puzzles so I joined him.

Some ten minutes later Dr. Brady walked by and asked, "What are you doing there? You're supposed to be with me in the OR. Are you here to learn surgery or goof off?"

"Well, I…I…" Quickly, I got up and hurried after him. As I looked back I gave Al a grimace.

He, in turn, had a look on his face that was partly, "I'm sorry," and partly, "this could only happen to you."

There were many other faces and cases in that third year of medical school, most of which have faded into the mists of time. When it ended, I had definitely been inaugurated into a doctor's life. It was challenging and a little overwhelming. I came to see the wisdom in perseverance, but doubts still plagued me. The final year of medical school started in September, but 48 weeks of the third year wrapped up at the end of August, leaving a very truncated one week summer vacation. "Welcome to the real world, young Dr. Casey!" But of course, the fourth year of medical school was purposely kept light, it being understood that the frenzy of internship would be following hard after it. The fourth year also was the time for students to pick their choice of specialty. All this happened through a process called "the match." Since some prestige residencies received too many applicants (Johns Hopkins, Harvard, The Mayo), the match ensured that everyone got placed somewhere. A medical school education was too precious to be allowed to expire. You might not get your first choice, or even your second, but you would begin internship somewhere. It worked almost like the college draft for professional football.

Well, I decided not to enter the match. This was a drastic step which almost assured that I would end my medical career with graduation. I did it for two reasons. The main one was that I just could not reconcile myself to devoting my life to medicine. The second reason was that I didn't want to get placed somewhere so far from my home and friends that I would feel stranded. I poured out my angst to Doreen until she got tired of hearing it. "Well, quit," she said. "What do you want me to do?"

I didn't know what I wanted her to do. I did love her, but I was afraid to commit myself to marriage, and for some inexplicable reason, perhaps jealousy, my male friends at church kept encouraging me to break up with her. The end result was to catapult me into even deeper indecision. On top of that, I had yet to tell my parents about the seeming reckless endangerment of my residency training. All this mental and emotional baggage accompanied me into that last year of schooling.

The final year of medical school is almost exclusively elective. The only requirement was one month in family practice, and even there you got to pick the location. For me, I definitely needed some place where I could get alone and sort out my issues. Rutgers sponsored a program where a student could do his four weeks of family practice in a physician shortage area. A majority of these were in urban inner city locations, but I chose a rural locale, Millville, in extreme southern New Jersey. Doreen was not happy about it, knowing it required me to stay in Millville the whole time, except weekends, and rightly surmised that I was distancing myself to get my thoughts in order. Before leaving, I got up the nerve to tell my mother that I might not pursue medicine after graduation. She thought for a minute, then answered, "With an attitude like that you'll never win a Nobel Prize."

I never said I wanted one!

When I parted with Doreen on a Sunday afternoon to begin the long ride to Millville, a thunderstorm was looming over Edison, mirroring my "stormy" departure. "I'm not going to wait forever, you know," she said to me.

I was in a very sullen mood as I left, but a few miles into the ride the storm clouds parted to reveal the most beautiful complete rainbow I had ever seen. I was almost in tears as I heard the Lord say to me "I'm faithful and I'll take care of you. I'll always be there, like my rainbow. Don't worry about a thing."

When I arrived in Millville, to my amazement, all the local people spoke with a Southern accent! I checked in with my preceptor, Dr. Charles Mintz, an extremely busy family doctor who looked much older than his stated age, which generated more fodder for my career concerns. He was, however, a very likeable person with a pleasant sense of humor. I never saw anyone move from room to room as fast as he did, and despite his aged countenance, I had a hard time keeping up with him.

I saw firsthand, as the course had intended, how a doctor's office runs on a daily basis. He saw patients, checked the mail, made and took phone calls, gave orders to his employees and advice to his patients. It was the chief cook and bottle washer concept raised to a new plain. Yet, little did I realize at the time that Dr. Mintz' lot would be my destiny.

In addition to his busy office Dr. Mintz, unlike most family physicians today, did hospital work. In fact, he was one of the big shots at the local hospital and wielded considerable political clout. The Harvey Rothberg of Millville. One morning I joined him at grand rounds, the weekly medical lecture, and to my amazement the talk was about an exciting new diagnostic procedure for heart disease, cardiac catheterization. How strange, I thought. At Rutgers this procedure had been done routinely for quite some time, and then it dawned on me, my father, despite his major heart attack, had never had one. I resolved to address this deficiency in my father's health care in the future, but at the moment I just pondered the trickle-down effect of medical knowledge, such as what was regularly done in a university could actually be breaking news in the backwater communities.

Millville Hospital graciously provided me a room and free meals (in the hospital cafeteria). The room was actually an abandoned hospital room with a hospital bed, not the most comfortable. It wasn't a luxury accommodation, but at least the room wasn't caked with dust or crawling with ants, and since night duty was not a course requirement, I usually got a good night's sleep.

Hospital cafeterias are famous for their unpalatable menus (except for the Princeton Medical Center) and Millville was no exception. Free food, however, is not easy to pass up, so I made good use of my privilege. One evening I arrived late and the cafeteria was empty except for me and the on call radiologist. I was already seated when he came up with a tray, introduced himself and joined me. I told him I was thinking about Internal Medicine.

"That's great," he said. "All the specialties have their significance, but I still say the internist is the prince of medicine."

The prince of medicine! The way he put it, it sounded almost reverent. Who wouldn't want to be a prince? I think that his comment really helped carry me through my doubts into accepting the challenge of doctoring. I thanked him for his encouraging words and we parted.

Dr. Mintz had a thriving suburban practice, but the course included time spent in a satellite office in the true physician shortage area of Port Norris on the

Delaware Bay. Here the local people subsisted on a fishing economy, but the fishing industry in the Delaware Bay area had been in a slow eclipse for many years, leading to the widespread and endemic poverty in the area. As part of my rotation I got to accompany a nurse who did home care visits subsidized by the state, and got a chance to see firsthand the great need of these people in this rural enclave of the northeast surrounded by a sea of prosperity.

In one home there resided a retired minister and his bedridden wife, both well into their eighties. She was quite incapacitated, but he, though advanced in years, was clear-minded and very lucid. On our visit, he continually dictated his needs to the nurse and outlined his plans for his wife's recovery. I was humbled by his incredible devotion to her, however unrealistic his goals were.

A few miles away from Port Norris, right on the Delaware Bay, was situated the town of Shellpile. Shellpile was a name given to the place by the local people because it was, well, a pile of shells! To the right and the left for several miles were snowdrift-high piles of oyster shells seemingly on permanent display. As I completed my externship I marveled at this silent testimony, even in decline, of the eloquent fertility of this planet we inhabit. It brought to mind the words in the book of Genesis, "...And God created great whales, and every living creature that moves, which the waters brought forth abundantly... And God saw that it was good" (Genesis 1:21).

So I came back home and prepared to face the three issues in my life that were rapidly approaching a culmination: my choice of career, how to tell my father, and my relationship with Doreen. Though our feelings for each other were often strained, we genuinely loved one another and she bore my indecision with patience (as much as her Italian female genetics allowed her). It really was only a matter of time before I popped the question.

As far as my career went, I had to concede that I was so far along in my medical training that it would be insane to drop out now. Deep inside I knew God would help me through any circumstance, but alas, I just didn't have the faith to take hold of it. I remember watching a Christian TV special back then, and at one point they interviewed a young medical student who confidently shared his plans to complete his training and then go on the mission field as a missionary doctor. So there I was mired in self-doubt and indecision, alienated from parents and friends, while this self-assured brother in the Lord was striding towards spiritual and temporal excellence. It was time for me to make my way back to the medical tower roof for another interlude of tranquility and introspection.

How peaceful everything appears from a height. As I looked straight down to the parking lot from my perch in the building, I saw people coming and going, seemingly untrammeled by the weightier issues of life. Of course I knew better. Everyone has their moment of crisis. I had asked God once to give me grace to endure my day of trial and now, I thought, it had arrived; but I was wrong. My true time of crisis was years in the future. And then, the Millville radiologist's words came to mind, "The internist is still the prince of medicine." I came to see that it was the right thing to continue my medical career, and that Internal Medicine would be my field. There were plenty of hurting people right here in America, I thought. How better to fulfill God's high calling than to be a provider here of physical as well as spiritual healing. My conflict resolved itself again, at least for the time being, and I confidently descended the stairs to rejoin my fellow human beings on the pavement below.

I had wisely put off telling my father about my thoughts of quitting. I well remembered his reaction after his heart attack, but Mom already knew so I finally spoke up. By then, however, I was pretty much resolved on continuing. (I didn't let him in on the fact that I was unmatched and likely not to have a place to continue my training.) Dad, it turned out, already knew of my doubts (How do parents know these things?) and was relieved to hear I had regained my confidence. So with a renewed vision of my chosen path, I resumed the final year of my medical school experience.

The fourth year was basically a series of electives, each lasting one month. Family practice, as mentioned previously, was the one prerequisite. Otherwise, you were free to choose from a bewildering variety of courses from various specialties. Most of my choices centered on Internal Medicine, but I did take one surgery course, and learned a great lesson. It was winter time, and New Jersey had one of its famous blizzards. There had to be ten inches of snow on the ground and it was still falling, and of course, my car wouldn't start. I had an 8:00 A.M. surgery case to assist on and had to be there. Fortunately, Dad was able to give me a lift to the hospital, but in all the rush I hadn't eaten breakfast, plus I was a little wasted from digging both of my parents' cars out of the snow.

As the operation began I was in my usual position, holding the retractor, when the same sensation came over me as when I was assisting Dr. Finklestein, only this time I fought it until I literally was about to pass out. Everyone in the room could see I was in distress, so I was released, a scrub nurse dutifully taking my place. Lightheaded and in a cold sweat, I made it to the main corridor of the operating room when the full sensation overwhelmed me. I held onto consciousness by a slim margin. Everything around me appeared like it was swimming and constricting into a tunnel. I could feel myself reeling like a drunken man. I prayed, "Dear Lord, don't let me pass out in here." Everyone was so busy they did not seem to notice my strange behavior. By the grace of God I made it to the doctor's lounge and flopped onto the couch and propped my legs up to restore circulation to my brain. After about ten minutes it was over. I experienced a common cause of faintness called vasovagal syncope, except that I never did pass out, which I attributed to God's mercy.

As I lay there recovering from the episode, one of the anesthesiologists who was dressing out asked me if I was alright. After I related the incident to him, he pondered quietly for a moment then said, "Do yourself a favor, don't go into surgery."

Another elective I took at Muhlenberg Hospital was cardiology for which I was eminently better suited. Doctors Fertig and Lomnitz ran the course and were easy to work with, but mostly I spent time with a young new associate who had recently come aboard. He was a hotshot from Albert Einstein Medical Center in New York, and never ceased to proclaim how over-qualified he was for the mundane Muhlenberg Hospital position. I remember a cherished pearl of wisdom he passed on to me from his early training. When he was starting his cardiology fellowship at Albert Einstein, his professor took him aside and asked, "Do you want to be a real doctor or just a schmuck like all the rest?"

In other words, don't just settle for mediocrity, but strive for excellence. He definitely impressed me with his advice, and I agreed that I didn't want to be a schmuck either, even though I wasn't quite sure back then what a schmuck was.

Despite all the intellectual challenges presented to me, I couldn't get my mind off Doreen. I knew the time for making a life committing decision was approaching fast and I was still hopelessly muddled. Should I propose marriage or shouldn't I? Ironically, one day at the ICU nurses station I overheard two interns conversing. It seemed that one of them was in kind of the same predicament as me. He was in love with a girl, but was not sure he should marry her. I listened more closely. It seemed that the young lady had diabetes (the brittle insulin dependent type) and being a doctor, this young man knew all too well the dire complications of the disease, especially later in life and the cost of medical treatment. He just could not see himself living his life dealing with her illness.

Wow! That poor girl. I slumped back in my chair. If he really loved her, I thought, it would be his joy to stand by her through all her trials and suffering. That's what true love is, isn't it? The Bible calls it "agape" love. Love that reaches out and gives, not asking anything in return, like the way God loves us. After all, he wasn't buying a video game, he was uniting his heart with a living human soul. In the end I had to feel sorry for this intern, for he didn't know any better. You see, without a God perspective all life comes down to whatever we can get out of it for our own good. He was obviously thinking of his own happiness, but when I became a Christian it was clear to me that I must walk like Jesus himself walked, who said of himself: "...The son of man came not to be served, but to serve, and to give his life a ransom for many" (Matthew 20:28). Selfless service and sacrifice have become dirty words in our pleasure driven, narcissistic culture, but the true Christian way is the way of service and of "agape," selfless love. Paul the Apostle summed it up, again pointing to Christ's example, "For God showed his great love for us that while we were yet without strength (helpless in our sins) Christ died for us" (Romans 5:6). When I married, that was the kind of love I wanted to have. I never saw that intern again, but he certainly taught me an important lesson on a supremely important subject, love.

There was no question I was moving in the direction of Internal Medicine, but I tried to take electives in other specialties to round out my experience. Pediatrics was an interesting elective, but definitely not as intense as medicine. It was virtually all office based and preventive health care. This is due partly to the amazing resilience of children and also to the incredible advances in disease prevention and treatment in modern times.

When you read in the history books about the appalling death rate among children in generations gone by it leaves you breathless. Johann Sebastian Bach buried six of his twelve children before even reaching the prime of life. We must be eternally grateful to the pioneers of public sanitation, vaccination and antibiotic development, for the preservation of life and health among the most innocent of humanity.

One day I was observing in a pediatrician's office in affluent Morristown when a delicate looking toddler girl was brought in for her vaccination. The doctor asked me if I would like to administer the shot. As I approached that little child I observed she was so fair that I could see the veins coursing beneath the surface of the skin. She appeared as delicate and fragile as a china doll. I figured I'd better use a very light touch with the needle. A little too much force and the needle might go right through her. So as she sat on her mother's lap, I cleaned her thigh with an alcohol wipe and applied the needle with what I felt was the right amount of force, but to my complete surprise, it bounced off her leg without even breaking the skin! This mishap was followed, needless to say, by her ear-piercing scream. Children really are tougher than they look, I thought, as I excused myself and incontinently retreated into the pediatrician's office. Her doctor accepted my apologies with a slight grin on his face and went back to the now hysterically crying child to finish the job. Adult medicine was looking more and more attractive to me.

I took Infectious Diseases at St. Mary's Medical Center in Newark, New Jersey, during Christmas time. Being a Catholic hospital, they observed the holiday season with all the trappings of a Charles Dickens novel. All employees and medical staff were treated to a free meal in the hospital cafeteria, and the serving line must have stretched for a quarter of a mile. Each department had a cozy, friendly Christmas party with an open invitation.

The Director of Infectious Diseases was Dr. Leon Smith, an imposing patriarch at the hospital. I did a research paper on cutaneous anergy while under his tutelage, which supposedly was published, although I never saw it in print. A human dynamo brimming with mental energy, he was living proof that hyperactivity was not limited to the practice of surgery.

Some specialties held more interest for me than others. Ophthalmology and neurology were okay. Student health allowed me the opportunity to work at my old stomping ground, the Rutgers College main campus in New Brunswick, at the student infirmary. Sad to say, probably ninety percent of what I did there was treat sexually transmitted diseases, and I got pretty good at identifying bacteria under the microscope. There was one notable exception, a young man who presented with profuse vomiting and diarrhea. He probably had contracted the notorious Rota Virus since it was spring time, when the virus usually became epidemic. He was so dehydrated he couldn't stand up without passing out. I told my preceptor that the student needed hospitalization, but he didn't believe me until he saw for himself. They obviously rarely saw kids that sick in their normal duties. It was decided to keep him overnight in the infirmary on intravenous fluids and if unimproved after twenty-four hours then transfer him to the hospital. I was put in charge of his care, my very first inpatient case. The student did well and never had to be admitted. As for me, that was my opportunity to meaningfully direct the care of an acutely ill patient to recovery. My first, but by no means, my last.

Dermatology was a very interesting course under the capable direction of Doctors Christopher Papa and James Berger. I took this elective along with fellow student Cliff Lacy. Cliff was a congenial, good-natured person. Like me he tended to joke, so together we had a good time. Cliff became an extremely conscientious and dedicated doctor as I came to know him during the three years of residency we completed together at Rutgers. He is now a Professor of Cardiology at Robert Wood Johnson Medical School, and an alumni magazine is hardly published without mentioning some new honor he has received. At one point I shared my career concerns with Dr. Berger, who though not quite understanding my motivation tried to encourage me to at least be confident in my choice, whatever it would be. He did, however, make a plug for his specialty.

In my radiology elective I became familiar with what was then a new breakthrough X-ray procedure, the CAT scan. Today, almost everyone under a doctor's care has had a CAT scan (I've had two of the abdomen for kidney stones), but back in 1979 they were only available for imaging of the brain, and the quality of the pictures was greatly inferior to those generated by today's powerful machines. Even so, it represented a quantum leap in the diagnosis of diseases of the brain. Prior to the CAT scan, the only way to diagnose brain pathology was by detailed, laborious neurologic exam, cold calorics (injecting cold water into the ear canals to analyze eye movements) and risky arteriograms. A book we all had to practically memorize back then, Plum and Posner's "Diagnosis of stupor and coma," has now been all but relegated to the history of medicine.

The learning process in the fourth year was just as intense as in the third year, but much more leisurely. There was no on call to contend with and weekends were usually free. Of course we all knew that the intensive first year of postdoctorate training, internship, lay at the end of that rainbow, so we enjoyed the respite while it lasted. Except for me. I had finally come to grips with my calling to medicine, but since I was not in the match program, I had no internship to go to. I resolved one day to go speak with Dr. Hadley Conn, the Chief of Medicine at Rutgers Medical School.

Dr. Conn was an aloof patrician, the descendant of a whole line of physicians, some of noteworthy fame in the medical history books. Because of this seeming air of superiority, he was shunned by many of his peers. When I met with him and shared my situation, and that after a long struggle I had decided on

Internal Medicine as my career path, he was delighted, and offered me a position in the Rutgers affiliated residency program. Thanking him for his generosity, I breathed a sigh of relief. Now I was free to deal with the one remaining challenge in my life, my relationship with Doreen.

Things improved between us in the fourth year, since I had more time to devote to her, but the squabbling continued on and off. This was partly due to the pernicious effects of gossip. No relationship in history that I'm aware of had more unsolicited advice from acquaintances on all sides. Because, out of conscience, we steadfastly refused to become physically intimate, Doreen's friends barraged her constantly with doubts about my sexuality. And my friends, because she didn't practice her Christianity to their specifications, inundated me with doubts about her spiritual commitment. You'd think we were Hollywood celebrities from all the buzz our dating generated. As I look back, I can only conclude that the ugly face of envy was behind most of it.

Now most of the people who influenced Doreen were acquaintances through family members who were not necessarily coming from a biblical perspective, although there was a pastor who suggested to her that I might be struggling with sexual identity issues. But my friends were approaching me with the pretense that they were doing it out of Christian concern, which made their advice all the more deadly.

The chief proponent of this was an older woman named Pat, who held a Bible study in her home that I attended. She was relentless in her proclaiming that Doreen was not the girl for me and that our relationship was not God's will. In all of this confusion and false accusation, our love for each other could not blossom into the beautiful thing God intended. Because I trusted my Christian friends and refused to believe their motives were tainted, it began to drive a wedge into our relationship. "A sound heart is the life of the flesh: But envy is as rottenness to the bones" (Proverbs 14:30).

Looking back, I wished I would have approached all this with a more mature attitude than I did, but I was naïve to human relationships, having been cloistered most of my young life in academia. The whole thing reached a tragic denouement at medical school graduation.

The Rutgers and Newark campuses traditionally held a joint graduation at the Garden State Arts Center, a vast open air amphitheater off the Garden State Parkway near the Jersey shore. It was a showcase of state pride, New Jersey's brightest students garnering the supreme achievement of a Doctor of Medicine Degree.

The governor was there, and I believe a congressman or two. But sadly, Doreen was not there to share my great accomplishment, and it was all my fault.

All of the negative talk along with my career vacillations generated increasing tension between us, and on the morning of my graduation I picked her up to go to the arts center, but we had an argument in the car. I brought her back to her apartment and left her, saying maybe it was best that we not see each other anymore. How could I be so stupid? I asked myself. I was throwing away happiness with both hands. Despite having done it, and despite the hearty approval of my so-called friends, I knew I did the wrong thing. I left her in tears. She was obviously looking forward to sharing my success. As I look back some thirty years later, I can see how my obdurate attitude planted the seed to her inability to embrace my career over the years.

With my head and emotions spinning from this debacle, I proceeded directly to the graduation to take my place in the ceremony. "Where's Doreen?" my mother asked.

"She's not coming," I said, sullenly.

"Oh," she said.

As we took our places in the graduation line, we saw up on the hill a bedraggled, worn-out young man looking ten years older than his real age. "Who is that?" someone asked.

"Why, it's Mike Spedick! He was just finishing his year of internship and is here to see his fiancée, Debbie, graduate."

I gaped at him in horror. Is that what's going to happen to me in the next twelve months? Suddenly the line of graduates going up to receive their diplomas morphed into a line of condemned inmates marching to their execution. Well, enjoy the moment, I thought, even though it won't last long.

Later, at a medical school reception, everyone was in a festive mood, except, of course, me. I saw Al Kelsey and Larry Swayne. We congratulated each other. Then I tried joking with Larry, partly to cheer myself up. "Well, now we finally get to pay off all those student loans we racked up."

"Not me," he said. "My dad paid for the whole thing."

"Oh," I said.

I forgot his father was a doctor, back when they actually made money.

I made my good-byes to the others I knew best and left. My father was having a reception for the family anyway, at Riggio's Restaurant in Newark, and up to it or not, I had to be there.

"So where's Doreen?" my cousin Joe asked. I never realized how much everyone had come to expect us to be together. Now I really began to regret my rash decision, but Dad was ecstatic, despite her absence. That day was practically the climax of his career as a father, and also the fulfillment of his word of promise to my grandfather. At one point, Frank Riggio, the restaurant owner, who was a close friend of Dad's, asked me to play act a popular TV ad of that day. It was a beer commercial, and though he knew I was against alcohol use, he begged me to do it. I felt that to honor my father at that moment I had to violate my personal convictions. So he gave me four bottles of beer and I went up to my father, handed him one and smiled, saying, "Here, Dad, this Bud's for you."

Dad smiled back and said, "Thanks, son."

So in a small tavern on an obscure corner of some forgotten street in an insignificant urban neighborhood, a family celebrated a rite of passage as the world around it, oblivious to its rejoicing, dizzily spun into the unknown future carrying them all along with it.

After graduation I had just three weeks to get my affairs in order before the all consuming internship began. The first thing was to get away from everyone to think things out, so I grabbed who I perceived to be the most unbiased person I knew, my old friend Mark, and took a trip to Maine and Nova Scotia. After listening to me lament for three days he said, "Well, for heaven's sake, just marry her!" So I took his advise and did, but not until after starting internship.

Internship, the first year of post-doctorate training, is the most intensive experience in a doctor's entire career. For the first time you're directly responsible for a patient's well-being. And, although you work as a team with a second- or third-year resident and an attending (i.e. Dr. Benson), you are the first responder, and often the immediate issue of life and death lies in your hands. Every primary specialty from pediatrics to psychiatry has an internship year, but it is the intern in Internal Medicine who is the prince (in waiting) of medicine.

Chapter Four

INTERNSHIP AND STARTING A FAMILY

"Let thy fountain be blessed and rejoice with the wife of thy youth."

PROVERBS 5:18

Internship for me began at Raritan Valley Hospital early on July 1, 1979. I would be there for the next three and one-half months, and then have a two week vacation before moving on to Muhlenberg Hospital. The two weeks off was for my marriage and honeymoon.

After returning from my trip to Maine, I went straight to Doreen's apartment, begged her forgiveness and promised her I'd be back with a ring. I don't think she quite believed me, but she gave me a chance to prove myself. I was, however, in earnest, and went out and used the last seven hundred dollars of my student loan money to buy a nice engagement ring. The diamond was not too big, but was of a superior quality. Now I really wanted to surprise her, so I also bought a three-dollar brass ring at a mall kiosk, then asked her out to dinner. Halfway through the meal I told her I loved her and wanted to give her a token of my love and ask a very important question. So I presented her with a little gift box in which, upon opening, she found the cheap brass ring. "So what is this?" she asked.

"Just something special for you."

She kept looking at it, trying to guess what I was up to. "Wait a minute." I said. "I have something else." I got up and went to the car and came back with another gift box. She opened it to find the diamond ring that cost me my last penny. "Doreen, will you marry me?"

After a fleeting hesitation she said, "Yes." Then I looked up and saw all the waitresses watching me with approving nods, as if to say, "Well, it's about time you wised up!" So we set a date, October twentieth, at First Baptist Church of Metuchen, New Jersey. "Whoever finds a wife finds a good thing and will obtain favor of the Lord" (Proverbs 18:22).

Buoyed by this decisive move in my private life, I started interning. On the first day I arrived at the hospital and proceeded down the usual long corridor and came to the Department of Medicine conference room for morning report. It was then I met the Chief of Medicine, an old, crusty neurologist, Dr. Hahn. Dr. Hahn was brutal on his interns. He knew his job was to take a bunch of glorified medical students and turn them into doctors, and he did it with the tenacity of a marine drill sergeant. He also looked very intimidating; tall, thin with a wild mantle of gray hair and a hoary gray beard. He gave all the appearance of an Old Testament prophet rather than a modern day physician. There would be no trifling with Dr. Hahn, as I would soon find out.

After report, the former interns, now second year residents with more seniority, turned over to us their active patients. It was not unusual to have more than twelve patients at any one time under your care, and Raritan Valley was far from being the busiest hospital. To come in early, see all your patients, attend morning report, round again with your attending physician, attend lectures, take admissions, respond to emergencies which popped up continually and work overnight every fourth day, you could see how busy a typical work day could be.

I recall my very first admission. Bill Byra, my resident, notified me of the patient's location. In medical school we learned to take a good history and do a thorough physical exam, but to do it right and to do it quickly was the primacy of the intern. I thought I was doing pretty well until it came to the rectal exam. "Okay, turn over, Mr. Smith so I can check your rectal area." I donned the latex glove and did the exam.

"Ow!" he cried, "What are you doing back there, Doc? You're killing me!"

Then it dawned on me, "Oh my gosh, I forgot the lubricant!"

Every hospital medical staff has its own unique individuals, and Raritan Valley was no exception. In addition to the congeries of full-time faculty there was Dr. Paul Coccia, whose private practice was so big that half the patients in the hospital at any one time were his. He was a good natured fellow and had complete trust in the medical school faculty and residents, giving us complete autonomy with his patients. There was also Dr. Goldberg, who was well past retirement age and very hard of hearing. We nicknamed him "tip of the ice, Berg" because his patients always had a multitude of problems in addition to the one for which they were admitted.

My first public holiday on call was Labor Day and it was busy as expected (complications of too much alcohol, heat exhaustion, etc.). Late that evening, a patient arrived in the E.R. He had been working hard marching in the broiling sun all day and imbibing at a local outdoor festivity. By evening, he felt a strange sensation which developed quickly into an excruciating headache and projectile (that is, sudden forceful) vomiting. His blood pressure was sky high and he had a stiff neck. These were all signs of a devastating brain condition known as a sub-arachnoid hemorrhage, easily diagnosed today by a CAT scan or MRI, but back then the only certain way to make the diagnosis was by doing a risky spinal tap. I had been a doctor exactly two months by then, and spinal taps were difficult procedures even in seasoned hands. I had tried and missed a couple of times before, but this time a successful outcome was crucial. So at 2:00 A.M., with the whole team of doctors and nurses gathered around the bed in ICU, I prepared the patient for the procedure. "Lord," I prayed. "Help me get the needle in right the first time." After cleaning the skin surface over his lower spine and establishing a sterile field, I slowly pushed the needle through the interspinous ligament moving down to the spinal canal. When I thought I passed the tip into the canal I slowly withdrew the stylus; nothing. Replacing it, I pushed the needle a little further in and again removed the stylus. The second time I could see the fluid coming out, so I carefully attached a graded cylinder to the spinal needle to be able to measure the intracranial pressure. Rising inside the cylinder before me was the column of spinal fluid, tinged frighteningly red with blood, pulsing with every beat of his heart due to the pressure of arterial blood leaking into his brain cavity. I breathed a sigh, took my samples for the lab then pulled the needle out. "Thank you, Lord God, for your faithfulness."

The diagnosis of hemorrhage was confirmed. We worked on getting his blood pressure down and got ready for the next step, angiography, to discover where the bleeding originated. Again in the absence of today's technology, though risky, it was the only option. The next day under "angio" we saw the culprit, a small berry aneurysm in the front of the brain. What this man had was a warning bleed. A true hemorrhage would have killed him instantly, so there was a chance now to save his life.

Today he would have a catheterization with an embolization procedure, and be home the next day. In 1979, he would need to be medically stabilized in preparation for major brain surgery to place a clip on the aneurysm to prevent a second, most likely fatal bleed.

Unfortunately, the patient never could get stabilized. He had one complication after another. One problem would be solved, and then two more would crop up. He was still in the hospital when I went off service in mid-October. I remembered one of Dad's pearls of wisdom, "As a doctor you'll lose more patients than you'll save, so expect disappointment, but don't let it discourage you from staying the course."

The routine of medical training continued. Dr. Hahn ran morning report like a board meeting at which he was the CEO, and a particularly cantankerous one at that. He loved to grill the interns, and I was no exception. Unfortunately, I had inherited some of my father's pugnacious attitude. One morning I was presenting a case and omitted the rectal exam. Well, Dr. Hahn jumped on that immediately. "You mean you didn't do one?" he thundered.

I offered my excuses, but he was nonplussed. In frustration I snapped back, "Well, I guess I'll have to order a rectal consult."

Another time he demanded a detailed report of my rectal exam, so I obliged him with a colorful and graphic description, which got everybody in the room rolling their eyes. He winced at my display of defiance, but bided his time. He would ultimately get even with me, as I will come to relate.

One of the better professors at Rutgers was Dr. John Kostis, Chief of Cardiology, very knowledgeable and a great teacher. With the assistance of his capable lieutenant, Dr. Abel Moreyra, he made cardiology at Rutgers one of the more progressive specialties. When you took call on Sunday's at Raritan Valley you would typically admit four to six patients of his for cardiac catheterization on Monday. I was on call one weekend when my father paged me. He had noticed a slight flutter in his chest that morning. No chest pain, but he was startled enough to call. "Come over to the hospital," I said, "and I'll run an EKG."

It turned out he was having a lot of abnormal skipping in his heart beat called premature ventricular contractions, often a sign of serious underlying heart problems. I recalled the Millville conference and the fact that, despite his heart attack, Dad had never had a catheterization, something all but taken for granted today. Dr. Kostis was in the hospital that day and when I discussed all this with him, he reassured me, "We'll take care of him. Oh, and he'll need a catheterization."

Doctors Kostis and Moreyra became Dad's cardiologists for a long time thereafter, but the catheter revealed how extensive his heart attack was. Fully twenty percent of his heart muscle was gone, but by changing his diet, quitting tobacco, and losing weight, he was able to keep going another twenty-five years.

One of my last night's on call at Raritan Valley, an older middle-aged man came in to the ER having just suffered a massive stroke. Even without the high-tech, diagnostic tests of today we all knew his brain was in the throes of death, but his longtime wife (by common law, not marriage) came to the bedside, tears welling up, stroking his head, and calling out his name over and over. He was totally unresponsive, but her plaintive wail, as she felt the slim thread of his life slipping from her hands, was enough to pierce the most hardened heart. I stood there in silence. There was nothing I felt confident to say to her, nothing I or anyone could do but commend them into the hands of a merciful God for better or for worse. For the past thirty years, the multiplied voices of grieving loved ones have echoed in my heart, and I expect will be with me till the day I die. Being a doctor has taught me one thing if nothing else; that in the end, when all human effort has been expended and there is nothing left to give, there is God. August Toplady said it best, "…could my tears forever flow, could my zeal no respite know… Rock of ages cleft for me, let me hide myself in thee."

My wedding day was fast approaching and Doreen and I had a lot to do, so I planned to take an elective in October. You were allowed two thirty-day electives during internship. The one I chose for October was hematology. Hematology, the science of blood, is a fascinating subject. The Bible says that "The life is in the blood," and as if to certify this bold assertion, scientists long ago learned that human cells in culture will continue to live if given nothing else but a regular supply of blood. I was privileged to be able to do that elective under the renowned Chief of Hematology, Parvin Saidi.

It was good for me that I had an elective that month. It allowed Doreen and I to get our apartment together, gathering furniture, rugs, etc., all at discount prices, of course. We were married by Pastor James Miller, had a small, mostly family reception and I brought her to our apartment. In the spirit of Sir Walter Raleigh, I picked her up and carried her across the threshold, and then in the spirit of Moe, Larry and Curly, I stepped on her bridal veil and tore it in half.

We had a simple but idyllic honeymoon. I drove to Florida and we did lots of touring. We also visited my cousin, Rosemary, who had just had a baby in Charlotte, North Carolina. When we got home after a twelve day trip, I actually had a couple more days off before starting my next rotation at Muhlenberg Hospital. Like a dutiful house officer, the first chance I got, I went to see the Chief Resident at Muhlenberg to get a copy of the duty roster and call schedule, when he popped a very unpleasant surprise on me. It seemed that Muhlenberg had expected me a week earlier since no one from Raritan Valley notified them that I was on vacation. Since they had to pull an intern from another hospital to take the call assigned to me, I now owed two extra nights of call because someone didn't do their job right. The result was that across the Thanksgiving Holiday I would be working overnight every other day for a week. I could see myself so sleep-deprived that I might end up like George Reilly, a fellow house officer who fell asleep at the wheel driving home after being up all night and crashing his car, losing a leg in the process. It wasn't fair, it wasn't right, and it wasn't going to change. I was stuck.

A few days later I was called to Dr. Conn's office to be told my evaluation from Raritan Valley Hospital was so bad that I was being recommended for an additional six months of internship beyond the customary year. Dr. Hahn had gotten his revenge on me! When I came home after all this I was practically in tears. Then I complained to Doreen that she had burned the tomato sauce for dinner, and now we were both in tears. The honeymoon was over with a vengeance! All I could do was pray and ask the Lord to give me the strength to go on, to do the best job I could do and to help me overcome the obstacles I faced. And He did.

Since my last stint at Muhlenberg Hospital, the house staff's rooms were at least improved. They were now in the actual hospital building. No more dust bowl to contend with, and there actually was a TV lounge, not that there was any time to enjoy it. On the first day I met Dr. Johnson, the Chief of Medicine, a soft-spoken, kindly gentleman who put me at ease after my debacle with Dr. Hahn. Unlike Raritan Valley, here I would be mostly working with private practitioners, not medical school professors. I was teamed up again with Bill Byra. Bill was a great resident to work with. He was patient, affable, and a good teacher by example. Somewhat high strung, he could get a little unhinged if something unexpected happened, which usually did.

Muhlenberg Hospital was located in Plainfield, which was centered in the densely populated urban/suburban sprawl of northern New Jersey, an outskirt of the greater New York City metropolitan area. It serviced a large population, and as you might expect was a very busy place. Night call required two intern/resident teams to handle all the admissions.

One memorable case was a young woman who came to the ER with a rash on her face. The emergency physician diagnosed poison ivy, gave her a steroid cream and sent her home. The only problem was that it was November and poison ivy was usually gone by then. In actuality it was shingles. What he failed to take note of was that this patient was on chemotherapy for Hodgkin's disease and because her immune system had been temporarily wiped out, the shingles, a particularly nasty virus infection, flared up. On my night of call she returned to the ER, this time covered from head to toe with a blistery red rash. She looked like pictures of smallpox victims you would see in a history book, as we have today. We had to use an experimental, very toxic drug called Adenosine Arabinoside. It worked, but it was a miracle her bone marrow wasn't permanently destroyed.

One other case was not so rewarding. A morbidly obese middle-aged woman was brought to the emergency room, dehydrated and massively swollen. She apparently had recently lost her husband and had gone into a deep depression. She stopped eating and never got out of bed. She literally shut down. By the time she reached the hospital she was in pretty bad shape. Intravenous fluids were started and a nutritional assessment ordered. A psychiatrist was also called in for consultation. For some reason, however, despite all our efforts she failed to improve. Detailed examination was hampered by her enormous girth, but after some effort we located the problem. She had an enormous decubitus ulcer (bed sore) in her groin area that had become infected, and had practically eaten its way down to her internal organs. Given her massive obesity and lack of motivation to help herself, this lady's prognosis was grim. I knew I had to help her, but the situation stymied me. It was another case of solving one problem and two more arising. All my resident could do was yell at me to do a better job.

One day I sat at the bedside. The patient as always just stared up, expressionless, at the ceiling. "You know," I said, "God doesn't want you to die. He loves you and wants to help you."

Well, for the first time, she responded and looked at me with tears in her eyes. "I know," she said. "I loved my husband and now that he's gone I don't want to live anymore. I want to go to heaven to be with him."

I wasn't expecting this response, but had to admit her logic was unassailable. If I kept her alive it would only be to make me look good in morning report, and make my resident happy. It seemed wrong somehow for me to override her deepest wishes for the sake of academics. The whole concept of comfort care and hospice was well in the future. In the 1970s we were still oriented towards aggressive medical care with no exceptions. Her devotion to her late husband was humbling. After praying together I left.

Not long after that meeting, I had been reassigned to another ward of the hospital, but once, while on night call, the operator announced a code blue, indicating that someone had a sudden cardiac arrest. Upon arrival to the hospital room, I found it was that poor widowed lady. Needless to say, she never made it and was pronounced dead. When I got home the next day, as I was relating the whole story to Doreen, my emotions overwhelmed me and I dropped my head into her lap and cried like a baby.

There is no end to the variety of diseases you see as an internist. I learned the hard way never to expect the expected and to approach every patient with an open mind. A resident once told me, "Don't let anyone rush you. When you examine a patient, take as much time as you need so you don't miss something important." Good advice!

One night I was called to see someone else's patient for some minor complaint. When I entered the room it seriously smelled like a bakery. This patient had advanced cancer, and that, combined with extensive antibiotic use, allowed Candida or yeast to multiply all over her body. In medicine we call this opportunistic, that is, yeast cells took the "opportunity" of her weakened immune system to overgrow her body. A quick evaluation revealed nothing serious so I wrote a note detailing my visit and left, but the patient had a haunted look on her face I couldn't easily forget. Later that night, a code blue was called, and when we arrived at the room it was the very patient I had seen earlier in the day. She never made it. Did I miss something? As best as I or anyone could see I didn't. I supposed it was a moot point since the lady was terminal with cancer, but the whole affair left me a bit shaken.

Code blues are practically a daily occurrence in a large urban hospital and it became so easy to detach yourself from it all and not empathize with the great emotional upheaval families often felt. The day I cried in my wife's arms, I guess all the pent up feeling just let go. "I know honey, I know," she said, consoling me. "But you're so overworked, you need a break."

I did need a break, but none would be forthcoming. I still owed a couple of days of night call because of the scheduling mishap. Being on call every other night for one week was a true test of endurance. When I was twenty-six years old I just barely made it. If I did it now, I would be the next code blue.

I got off Christmas that year and Doreen and I were able to enjoy it as a married couple together, but I still had two more days of call and took one between Christmas and New Year's Eve. The trouble was, I came down with a stomach virus that day and developed a severe case of diarrhea. I was leaving the day after New Year's Eve for my new rotation at Middlesex General Hospital, so I had no choice but to work that day. And to compound the situation I was posted to ICU, the busiest ward in the hospital. *Oh woe is me*, I thought. *Lord, only you can help me now! Please don't let it be busy.* And thank God it wasn't. I had one admission during the day, but got through the entire night call without admitting one person, which was unprecedented, truly a token of God's mercy. I had to check a few minor problems in the ICU, but these were resolved quickly, allowing me to get back to the bathroom where I actually spent most of my night. By the early morning there was nothing left in me to evacuate. I got up from the commode, cleaned up, and when I reached for my pager on the shelf above the toilet it slipped out of my hand and fell in! "Oh no!" I murmured. Quickly fishing it out, I cleaned and sanitized it the best I could. By some miracle of Providence it was still working. Later that morning I handed it over to the relieving intern. The toilet incident forever remained my "dirty" little secret; that is, until now.

I had one final on call before leaving Muhlenberg Hospital, and that was New Year's Eve. Doreen wasn't feeling well and her period was late. Had she caught my virus? To be sure, I brought a urine specimen to the hospital for a pregnancy test. At dinner that evening my fellow interns bemoaned the fact that as newlyweds Doreen and I couldn't welcome in our first New Year together, but we never were party types and we did have Christmas together which, with its more spiritual significance, was our holiday of choice.

It was early evening when I checked with the lab for her urine result, and then called her at home with the news "Honey, Happy New Year, you're pregnant." Silence.

"Are you sure, could it be a mistake?" she asked.

"No. They ran it twice." More silence. We hadn't planned on this, and I knew she needed time to absorb the impact of this revelation. "Well, I have to go, being paged. I'll call you later. I love you, bye."

There were times when a page came in handy. Some hours later, at midnight, I called back to really wish her a Happy New Year and found her bawling. "We've hardly been married. It's not fair." Well, she needed a lot of hand holding, but eventually, like most expectant mothers, came to cherish the miracle of God's procreation incubating in her womb.

The final six months of internship would be at the place of my first light, Middlesex General Hospital. I narrowly missed Princeton Medical Center, the ultimate proving ground for internship, but Middlesex wasn't going to be a cake walk either. My electives were used up, so outside of five days of vacation I would be on call every third night from New Year's Day to the end of June. I decided to put a calendar up in the kitchen where I crossed out each day as it passed as if I were completing a prison sentence. Apart from this veiled gesture of contempt, I was prepared to do a good job. After all, I was still under consideration for an additional six months of training.

The rotation began as all do, with morning report. When the patient census was high, however, it was necessary for the actual change of hands to occur much earlier out of time necessity. For my first three months at Middlesex the chief resident was Tony Scardella. Tony, a fellow paisan, was a genuinely nice guy on top of being a good doctor, but he took very seriously his appointment to lead the house staff and was unsparing with us. A morning report hardly went by where he didn't ream us out for some reason or other. Again, it was all a part of the hardening process. Several faculty members were typically in attendance, presaging the hospital's future position as the core teaching facility for the medical school.

For the first time, I actually had a regular medical student of my own to tag along. One morning we went down to radiology to review some X-rays. I put the film up on the view box and began to teach the student, pointing out subtleties to look for in making a diagnosis. Dr. Finklestein happened to be standing nearby waiting for some X-rays of his own, listening attentively, then broke in, "Where did you learn so much about reading X-rays, Salsano? When you were a student with me you didn't know squat!"

I smiled back and took his comment as a high compliment, which in doctor's boot camp parlance it probably was.

There was no question, Middlesex Hospital was being upgraded to become the University Medical Center. The ER was new, although the doctors were the same, including Dr. Soto, who seemed shorter than ever. A new parking deck was being built and for the first time house officers and students were issued parking passes. The on call rooms, however, were exactly the same. One night in the dead of winter I found the only unclaimed bed, which happened to be situated under a transom window that was stuck open, and a steady stream of snow and fine ice particles was drifting down onto the bed so that half the blanket was covered with frost. I knew as a doctor I needed to get hardened, but I didn't expect to be frozen too! I mumbled some deep oath to myself then curled up on the dry side of the bed to get a quick nap, thankful, I suppose, that there was any bed at all.

There was one memory of night duty, however, that I recall fondly. New Brunswick was a city full of churches, as Dr. Wiseman had learned to his great discomfort. Whenever I had Saturday night duty and managed to get up to the residents quarters for a few hours sleep, I didn't need an alarm clock to wake me, because daybreak was always accompanied by a chorus of church bells, first one church then another. I'm sure this was an annoyance to many, but to me it was an encouragement. There is something peaceful and reassuring to awaken to church bells on a Sunday morning, as if God were saying, "Don't worry, I'm here. You can face the day because I will be there to help you." I will always remember the church bells.

Doreen's pregnancy was coming along well. I had asked Dr. Bakshi at Muhlenberg Hospital to be our obstetrician, and she was delighted. I was thinking about some kind of clinic job so I could be home with my family. Once a doctor completes his first year of residency he takes the board exam for licensure. Armed with his license, you might call him a G.P., or general practitioner. That's not true today though. As a G.P., about the best you could do was work in a government run clinic somewhere, but I didn't let the thought go entirely.

I made it, in one piece, to my last week off at the end of February. I mainly used the time to catch up on my sleep, though we did take a three-day trip to Mystic, Connecticut. The old seaport had a haunting beauty under the gray New England winter sky, and the restaurants were good and not too expensive. This latter attribute was very important, because back in 1980, as an intern, my annual income was about $15,000. And when you consider that my average work week was about 100 hours, my pay scale was around $1.50 per hour! I actually made better pay working part time in the Foodtown deli!

Working every third night continuously for six months (excluding my week off in February) was a marathon experience. The day after call you're pretty much exhausted, but can usually make it through the regular work day to get home and crash. At least, for that day, you were taken off the admission hit list since you needed time to consolidate the care of all the admissions you received the night before. The next day was okay and you almost felt normal, but by day three the whole process repeated itself.

One E.R. call involved a dope pusher fleeing the police. He was known to be in possession of several bags of heroin, but in the car chase he lost control and crashed. A detailed search could find no heroin. The young man was in critical shape in ICU on mechanical life support when days later a nurse discovered he had actually swallowed the bags when they regurgitated up from his stomach. I remember another young man distraught over financial trouble who tried to commit suicide by drinking "Pine Sol." It never came close to killing him, but scoured his lungs and brought on seizures. The half empty bottle of Pine Sol was put conspicuously on display in ICU for days after his admission.

One case that really gripped the imagination was presented at morning report. It seemed that a teenage boy, diabetic, on insulin, had broken up with his girlfriend. As he lay in bed, totally heartbroken over it, he decided life was no longer worth living, so he gave himself a massive insulin injection in a suicide attempt, but the insulin he injected had a long half-life and would take hours to kick in. As he lay there watching the clock he had a change of heart and decided that he wanted to live after all, but he didn't know how to counteract the insulin. Then he got an idea: "I'll eat a box of "Dunkin Donuts!" So he went out and bought a dozen donuts and wolfed down every last one. Now what brought him to the ER wasn't the low sugar from insulin, it was an upset stomach from the donuts. In fact, his blood sugar, when tested, was actually high. This would seem to prove that in the eternal struggle between insulin and donuts, the donut wins.

House officers, interns and residents had to always be ready for emergencies. One day a stat call came from ICU. I was the first to arrive and went to check the patient. He had an ashen gray look to his face, and his eyes were bulging as if in sheer terror. I tried to question him, but he couldn't respond, so I went to check the chart. While trying to retrieve the chart he went into a cardiac arrest. We worked to revive him for a long time, but in vain.

The autopsy later showed he died from a massive pulmonary embolism (blood clot to the lung). I still vividly recall the look on his face, sheer terror, as if I were staring face to face with death itself. "For we spend our years like a tale that's been told…and our strength fails and we fly away"(Psalms 90:9-10). Dealing with sudden death happened so often in an intern's line of work, it eventually became routine. I heard once that an intern directed a code with his white jacket on, suspended from a coat hook!

And finally, there was a patient whose name raised cries of despair from all the interns, Avery Shatz. Avery was an insulin dependent diabetic who would randomly stop his insulin, become deathly ill, be brought to the emergency room and end up being hospitalized. He actually helped us all to learn to treat diabetic emergencies, but the only problem was he always turned up at the worst possible time, just as you were going home, changing shift or wrapping up your morning's work. Everyone in the Rutgers program got a chance to treat Avery Shatz.

While all this pandemonium was going on at the hospital, I still had a pregnant wife at home who needed me. One day I got home from work and she was sitting at the kitchen table in a full blown crying jag. Nothing I said would console her. Finally, I called my mother-in-law, and asked, "Gloria, what should I do?"

She said, "Just get her out of the apartment. Take her for a ride."

So I got her in the car and drove to Princeton where we found a lovely outdoor café. We had a nice dinner under the stars, which turned out to be the perfect cure for her melancholy. One day I came home and found her leafing through my embryology textbook. "Don't worry, honey," I said. "All those scary pictures represent very rare defects."

The difference between Middlesex General and Princeton Medical Center as far as night call was that at Princeton you never slept at all but at Middlesex you managed to just doze off only to be awakened by a call from the operator. One night on call, particularly exhausted, I flopped onto the bed and fell asleep immediately, and then the phone rang. Half-dazed, I picked up the receiver. It was the operator, saying "Dr. Salsano?"

"Yes."

"Hold for a call."

This always meant the emergency room and an admission, but it was Doreen crying, "I can't feel the baby move and I saw some blood! Les, what should I do?"

"Wait…Doreen…are you in the emergency room?" (Oh my gosh, they want me to admit my own wife!)

"No, I'm home and I'm afraid the baby is dead."

Well, we prayed about it and soon she felt the familiar kicks again. The blood was probably from a moment of intimacy we had the night before. So I did two things when I got home. First, I gave her a big hug and a kiss, and then I hid that darn embryology book.

The "donut case" was hard to top, but someone did it. One quiet Saturday afternoon an elderly man was sitting in his living room, relaxed on the couch watching the ball game from his TV on the opposite side of the room. All was total peace and serenity … when suddenly a car literally came crashing through his living room wall, smashing the television set and catapulting him and everything else in the room into a jumbled heap! It turned out that the driver of the

car had suffered a stroke and lost control of the car which veered onto the elderly man's front yard and right through the front of his house. All involved par-
ties were brought to Middlesex General's ER. Remarkably, the man whose house
was demolished was unhurt and was actually sent home. However, the shock of
the event, quite undetected, had thrown his heart into a tachyarrythmia (a rapid,
chaotic heart beat), and he was brought back to the emergency room later that
evening, having now suffered a massive stroke. No Hollywood director could
have concocted a more incredible scenario. That poor man was still in the hospital months later when I completed my internship.

I had become a fixture at Middlesex Hospital during my six months there and
was paired with several different residents. At the midway point of my rotation,
I was teamed up with none other than the big guy himself, Eric Jackson. You may
recall, he and I first met when I embarrassed him at medical school orientation,
and he never let me forget it. "I was wondering what you were trying to pull back
then, Les," he said.

We worked together for a good two months. Eric actually began his internship at Mount Sinai Hospital in New York City, but I think for family reasons he
came back to Rutgers to finish his residency.

In those days we all wore short white jackets to distinguish ourselves as house
officers. Of course, no jacket was big enough to fit on Eric. When he wore his
jacket it gave all the appearance of an optical illusion, as if the jacket were reced-
ing from your view or that he was advancing toward it. Sharp-witted as ever, and
a tough customer to cross swords with, Eric certainly made the two months go
by quickly. As my senior resident he had a lot of control over my workload, and
never ceased to remind me of it. His favorite saying was, "Now, Les, you do what
I tell you, or I'll hurt you bad. I'll hurt you bad."

A lot of good natured kidding went on between interns and residents, even
to some extent between house officers and attending, but it seemed that no one
could please Dr. Kerpelman. He could be nice, as our one-time meeting in the elevator showed me, but he always seemed to be at odds with some house officer or
another. Tony Scardella, of course, had to field all the complaints and was sick of
hearing them. One time in frustration he blurted out, "Well, if you want to get
even with him, call him up and bother him at two in the morning when he and
his wife are…" (well, you know). As far as I know, no one took him up on his suggestion.

The whole Dr. Kerpelman thing reached a hilarious climax one Monday morning on the medical ward. Warren Sacks was an intern, who was a particularly laid-back individual. It seemed nothing could faze him. It so happened that he admitted one of Dr. Kerpelman's patients over the weekend, and although it was customary to be criticized by this attending for something or other, whatever Warren did, Dr. Kerpelman was beside himself with fury. Nurses and residents could hear him yelling from the other wards as he approached. "Where's Warren Sacks? I want Warren Sacks!" When he got to the main teaching ward, he started grabbing interns indiscriminately. "Are you Warren Sacks?" he would ask. The startled house officer shook his head no. He then grabbed another hapless intern, "Are you Warren Sacks?" Again the answer was no. He then set his eyes on the next victim and charged up to him, but this time it really was Warren Sacks! Dr. Kerpelman grabbed his lapels and looked him in the eye. "Where's Warren Sacks? Have you seen him?"

"No, I haven't seen him for days!" Dr. Kerpelman let him go in disgust and stormed off, leaving the nurses in stitches.

For all the noise he made, Dr. Kerpelman actually was an anomaly, for much friendly and beneficial intercourse went on between house staff and attending physicians. They taught us a lot, and our eagerness to learn stirred up renewed confidence and vigor in their own careers. Dr. Van Avery was a permanent fixture. Gary Gartenberg, newly come from Infectious Disease fellowship, was a great teacher. Matthew Morton, the peripatetic neurologist, popped in regularly, and Doctors Chinchilla, Lifshutz and many others taught us well, not to mention the growing faculty of the medical school. It was, however, without any doubt, that the great triumvirate of cardiology: Doctors Reitman, Keller and Sicherman who, outside of the full time faculty, contributed the most to the education process.

Dr. Barnes Keller was as always the most directly engaging. His EKG conferences continued to be popular for the serious learners, but he was somewhat unapproachable. An irascible nature coupled with a hectic schedule gave him a semblance of aloofness not totally deserved. Dr. Norman Reitman was the grand old man of the Middlesex Hospital medical staff. One of the first board certified internists in the state of New Jersey, he was very easy to approach, and I learned much about the practical end of being a doctor from him. Dr. Jay Sicherman was a fountain of energy and the resident's friend. A good teacher by example, he was the most interactive of the group. For some reason, I was always getting into trouble with Dr. Keller. When a patient of his had an attack of gout, I started a medicine that shot his potassium way up. He turned out to have a rare kidney disorder called Hyporeninemic Hypoaldosteronism. It was a great learning experience for me, but Dr. Keller was ticked because he had to keep the patient hospitalized a week longer than he had planned because of it. One other time I admitted his father-in-law with a slight case of heart failure. Dr. Keller warned me, "Look, Salsano, just give him a little Lasix and some oxygen. I just want to keep the wife happy." By then, however, I was intent on proving my medical abilities to him, so I got a little more aggressive with the treatment, which pushed the poor man (he was close to ninety) into azotemia, a form of kidney failure. Dr. Keller was able to send him home, but the next week I overheard him complaining to a colleague that because of my treatment, he had to make regular house calls on his father-in-law to correct the kidney problem. I made myself scarce. The worst blunder of all, however, had to be the infamous "Lukens tube" incident.

It was the end of a busy day and the beginning of night call for me when Dr. Keller had me paged. "Salsano," he said. "I'm sending over an elderly guy with an early pneumonia. He's not in too bad shape, so please, don't do anything drastic. All he needs is some antibiotic and some IV fluids. You get me?"

"Yes sir, Dr. Keller," I responded. "You can count on me. I'll take good care of him." The patient was very pleasant with a mild case of Alzheimer's disease. He was coughing, with a slight fever and a little shortness of breath. I was mindful of Dr. Keller's instructions, but after two fiascos, I thought I'd better do this one right. I had a medical student by then, and I also felt that it was important for the student to see me approach the patient academically. The first step was to obtain a good cough specimen for culture. I tried every maneuver to get one: ultrasonic nebulization, chest percussion, but nothing worked. It was almost midnight and we still were trying. "Okay," I told the student. "Let's try the Lukens tube." This ungainly device belonged more to the dawn of modern medicine than to the latter twentieth century. Basically, a rubber suctioning tube was put through the nose and down to the upper airway. Intense negative pressure was then applied to extract a specimen of sputum which was collected in a sterile glass tube for culture: the Lukens tube. But the procedure was uncomfortable, and when I did it to this demented elderly patient he went off on me. I didn't know it at the time, but he was a Polish immigrant who had served in the Polish Army in World War II, was taken prisoner by the Germans, and suffered some untold horrors while in a concentration camp. In his mind that evening, I literally became his resurrected Nazi tormenter. Nothing I did or said would calm him down. He wouldn't let anyone touch him. We were all monsters, sadists, and torturing fiends. At two in the morning, no treatment had been started and I sat at the nurse's station head in hand saying, "Now what do I do?" I had no choice but to wake Dr. Keller. With great diffidence I dialed his home. He picked up the phone sleepily. "Yeah?" he muttered.

"Dr. Keller, it's Les Salsano, I tried to get a sputum specimen with the Lukens tube on your patient, and now he's having a fit. He won't let anyone near him and he's demanding to speak with you."

A long interval of silence followed, then slowly, he answered me. "You had to use the Lukens tube, didn't you? Alright, put him on the phone."

After whatever Dr. Keller said to the patient, I'm sure his voice was reassurance enough, we were able to start treatment, but I was not, by Dr. Keller's express order, to enter his room under any circumstances. Finally he had to be sedated with a high dose of Haldol, a commonly used tranquilizer for confused elderly patients back then (we all referred to it on the wards as vitamin H). When the patient was ready for discharge, I dropped by his room to find him fully dressed with a sports coat, tie, and even a fedora on his head, lying in bed stiff as a board from all the medicine in his system.

As spring arrived, the hospital census was up and all the interns were busy. Eric was hitting me with one admission after another and I was straining to get all my work done. And then he started riding me. "Les, did you do this? Les, did you check that?"

I finally snapped back, "Give me some slack. Can't you see how much work I have on me?"

Almost expecting my outburst he fired back, "Well, you know Les, my heart bleeds for you. I mean my heart f____g (expletive) bleeds for you!" I then calmed down, since our confrontation was obviously going nowhere, and besides we had to work together that night.

It was a typically busy call with lots of admissions as well as problems on the wards. By midnight, things had settled down and I entertained a reasonable hope of getting a nap, when Eric paged me. "Les, I've got an admission for you...it's Avery Shatz."

Groan... Avery Shatz! It figured! He was back in diabetic crisis, having taken one of his regular insulin holidays. When I approached this unfortunate young man's room, I came with a real attitude. I resolved that I would talk some sense to him and put an end to the absurd ritual of constant hospitalization. "You know, Avery," I said, "you can't keep doing this to yourself. Letting your diabetes go like this is wrong. You need help. Do you know who can help you?"

I was about to make my case for a psychiatrist when he looked me in the eye and said, "Yes, I know. God." I was dumbfounded at his answer, but more than dumbfounded, I was ashamed. Of course God could help him, but I was too self-absorbed with my own immediate concerns to see it. Avery Shatz had brought me back into a proper focus.

At morning report the next day, still pondering Avery's words, I presented all the admissions from the night before, including, of course, his own. Tony Scardella was in rare form that morning. The Chief of Medicine was in attendance, which usually meant something important was in the works. I was very tired and very bored as Tony launched into his tirade. "Now everybody listen. We're having the second year students here today for physical diagnosis, and I need every one of you to give me the name and location of a patient with some interesting physical finding." He was working up to an ultimatum. I could feel it. "I know you've all got patients that are suitable, so I want their names before 9:00 A.M. and don't give me any of your s—t (expletive)!"

"Okay," I said, jumping in. "I'll give you Shatz!"

I could hear Eric's booming laughter from the back of the conference room, and then everyone else joined in. "Okay Les, if you want to do that to those poor students, go ahead." Tony tried to recover the initiative, but my riposte carried the morning. Actually I felt bad that I took advantage of him, but my excuse was sleep deprivation. Anyway, everybody needed a good laugh, myself included.

I wanted to go to Easter sunrise service that year, but I was on duty so I asked my resident if he would cover me for a few hours that morning and he agreed.

It turned out to be a very tranquil day until midnight. A woman who was overwhelmed by smoke inhalation in a house fire was brought in by ambulance. Inhaled combustion products are very toxic to the lungs. It's not so much the heat as it is the toxic chemicals released from burning plastic, paint and varnish. The mucus lining of the lung literally blisters off, and the lungs collapse like empty water balloons. I was up all night tending to this patient in critical care. By morning, we had stabilized her condition and it looked like she would survive. That was more than I could say for me.

Dr. Jerald Ansel, the new chief resident, called me to his office the next day. "Les, never take off and leave your hospital duty to someone else. When you're on duty, it's your job to be there!"

"But, I...."

"Look, no buts. I'll have to write you up if it happens again."

I took his threat seriously, especially since my diligence up to that point had led Dr. Conn to release me from the extra six months of interning, but, I thought, all I wanted to do was go to church with my wife. A leave of absence was more and more looking to me like a viable option.

Meanwhile, caring for the sick and the indigent continued unabated. I could really understand how the New Testament could say that Jesus labored far into the night healing all the sick that came to him. As long as life as we know it exists, there will be the poor and the sick. I found that, in order not to be overwhelmed, I needed to draw on the infinite resources of an infinite God.

My ICU patient admitted on Easter, the woman in the house fire, could never get well enough to come off the ventilator. We tried everything to reestablish normal breathing. One day I went into the room and she was wide awake. I asked her to breathe as hard as she could and listening to her lungs heard very good air movement. The breathing tube in her throat, however, needed to be repositioned a little, so I got a scissors to cut and re-tape it, but as I was cutting away the tape that anchored it I accidently cut the small hose that went to the balloon which held the tube in place inside her airway. Now she had to either breathe on her own or have a respiratory arrest. I held my breath and silently prayed, and thanks be to God she was breathing fine, so we did a quick extubation and she went on to a full recovery. The next day in the hospital library I was bragging about the incident to my fellow house officers. "God must have been guiding my hand when I cut that tube because it all worked to the good." Astute George Reilly was ready for me and shot back, "Are you trying to blame someone else for your sloppy work, Les?" That time the laughs were on me.

It was during the whole whirligig experience of internship that I became acquainted with the "lipstick" sign. That is, when a female patient begins applying makeup and worrying over her appearance, there was a strong correlation with a complete recovery. It happened one day that an elderly woman patient was feeling better and asked the nurse for her cosmetic bag. While passing her room during teaching rounds, our attending smiled and pointed her out. "The lipstick sign," he affirmed proudly. Well, about ten minutes later, a nurse ran up to our group to tell us that very patient had just suffered some type of seizure. We rushed back to the room to find her conscious and sitting up in somewhat of a daze. She had lipstick smeared all around her mouth and face, but ironically, none on her lips. "Well, I guess I was wrong," the attending doctor said. "She's not ready to leave the hospital yet."

I thought for a moment and said to a fellow intern, "I guess we should call this the reverse lipstick sign." And sure enough it was!

The learning in medicine never stops, nor does the endless critiquing by your peers, but that is how the conscientious doctor learns humility. One night a patient from the Rutgers Community Health Plan, a local HMO, came into the emergency room. He had been started on a diuretic, a fluid pill, a few days earlier for high blood pressure and was now having uncontrollable muscle twitching and restlessness. Laboratory tests revealed he had a critically low sodium count of 108, and was at risk for either a major convulsion or cardiac arrest. A low sodium count is not uncommon with many drugs that exert an effect on the kidney, but a count this low usually meant something else was going on (normal sodium is about 140). Upon taking a history from his wife I learned he was a recovered alcoholic, and to keep away from the bad stuff, he had taken to drinking ice water by the pitcher full. His kidneys were already being overworked when the addition of the diuretic became the last straw. To avert a seizure or worse, I had some critical decision making to do. I decided to use a risky treatment called hypertonic saline infusion, since it was the only thing that could bring his count up quickly enough to avoid a disaster. To avoid the potential complications (heart failure, brain edema), I had to carefully calculate the rate of increase of sodium in his blood. Using equations I long ago jotted down in my personal handbook for just such a circumstance, I plotted the dose and began the treatment. I personally checked on him every hour through the night and by morning his blood level had risen past the crisis point and he was in the clear.

I entered morning report confident that my successful treatment would garner the praise of my professors, but not so. Although many in attendance nodded in approval as I presented the case, one professor of medicine blasted me. "Why wasn't this patient put on Loop Diuretics? He was clearly already volume overloaded. Hypertonic saline, by its use, was putting his life at risk."

I countered that I was monitoring him closely in ICU, and that using another diuretic might worsen his already severe electrolyte imbalance. The professor, however, was not impressed. "This patient was in volume overload and proper treatment was to use a diuretic in combination with other modalities."

When morning report was over, my confidence was effectively deflated, until Dr. Jerald Ansel came up to me and said, "Don't let him get you down, Les. He wasn't there, you were. You saved that patient's life." His kind words lifted me up. "Pleasant words are like a honeycomb, sweet to the soul, and health to the bones" (Proverbs 16:24).

As my year of internship neared its close, I had a final meeting with Dr. Conn, at which time I announced my wishes to take a year off from residency to be with my family. He congratulated me on my superior record since Dr. Hahn's negative assessment, but could not bring himself to support my decision. He did, however, wish me luck in my venture. There were still several night calls to do, and still many things to learn. Eric Jackson and I were paired one last time.

It was about midway through the night and we were sitting in the ICU with the medical student by the printer terminal pretty well exhausted. As I stared blankly at the printer dashing off pages of data in seconds, I again marveled at the march of technology in just two years, then Eric snapped me out of my daze. "Do you remember when you floored Tony Scardella with your Avery Shatz comment?" he asked. (For some reason that episode had really gotten to him.) "Let's have some fun with the hospital operator." He picked up the phone and dialed, "Operator, please page Dr. Avery Shatz to the ICU."

We waited a minute and sure enough the intercom blared, "Dr. Avery Shatz, please call ICU." A few minutes later he tried again. "Please call, Dr. Shatz, stat!" And again the operator blared, "Dr. Avery Shatz! Dr. Avery Shatz! Please call ICU, stat!"

Eric, the medical student and I got a big laugh out of it, but the nursing supervisor who was watching us sure didn't. "You know, that's improper use of critical hospital personnel. I'm going to have to write you up."

Eric, who always had a maverick quality to his nature, just blew it off. "She's just a nine-to-fiver (not totally true), and has no appreciation for the stress we all work under (almost certainly true). It's important for everyone to unwind once in a while." (Boy, did I think, amen to that.) I never found out if Eric did get in trouble with the administration, but having been there, and done that, and survived, I was pretty certain he would too.

After almost one year as a full-fledged medical doctor, I was beginning to feel confident in treating illness. One time I shared with Dr. Sicherman how what once was a mystery to me I now had mastered. "That's right, Al," he said. "When you finally learn it, it all makes sense." Of course, no sooner did I make that boast than my one and only case of polyarteritis nodosa came in and I was right back to square one.

In one area, the area of cardiopulmonary resuscitation, all interns quickly became master practitioners because we did it practically every day. In a typical hospital cardiac arrest residents ran the code while interns did chest compressions, although often roles were switched. One day, a patient coded on the regular hospital ward and we responded. Most of the time the patient was totally unresponsive, but not this time and it was extremely unnerving, for when heart compressions stopped, the patient was unresponsive, but when they were resumed he partially regained consciousness and began to frantically flail and grasp. I remember as if it happened yesterday his reaching up and grabbing my jacket briskly even as I pumped on his chest to save his life. In the end he didn't make it, but the incident left me feeling the closeness of death as if I were grappling in hand-to-hand combat with a mortal enemy. There's no question that the practice of Internal Medicine often aspired to melodrama of the highest order, but after one riotous year, I was ready for a break!

Doreen was almost to the end of pregnancy and I believed it was important for me to have a regular job once the baby was born. In ancient Israel, Moses decreed the custom that a newlywed husband would not be required to serve in the Army for an entire year, so as to be available to his new family at the onset. The U.S. Public Health Service was looking for a medical officer for their Staten Island Hospital day clinic. I applied and got the job with a modest income at first of $27,000 annually, but no nights or weekends. When I got my license and wrapped up internship, I bid Rutgers farewell, but not forever.

What a change it was for me! A regular day job, with no weekends, no night call, and reasonably good pay (certainly better than my below minimum wage intern's salary), it seemed too good to be true, and it was. Society does not invest so heavily in the perfecting of its health care practitioners to squander their talents in a nine-to-five job. Doctoring, in the end, still meant being available at night, on weekends, in an emergency, like it or not. But I was determined to at least have my year away from it.

Doreen and I had taken an apartment in Highland Park, New Jersey, across the river from the main Rutgers campus. The U.S. Public Health Service Hospital was on Staten Island, New York, a mere forty minute ride barring traffic mishaps. The hospital was built on a gentle bluff overlooking the Lower New York Bay not far from the majestic Verrazano Narrows Bridge spanning the waters to Brooklyn. My official title was Ambulatory Care Officer.In other words, I was a day clinic doctor, which in a federally subsidized facility meant I would see anyone and everyone who walked through the doors. The ride to the hospital was pleasant. Staten Island is the forgotten borough of New York City and in many places it was downright picturesque, although in some areas the squalor of a large urban enclave was evident. The U.S. Public Health Service Hospital on Vanderbilt Avenue and Bay Street was a stately old edifice from the early twentieth century. It was known locally as the Marine Hospital because for much of its existence it served the Naval and Merchant fleet's health needs, especially those stemming from Marine disasters. It had a nice grassy campus to lunch on and a lovely view of the lower New York Harbor. Once inside the hospital, however, it was medicine as usual. The uninsured sick and homeless of New York's teeming masses were at our door if they were willing to make the ferry ride over from Manhattan. We also continued to care for the Merchant Marine as the hospital had done since the early days of World War ll and for the active duty military personnel from all over the greater New York City area.

The Merchant Marine was a particularly rewarding group to care for. These men, often after six months at sea, would arrive in port and check-in for their health needs. They were a hearty group, friendly and well-mannered, at least to their doctors. They knew they were getting free health care, and to show their appreciation they would often bring exotic gifts from overseas and present them to the medical staff. I still have a wall mounting of two South American moths, simply huge, that regularly draws the admiration and wonder of patients and other visitors to my office.

Having a child opened up a whole new stage of life for me, and Doreen had our first child, a girl, on August 17, 1980, not two months after starting my new job. We named her Leah, after Jacob's first wife in the book of Genesis (not after Princess Leia, the "Star Wars" character, as I had to constantly remind people). Her hair was so red when she delivered, everyone gasped because she appeared to be covered with blood.

The summer Leah was born was truly a summer of change for me. First, of course, was my departure from residency. Most people considered it a foolhardy move that would ruin my career, but I was determined to follow my convictions. Besides, the Marine Hospital had a residency program of its own, and I might be able to complete my training there. Second, I now was able to fulfill a longtime aspiration, to become an active member of the Gideon International Bible Society.

When God became real to me as a college student at Rutgers, I was given a

Gideon Bible which I signed and dated, June 30, 1975, my second birthday with the Lord. Later that summer, a Gideon named Dave Hillman gave a presentation at First Baptist Church Metuchen and when he mentioned the Bible distribution at Rutgers, I excitedly waved my green Gideon Bible so high he couldn't help but see me. After the service he promised me that upon graduation he would hand me an application personally. He did, but internship effectively delayed my active participation another year, and now with my new job I was ready to get started. It was refreshing to meet regularly with a group of adult men for prayer and Bible reading, and to take part in the spreading of the gospel of Jesus Christ.

Well, it so happened that on a certain Sunday in August I was to meet a fellow Gideon at a local church to give my testimony. Doreen had been having some abdominal cramps for several days which were diagnosed as false labor, so I felt it would be safe to leave her that morning for a short while, but when I got back, my sister-in-law was there and my wife was in full-blown labor. I called Dr. Bakshi and rushed her to Muhlenberg Hospital. Leah was born about 7:30 P.M., with Dr. Bakshi commenting that it was nice to deliver a baby at a reasonable hour for a change. We were thankful to God for a healthy child and a safe delivery, but were caught off guard by the next challenge; colic.

For four months we waged a constant struggle with broken sleep, formula changes and inconsolable crying, but as unheralded as it appeared this brief return to the fray of internship departed.

By the time of Leah's birth I was settling in at my new job. It was in the Public Health Service that I began to display what many felt was my strength: the ability to communicate to my patients. Because of it people started to ask for me in particular when signing in at the clinic. In fact, most of the doctors in the ambulatory clinic were competent and we all had to work as a team to be able to see the large volume of patients who came through the door.

I really enjoyed my work at the Marine Hospital, but with a new baby and a family to support, I decided to join the commissioned corps of the U.S. Public Health Service, the uniformed service. This obscure branch of the military was created in the early years of our nation's history by President John Adams as a medical division to aid in the care of military and marine casualties. It still is active today in disaster relief, most notably recently as part of the federal response to Hurricane Katrina. My income in the Corps was better than in the civil service and for the one and only time in my life I actually had a military rank. I was a first lieutenant (the Public Health Service followed the Navy ranking system). It was a two-year commitment so I was distancing myself further from completing residency, although as it turned out, God had other plans. For the time being anyway, I now had the privilege of access to military facilities and military benefits. We often shopped on base (usually Fort Monmouth, New Jersey). Since I never spent time in the military (I just missed being drafted into the Vietnam War), I had to learn to salute the guards and not just wave at them.

Doreen and I both voted for Ronald Reagan for president that year (1980), contributing to his landslide victory with the high hopes he could turn things around in the country. As history proved, he certainly did, but ironically for me, one of the first things he did was to slash the Public Health Service budget and cancel my job! Of course, none of that seemed to matter at the time. My income was adequate to sustain our modest lifestyle, and we had time to spend together, taking the baby for a stroll in the park or on a weekend ride into the country. It was all so idyllic. I was able to be actively involved in the Gideon Ministry and even took part in a Bible distribution at Rutgers much like the one that had made such an impact on my young life. Being on the distributing end, however, I was able to appreciate the incredible antipathy to biblical faith when by the end of the day the grounds were covered and the litter baskets full with bibles indifferently cast away as worthless. Saint Paul could not have been more accurate when he told us that "The preaching of the cross is foolishness to them that perish" (1 Corinthians 1:18).

Back in Staten Island there was no end to the unusual patients I saw. The entire spectrum of large city denizens paraded through our clinic all imbued with the legendary New York City uniqueness and toughness. One man came in with an enormous ulcer engulfing practically his entire leg below the knee from poor circulation and equally poor hygiene. It was draining copious amounts of pus and smelled awful, but on closer inspection, to my astonishment, I saw in the crater of the wound dozens of maggots crawling about. Another patient, a young Vietnam veteran, was covered from head to toe with a mass of scar tissue nodules. He reminded me of pictures of small pox survivors. In reality he had been shot in Vietnam, not with a lead bullet, but one made of nickel, that being the only metal available to the Vietcong. It turned out he was allergic to nickel (the same thing that makes people react to cheap costume jewelry), but in his case the allergic reaction rifled through his entire body.

I remember well a cold day in late March, 1981. I was on my way into work, running late that day, when the air waves erupted with a bulletin that President

Reagan had been shot. John Hinckley came close to killing the new President that day. Months later I spoke to a house officer, who was on duty at George Washington University Hospital at the time, who said that when President Reagan arrived in the E.R. he had lost so much blood he was pale as a sheet and in shock with a collapsed lung. It was a testimony to his physical fortitude that he was able to recover so quickly. The only other thing I remember from that day was how a young Muslim patient in the clinic was convinced that Reagan was the Antichrist, having come back to life. And around the Marine Hospital at that time there were a lot of employees inclined to agree, as the budget cutting measures were beginning to take effect. It was very surreal. You couldn't get tests done; people didn't answer their phones, hospital staff were running back and forth in seeming mass confusion.

For me the choice was to stay in the commissioned corps and be transferred to an Indian Reservation or to resign and go back to residency. I wasn't sure if Rutgers would take me back, so I looked into several other programs, like Morristown Memorial Hospital and Nassau Hospital on Long Island, but everywhere the directors were suspicious of my motives for leaving residency in the first place. It seemed pointless to explain my spiritual convictions about family. It was universally assumed I was a quitter and unreliable. So Doreen and I prayed and one day it dawned on me; go talk to Dr. Conn, maybe he can help you.

Dr. Hadley Conn received me warmly, and after I related my Public Health Service experience to him he calmly assured me he'd be able to open up a residency position for me. My gratitude to him was not expressible in words. I guess the teacher in him saw something in me that showed promise, so as if by divine appointment I was back in the Rutgers fold.

Chapter Five

Residency and Starting My Career

――――――⌘――――――

"When I was a man I put away childish things."

1 Corinthians 13:11

After the helter skelter of the last months at the Marine Hospital it felt good to have a secure position again, but I was bracing myself for another round of sleepless nights and long weekends. It was amazing the transformation that had taken place in one year. Raritan Valley Hospital was closed down permanently. Middlesex General was now the university Hospital of Rutgers Medical School. Its bed capacity was greatly increased, and now there was a large parking garage adjoining the hospital. No more trudging down slushy side streets past twelve-foot high snow drifts. Even the on call rooms were now actually fit to sleep in, although the house officers rarely got a chance to use them (at least one thing hadn't changed). Because of this expansion at Middlesex it was no longer necessary to rotate residents through the various community hospitals, but Princeton Medical Center remained in the program, and continued to be the baptism of fire for the medical interns.

There were many new faces for me to meet when I arrived for my first day at Middlesex Hospital, and many old familiar faces, too. I also recognized several of my former students, who would now be working with me as interns over the next twelve months. Most of the faculty was the same. The new chief of medicine at Middlesex was Dr. Norman Edelman, former chief of pulmonology (lung disease) at the medical school, who now presided over morning report with his associate professor, Dr. Marie Trontell. He greeted me by name. I figured I had acquired some kind of good reputation. Cliff Lacy was now chief resident and brought his good natured temperament and insight to every morning report. Tony Scardella was still around, having advanced to a Pulmonary Fellowship, and had seriously mellowed out now that the administrative burden was off his shoulders.

The experiences of residency were not as sharp and intense as during internship. For starters, you had more elective time and less night call, and subsequently your interaction with the patients was not as direct nor as intense. The second year is a time when the budding physician perfects the skills he learned as an intern, and expands his knowledge and expertise in patient care. It took me a few weeks to get readjusted, but once over that hurdle it actually felt good to be back. I now was fully committed to forging ahead to the completion of my training and beginning my medical career.

I missed being with my wife at night, a fact with which many could commiserate. My tour of duty required me to do four months at Princeton Medical Center starting just before Christmas, and I was anxious to do it as a kind of personal vindication of my desire to get back in the swing of things.

Meanwhile at Middlesex General, I reacquainted myself with the various attending physicians, both new and old. Most prominent among the new doctors were the faculty neurologists, led by Dr. Roger Duvoisin, a nationally renowned authority on Parkinson's disease. Under his tutelage I learned much about that once obscure disorder of movement. All the intern-residents' teams had at least one of his patients on their service at any one time.

The science of cardiology was undergoing revolutionary changes in the early 1980s and the concept of acute intervention was becoming firmly established. This is the decision to abort an acute heart attack right from the start using potent intravenous drugs and invasive procedures to prevent or minimize damage to the heart muscle.

One Monday morning after a weekend off, I met my intern on the wards. He had been on call Sunday night and he gave me a rundown of all the new patients. One patient he had not seen yet had been admitted with chest pain. In the emergency room, his EKG was okay so he was sent to a regular bed for some non-emergent evaluation. Something told me to go see him first.

When I arrived at the room, the patient was pale and in a cold sweat. I ordered a stat EKG which now showed he was having a massive heart attack. I immediately called Dr. Burns, the faculty cardiologist, and we got the patient ASAP into the cath lab for coronary angiography. Dr. Burns found the blocked artery and successfully opened it, limiting dramatically the degree of damaged heart muscle. The next day in morning report he presented the case. "This man had occluded the main artery to his heart," he commented. "We used to call this type of heart attack 'The Widow-Maker.'"

By the next day, he was sitting up in bed eating breakfast in total serenity. By looking at him, one would never have suspected his close brush with death had ever occurred.

Modern technology has enabled educated men and women of high degree to perform unheard of surgeries, crack the genetic code, clone organisms and probe the very mysteries of life. But a doctor, in the true sense of the word, places the saving of life and the relief of human suffering ahead of fame, wealth and intellectual pursuit. "The fear of the Lord is the instruction of wisdom. And before honor is humility" (Proverbs 15:33).

Although the medical school faculty was becoming more and more dominant at Middlesex General Hospital, the residents still worked closely with the private attending on many of their patients. Dr. Chinchilla was a fixture at Middlesex.

One morning, after a busy night on call, I was telling my intern about how much I was looking forward to the day I could finally catch up on my sleep. When he overheard my comment, Dr. Chinchilla quietly said with the force of conviction, shaking his head, "You never catch up!" To the validity of that statement I present the last twenty-five years of my life as irrefutable evidence.

Apart from the shared loss of sleep and house staff camaraderie, interns and residents had quite divergent experiences. The focus of an intern's training is hands-on patient care, but as a second year resident you start honing your leadership skills, which are crucial to practicing good medicine. I had the opportunity to work with several good interns during my residency, but by far the most memorable had to be John Bleiweiss.

John was a good-natured, enthusiastic young doctor. His one fault was that his enthusiasm would often spin out of control, leading to unnecessary and fanciful testing and treatment. This overzealousness, unchecked by caution, would invariably draw criticism from his superiors like a lightning rod. Never had I known someone who was in such constant trouble with the attending physicians. After residency, John and I never met again, but in researching for this book, I was saddened to learn of his tragic premature death after establishing himself for many years as a caring physician in the state of New Jersey.

As I said before, cardiac catheterization and acute cardiac intervention were, in the early 1980s, revolutionizing the way we treat the number one killer in America, cardiovascular disease. As a consequence of this, Internal Medicine residency at the time was heavily weighted with cardiology training. Dr. Sicherman and his associates, Drs. Reitman and Keller, were known as non-interventional cardiologists, meaning they did not perform catheterizations, which in their day was not a part of the standard cardiologists training. It reminded me of an infectious disease specialist's answer when challenged that his specialty did not include a high-tech procedure. "Yeah," he said, "I guess we just have to use our heads." Such cardiologists as these were excellent teachers simply because they taught us to use our heads. Another great teacher was Dr. Gerald Weisfogel, who was the acknowledged local expert on EKG interpretation. He also was a young, eligible bachelor. The story goes that one time he stormed into the ICU saying, "Okay. Where is it? Has anybody seen it?"

The "it" he was frantically searching for turned out to be a little black book which according to one of the interns had all his important names and phone numbers, including several young women kept "on the hook." Upon finding the book, his relief could scarcely be exceeded by that of successfully rescuing a critically ill patient.

Of course Dr. Barnes Keller, the quintessential teacher, continued to instruct us in his own irascible way, and Dr. Norman Reitman dispensed his kernels of wisdom to those with ears to hear. One time, as I recall, we had a patient of his come in with chest pain. We ran every test in the book and attempted several medication trials, to no avail. The cause of the pain simply eluded us. So Dr. Rietman came in one day to see the patient and after hearing our report and assessing the situation he simply said, "You know what I'm going to do for his chest pain? I'm going to send him home."

He added that often, inexplicable cases of chest pain go on to develop into shingles, so always watch for the development of a blistering rash in the area of pain. I have made the diagnosis of shingles many times in this way, so Dr. Rietman was absolutely correct. On another occasion he was in a more reflective mood.

One evening, the intern medical student and I sat with him at the nurses' station, discussing the advances in medicine and the new technologies that were changing the way we practice. Dr. Rietman related to us a meeting he once had with a radiologist friend. As they sat in his colleague's office making pleasant conversation, Dr. Rietman noticed on the desk a stethoscope inside a jar with a sign over it, "Obsolete Medical Equipment." "Norm," he said, "Pretty soon our X-ray machines will be able to tell us things about the heart your exam could never uncover." How he answered him we weren't told, but Dr. Rietman, his eyes widening as a sign of his earnestness said to us, "What my radiologist friend said may be true, but when a doctor enters a patient's room and puts his stethoscope on the patient's chest, something unique happens. A bond of trust forms between you and your patient that no technology can duplicate." What a profound statement! Such talk could easily be dismissed as meaningless hyperbole if it came from anyone else, but coming from a man who practiced what he preached for some forty years of his life, they were words ringing with truth. To this day I have carried Dr. Rietman's vision with me, and have made it my own. I will be ever grateful to him for teaching me to be a real doctor.

The second year resident on night call continues in his capacity as supervisor of care. The ER will typically call you first. A quick assessment is done on your part, and when you determine the patient's need for admission you call the intern. After his admission exam you sit down together and discuss the plan of care. Of course this whole process varies greatly depending on the intern's level of training, his current workload, and the severity of the patient's illness. There are times when the resident physician will totally manage the case, at least during the acute stage.

One night I was called to see a patient, a young man brought in by the paramedics in a deep coma. Evidently he had been driving his car with some friends when he pulled over complaining that he felt "funny." He sat down on the side of the road and passed out. In the emergency room, he was completely unresponsive. Several etiologies were ruled out including carbon monoxide poisoning. I ordered a CAT scan STAT.

It was three A.M. That meant that X-ray personnel had to rush to the hospital to perform the test. I also put a page in for Dr. Matt Morton, the neurologist. I was extremely anxious, given the youthfulness of the patient. When he called back, I hastily grabbed the phone. "Dr. Morton, I've got a young guy here...who passed out...maybe a brain hemorrhage or something. My exam..."

I went on somewhat rambling when he broke in, saying "Calm down, Salsano! You sound like a f____g (expletive) patient!" He then said he would call in a neurosurgeon. So about thirty minutes later there we were: myself, the intern and the surgeon in the CT scanning suite, waiting for the pictures to be developed, and as they came out we could clearly see that they were...normal! The surgeon stormed off hurling epithets. Now what? A spinal tap would have to be done to rule out meningitis, but by then it was morning and I turned over care to the day team. It turned out that the patient eventually awoke, and all the tests were negative. I believe the final diagnosis was "hysterical coma."

Although he could be a bit abrasive at times, Dr. Morton was an excellent neurologist, and until Dr. Duvoisin joined the Rutgers faculty, he was practically the only neurologist we knew. No matter which hospital you were at: Middlesex, Raritan Valley or Princeton, he was the man you consulted. I can still see him now, bone thin, walking down the hospital corridor, black bag in hand, sucking on a lollipop. Once at Princeton Medical Center, I called him to discuss an adult patient who had an unprovoked first time seizure. All the tests, including the CAT scan, were negative. "Matt, what do we do?" I asked.

"Run a Mono test" was his answer in his flute-like voice, and sure enough it came back positive. The patient had developed Mononucleosis Encephalitis. I later asked him how he knew it was mono. "Because I'm a f_____g (expletive) genius, that's how!"

Okay, I thought, don't ask that question again.

By November I was ready for an elective, so I took Infectious Diseases. Starting in December I would be spending four months at Princeton and I wanted to get a good thirty days of rest before starting the ordeal. Like cardiology, the specialty of infectious diseases was poised on the brink of some revolutionary changes. The halcyon days of the wonder drugs, penicillin and streptomycin, were over. Bacterial resistance was on the rise, in spite of ever newer and stronger antibiotics. Strange new infectious illnesses were making their appearance, like Lyme disease, MRSA (pronounced Mersa), and Legionnaire's Disease, to name a few. And then, there was a yet unnamed illness which portended very ominous tidings for the future.

As early as the mid-1970s, cases of people with immune systems weakened for no obvious reason began appearing, mostly in major metropolitan areas. Healthy young adults, mostly men, were presenting to emergency rooms with previously little known conditions such as Pneumocytis Carinii Pneumonia and Kaposi's Sarcoma. Around this time I was called to the ER to evaluate a patient who had developed an allergic reaction to the sulfa antibiotic he had recently been given for pneumonia. I wasn't sure what to make of it since sulfa drug was not a typical antibiotic used anymore to treat lung infections. Plus, he was on six times the usual recommended dose. The patient was a homosexual and he did not want to stay in the hospital, so I sent him home. The next day in morning report, Dr. Melvin Winestein, head of Infectious Diseases, told me he was the one who started the antibiotic in the day clinic, based on medical reports of Pneumocystis, a hitherto rare parasite, found to be causing pneumonia in homosexual men in increasing frequency. Of course this mystery illness, which we now call AIDS, was at the root of all this, but at the time medical science was at a loss for answers. We were all like children blindfolded, trying to pin the tail on the donkey.

Before I completed my residency, this deadly viral infection had acquired a name, and an increasingly dark reputation to go with it.

So I wound up my rotation at Middlesex General Hospital. I enjoyed Infectious Disease and one day on rounds I mentioned to the professor a word I happened to encounter recently in a crossword puzzle. "So, how about ague?" I asked.

"Ague?" he asked, laughing. He kept laughing so intensely I began to blush with embarrassment. The day before I left for Princeton there was a sign on his office door "Word of the Day – Ague" (which means high fever, by the way).

I started my Princeton rotation in December, and had put a request in four months earlier for the Christmas holiday off, so you can imagine my utter dismay when I found myself scheduled for on call duty right on Christmas Eve. The acting chief resident was no help whatsoever, so I frantically tried to find someone who would be willing to swap call.

The Rutgers residency was the epitome of cultural diversity. But whether Jews, gentiles, Hindus, Muslims, Buddhists, agnostics or atheists, it didn't make a difference! Whoever I asked wanted Christmas off. Christmas had been stripped of all spiritual significance. It had become the world's holiday.

The next day as I complained to my peers about pulling duty on this day, I was consoled with reassuring words, "Don't worry, it's Christmas. It'll be slow. No one wants to be in the hospital on Christmas." But Dr. Trontell, the Assistant Chief of Medicine and herself a recent graduate of the Rutgers Pulmonary Fellowship Program, spoke otherwise. "Brace yourself. Christmas Eve can be one of the busiest days on the schedule."

Deep inside I knew she was right, but when I approached my wife with the bad news I encouraged her, "Don't worry, no one wants to be in the hospital on Christmas."

Princeton Medical Center was in the process of renovation just like Middlesex General, although on a lesser scale. It was, however, pretty much as I remembered it from three years before. I was privileged to work with an extraordinary group of interns at Princeton. There was Kevin Murray, with whom I would soon share my legendary Christmas Eve call, and Rick Guarino, a bright and dedicated former student of mine. John Bleiweiss was there, still a fountain of enthusiasm, but a bit more circumspect, and there was Bob Copeland. Bob was a great guy. He was smart and very conscientious. He also was a born again Christian and because of that we forged a special friendship during our time together at Princeton. Bob was black and never ceased to refer to his intern-resident grouping as the A-team, he being of course the Mr. T character. Bob was single and eligible.

Christmas Eve arrived and I left early for the hospital with Doreen and the baby both still fast asleep. Dr. Trontell's prophecy was about to be fulfilled, for even as I walked through the hospital doors, emergencies were awaiting me. Kevin Murray and I quickly reconnoitered, then he went off to take care of his current charges and I went to the emergency room. In all, we had twelve admissions that day, eleven of which were critical. Kevin and I met once at 10 PM in the snack bar (for dinner). The rest of the day and night was taken up by non-stop patient care.

Since time immemorial, essential services personnel like doctors, nurses, police, fire and rescue workers have tried to eke out some holiday cheer when on the job. At Princeton that year the ICU and CCU nurses all pitched in to make a wonderful potluck Christmas dinner to which house officers were cordially invited, but sad to say, it was the potluck that never happened. *Poor nurses!* I thought. They tried so hard by preparing a nice spread for us. Poor Kevin Murray, who had doubled his patient load overnight. Only insiders in the world of patient care, and their long suffering spouses, can truly understand the dedication and self-sacrifice that goes into the job of caring for the sick.

When I reminisce on such things, I cannot help but be scornful of the tassel-shoed personal injury lawyers and the outrageously paid insurance executives who parasitically feed off the true laborers in the field of medicine, the health care workers. This is a feeling I am constantly asking God's forgiveness for indulging, because I know that if I allow bitterness to take root in my heart, then I have lost the spiritual battle of life. "Lest any root of bitterness springing up trouble you, and thereby defile many" (Hebrews 12:15).

I was glad to get the holidays behind me that year. Princeton upheld its reputation as a busy regional hospital. One month, John Bleiweiss and I were paired up again and we actually worked well together. I had learned that a good resident looked out for the interests of his intern, but one time I goofed, ironically to the ultimate good of the patient. It was an older woman who had an unwitnessed blackout at home. In the emergency room her work up was negative, and I was called in. The lady had a history of alcohol abuse and had suffered several such falls over recent months. I reviewed the case with John. "You know, these people often hit their heads in a fall and are at risk for subdural hematomas (a type of brain hemorrhage) and are prone to seizures. Maybe her blackout was a seizure. Let's order a CAT scan of her brain." John agreed and went off to get things started. Our attending that month was Dr. Ken Goldblatt, a good physician, but a little high strung himself. He knew all about John's reputation for impetuosity, and unknown to me had put him on notice not to make any major clinical decisions without his approval. When he found out that John was ordering the CAT scan without his consent, he charged right over to the ER, took him into the conference room and blasted him royally. I sat at the nurses' station speechless and a little embarrassed as we all could hear Dr. Goldblatt's tirade. At one point I really believe I felt the countertop shake. "Well," I said, "I think I'd better get going." I slinked out of the ER to attend to my other duties. As it turned out, the patient, shortly after that confrontation, had a full-blown seizure right in front of everyone. And sure enough, the CAT scan did show a large subdural hematoma. John was vindicated, if a little wrung out.

The hospital library was the universal gathering place for residents on break and Princeton Medical Center had an excellent one. One day I arrived there for some repose and quiet contemplation when I noticed displayed prominently on the checkout desk a beautifully illustrated hard bound copy of Chaim Potok's Book "Wanderings, A History of the Jewish People from their Ancient Origins up to Modern Times." I had always enjoyed history, and my biblical world view naturally drew me to any book about ancient Israel and the Jews. It was fascinating reading, replete with exquisite photos and reproductions of biblical themes. Moses and the Exodus, the Babylonian exile, Judas Maccabee, the Roman Period, all wonderful accounts of God's faithfulness and the preservation of the Jewish nation. But then, the story turned to the medieval and modern eras and for the first time in my life I came face to face with the ugly specter of Christian anti-Semitism. I shared with you already how racism of any kind was alien to my upbringing thanks to my father's egalitarianism, but now I had to rationalize the unrepentant hatred for the Jewish people by those who shared my Christian faith throughout the ages. How strange, I thought, to hate the very people from whom Jesus Christ, who you worshiped, sprang. It was fruitless to brand all these people as non-believers. Some, like Martin Luther, were pillars in the history of Christianity. As I was beginning to see it, the real issue was human pride. Everyone has it, but a Christian, if he is to walk in the footsteps of his Savior, must repudiate it. When our self-esteem is threatened we instinctively react in anger and fear at whatever perceived enemy we see. For over a thousand years the Jews were forced to develop the skills needed to survive in a universally hostile world, but their ability to endure and to prosper incurred the envy of their gentile Christian neighbors. Many, though not all, responded in anger at this, and any positive witness of their faith was drowned in negativism. Jesus spoke very emphatically when he said, "If your eye be evil your whole body will be full of darkness…And how great is that darkness…Be sure that the light in you is not darkness" (Luke 11:34, 35). There is really no room in a Christian life for anti-Semitism or for hatred of any kind. "God is love," said John the Apostle, "And he that dwells in love, dwells in God, and God in him" (1 John 4:16). This all certainly called for some deep introspection. As Dr. D. James Kennedy once asked, "Christian, are you part of the problem, or are you part of the solution?"

The Princeton experience was an important part of our training at Rutgers. It was important to learn how to be very busy but still make clear-minded therapeutic decisions. When the operator announced overhead a code blue, you dropped whatever you were doing and ran to the scene of the event.

One early morning at the end of night call, the intern and I were just sitting down to have breakfast in the hospital cafeteria when a code blue was called in the surgical ICU. Upon reaching the ICU we found that the surgeons had matters well in hand, which was just as well, since I was too out of breath from running up the stairs to give orders anyway. Of course by the time we got back to the cafeteria, the kitchen staff had disposed of our uneaten food.

At Princeton I was to receive a sharp lesson in professional protocol and Dr. Harvey Rothberg would be my teacher. It happened that while on night duty I got a call from Dr. Rothberg. "Dr. Salsano," he began, "I'm sending a patient over to the ER with chest pain. Admit him for me and I'll see him in the morning. I have a terrible cold tonight, and I know you'll take good care of him."

"Yes sir," I said. "I'll look after him."

When the patient arrived I was called to the emergency room to make my evaluation. The first thing, of course, was to run an EKG, and as I stood there watching the readout my eyes widened in horror. This man was having a massive heart attack right before my eyes. I looked at his chart. He was barely fifty years old, and as if to crown the irony of the situation, he was my mother's boss at GAF Industries! His last exam was unremarkable. When I explained to Dr. Rothberg what was taking place, he simply assured me he would have a cardiologist see the patient first thing in the morning. Now it was three A.M., and that patient wasn't just having a "slight" heart attack. His EKG was showing M-Waves, also known by the house staff as "Tombstone Waves" because of the high mortality rate associated with them. The main artery to his heart was occluded with a clot and probably half his heart muscle was in danger of dying. I knew this man's life hinged on my making the right decision. Back in the early 1980s, very few hospitals, mostly university centers, were equipped to perform acute cardiac interventions. I began making phone calls first to Rutgers, then to Temple University in Philadelphia. The story was the same: intracoronary streptokinase (clot dissolver), the treatment of choice, was only available on a very limited basis, even at the university level, providing the patient was even stable enough to be transported there. I called Dr. Rothberg again, "Sir, this patient is going to die if we don't get him to a university hospital for thrombolytic therapy. He's having a massive heart attack!"

"Alright," he said, reluctantly. I could hear the irritation in his voice. "I'll be there shortly."

When he arrived at the hospital bedraggled and coughing from his head cold, I summarized my findings. He told me, "Dr. Salsano, this patient isn't going anywhere. I expect you to take care of him right here. I will have a cardiologist see him in the morning, and that's final!" I was properly chastened and did as he asked. And much to Dr. Rothberg's satisfaction, the patient had an amazingly uneventful hospital course, and went home in pretty good shape. Yet in one week he was dead. We were all surprised to hear this, myself included. Apparently, he got up from dinner one evening and told his wife he felt tired and went to the couch to lie down. He never got up. In retrospect, an acute cardiac intervention, if available, would have saved his life. Unfortunately for this gentleman, he had his heart attack about two years too soon. Yet Dr. Rothberg had followed a time honored principle of medical care, enshrined in the medical-legal justice system known as the "accepted standard of care." A doctor is only called upon to carry out his duty as the expected standard of his day dictates. Engaging in untried therapies may put the patient in jeopardy. In the end, a physician can only do what he can do. The ultimate outcome, whether life or death, must reside in the providence of Almighty God.

My riotous four months at Princeton ended and I was back at Middlesex General to finish my final two months of second year residency. Money was tight. It was ironic that in my final year of training when I could look forward to rest and refreshment, I now was committing myself to two nights a week working in a nearby hospital emergency room. Again, up all night, again separated from my family, although at least this time actually being paid for it.

I had two more months to go though, and they did pass quickly. My most poignant memory from that interlude was of an emergency room case that came in late one Sunday evening.

An older man who had suffered a long time from major depression had recently been sent home from the psychiatric hospital. Though pronounced cured, his wife had seen him relapse many times into suicide attempts. Though worried, but with the psychiatrist's blessing, she went to the city for the day. Upon arriving home, her greatest fear had been realized; her husband had asphyxiated himself in the garage with carbon monoxide. He was essentially dead on arrival and it was my job to tell the family.

As I approached his wife in the waiting room, I could see she was an attractive and well-to-do older woman. I will never forget the look on her face when I announced that her husband had died. It mingled utter dismay with undiluted horror. I knew she felt deep pangs of guilt over leaving him alone that day, and her grief was beyond conciliation.

No one ever chooses to be a part of human tragedy, but it is in the partaking of those moments of deep despair, in commiseration with your fellow travelers, that you develop a wonderful gift; the gift of compassion: "Because His compassions fail not, they are new every morning. Great is your faithfulness" (Lamentations 3:22).

So the second year ended. There were some moments of extreme tragedy like the suicide just mentioned, and moments of lightness like Dr. Agin's reaction to the word "ague." And of course there were moments when the serious and the silly mingled together. One such time happened when a patient had a sudden cardiac arrest in ICU. More than usual, there was mass pandemonium with different house officers calling out different orders. No one was in charge. Unfortunately, the patient didn't make it, and there were questions about the wrong medicine having been given. When Dr. Abel Moreyra, Assistant Chief of Cardiology, arrived like the *Detective Columbo* after the incident, he quietly surveyed the scene, reviewing the nurse's log, and detailing the course of events.

Everyone involved stood there in silence, quietly awaiting his pronouncement. Then calmly, he looked up and asked in his thick Argentine accent, "Okay, who giffa dis patient the Deege!"

My third and final year of residency had arrived. Most people not personally involved in this process only have a vague appreciation for how much education and time it takes to make a doctor. Counting my third year of residency, I had been in training for eleven years since graduating from high school. If I decided to go on into a specialty, that would have extended it another two to four years. Plus, as new technologies and procedures are developed many physicians go back to school for even further training. The truth is a doctor never stops training or learning. Continuing medical education (CME for short) is required by hospitals and insurance companies for participation, and the competent physician always needs to keep up to date for the sake of the patients under his care.

As a third year, senior resident you rotated through various medical specialties, but with far more direct responsibility for the patient's care.

The field of medicine has always been dynamic, growing, and in a state of constant flux. So also was the medical school faculty, new faces always appearing, but none in that final year was so intriguing as Dr. Michael Nissenblatt. Nissenblatt was a prodigy. He must have had a photographic memory, and though his specialty was oncology he would routinely expound on any and every topic in medicine and beyond. At first he was a bit intimidating, but after awhile you learned to take him in stride, and every so often (but not too often) you caught him making a mistake. It was all kind of theatrical and one suspected Dr. Nissenblatt did it tongue in his cheek. It was his "shtick," so to speak. One night he apprised me of a terminally ill patient of his and said with total confidence that I would be called at exactly 12:15 in the morning by the nurses to pronounce him. He was off by ten minutes.

Every so often a fourth year medical student joined our team, and I remember when an arrogant young hot shot who had assisted in some infertility research rotated with us for a couple of weeks. After three years of working in close proximity to life and death issues I had little patience for this kind of hubris. Once on morning rounds, with our attending physician present, this student was asked to talk about infertility to the team. During his talk he flippantly made a side comment, "We have made great advances in the diagnosis and treatment of infertility. It's amusing that there was a time when ignorant people actually believed that infertility was the result of God shutting up the womb."

Now, I thought, he was going too far. To take a potshot at biblical belief was unfair, especially when he knew as well as all of us that 80 percent of infertility cases were the result of causes unknown. He continued, "but now with modern technology at our fingertips we can do a battery of sophisticated testing and conclude…"

"that God has shut up the womb." I completed his sentence for him. Everyone laughed, and that young man, red with embarrassment, offered no rebuttal.

My final year of residency was mainly about three things: moonlighting to make some desperately needed income, finding a job once I finished, and preparing for the Internal Medicine certification exam. To pass that exam was the crowning achievement of three years of hard toil. As important as passing the board exam was to my future career, however, my immediate and pressing need was for money. My salary had increased 1,000 dollars each year of residency, but my family expenses far exceeded that, so I had to begin moonlighting, like so many others, in the emergency room. Saint Peters Medical Center across town from Middlesex General Hospital was well known for hiring residents to work the ER. Of course, the hitch was that you agreed to work nights and weekends, but the pay was good and the need great, so I took the job. Doreen was a little disappointed since we were looking forward to a year when we could spend some quality time together. I promised her things would improve in the future, but of course they didn't. Like so many of my colleagues, I have recited that promise a thousand times, even to this day, and it has yet to be fulfilled, and perhaps, it never will be. In any case, I long ago lost credibility with her in the matter.

Saint Peters Emergency Room at night varied from explosive activity to eerie silence. There were times I was even able to take a cat nap, but I was too wired up, so I sat at the nurses' station reading medical journals. By shift's end I was exhausted but intact. Once I got home, however, I would crash and six hours later awake to my normal sleep deprived baseline.

Meanwhile, back at Middlesex, ward work continued unabated. The curious immunologic disorder of a year before now had a name, AIDS, and a growing infamy and the causative agent, Human Immunodeficiency Virus, was about to be discovered. Originally we spoke of the "Four H's" of AIDS susceptible groups: hemophiliacs, heroin abusers, homosexuals and Haitians. The Haitian connection turned out to be a statistical blurb, while hemophiliacs and heroin abusers became minor risk categories with the safeguarding of the blood supply and the institution of safe needle programs in the large cities. This left the one group which turned out to be the single major vector of the AIDS epidemic; homosexuality. Homosexuality and AIDS were mutually inclusive, at least in America, and herein lay the seed of a major moral dilemma, at least for the church. Was AIDS a just punishment from God on sinners? Political correctness aside, homosexuality, although existing since time immemorial, had been for most of recorded history and in most cultures and religions a condemned way of life. Most would agree that drug abuse, prostitution and promiscuity, all directly or indirectly connected with AIDS were sinful, or at least self-destructive. So why not concede the obvious, that God was behind the AIDS crisis punishing the purveyors of it, just as he sent Joshua and the Israelites into the Promised Land to destroy the idolatrous Canaanites?

I once sat in the hospital library contemplating that great paradox of how a loving God could send evil and suffering. Homosexuals after all, are human beings too, and are often trapped in a cycle of addictive behavior. For the Christian who takes his faith seriously, however, this paradox has to be explained. The answer goes back again to a thorny doctrine of the early church called Predestination. There is much in the Bible to support the fact that God has foreordained (willed ahead of time) all our lives and all the events that make up the universe for all time. It only seemed logical to assume that if God is omniscient, and omnipotent, that this would be true. In the Old Testament book of Proverbs it is written, "The Lord has made all things for himself, even the wicked for the day of evil" (Proverbs 16:4). Okay then, this much is true, that God in His infinite wisdom predestined, or at the very least allowed evil to exist, whether it be the deeds of evil men or the ravages of disease and destruction.

All of this may seem a bit esoteric, but I can assure you that in my struggle against disease and death I have faced this dilemma every day. The ability to reconcile the love of God and the existence of evil has been critical to my faith and my professional calling existing together in harmony. I have never believed that a Christian must park his brain outside before entering the church.

God obviously allowed evil to come into existence and must surely have known it would soon flourish. Yet the Bible also says, "The way of the wicked is an abomination to the Lord" (Proverbs 15:9). As I contemplated this, I came to understand in it a most incredible truth. God, who is all powerful, has allowed evil to exist, though He hates it, because out of the evil He would bring forth something good and wonderful, and that if evil had not existed it would not have come to pass.

God's nature is to forgive, which we could never know if there never was anything to be forgiven for. A skeptic might raise an objection here, claiming that God is using us like pawns on a chessboard playing games with our lives, indifferent to the suffering He has allowed to exist in the first place. But here is where the Christian message becomes indispensably necessary. If God were an aloof far off deity who created us to endure suffering simply to prove something to Himself, existence would be a sad farce, but if on the other hand, God willingly became a part of His very creation to endure the same suffering and indifferent fate that is the birthright of all men, then there truly is hope. And, in Christ, that is exactly what God did. Not an aloof, uncompassionate deity, but a God of empathy and infinite compassion who tasted sin and death to become our Savior from it. By our act of faith in believing what God did on the cross of Christ, we are joining ourselves in the hope that one day God will deliver us from this veil of tears, and we catch a glimpse of the eternal plan as the apostle said, "...for we have a High Priest (Jesus) who can appreciate the feeling of our infirmities; but was in all points tempted (through suffering) like as we are yet without sin" (Hebrews 4:15). So if there was no sin, we would never appreciate one of the greatest attributes of the eternal deity; forgiveness. In fact, Saint Peter in his letter goes so far as to say that the angels who are sinless can't understand this aspect of God's nature, but wish they could (1 Peter 1:12). And though God's offer of hope often is rejected, it is graciously extended to all mankind. "...for many hear the call, but few are (the) chosen"(Matthew 22:14). AIDS is not a judgment from God, it is a consequence of human activities that have broken His moral laws, but He knew it would happen beforehand and predestined it to happen so that we, the afflicted, might have a chance to turn to Him for forgiveness and cling to Him in hope. I say we, because Christians have no claim to be some kind of superior class of beings. I am reminded of Saint Paul's wonderful statement, "Know ye not that the unrighteous shall not inherit the kingdom of God? Be not deceived, neither fornicators, nor idolaters, nor adulterous, nor effeminate, nor abusers of themselves with mankind..."and such were some of you", but now you are washed, now you are sanctified, now you are justified in the name of the Lord Jesus Christ and by the Spirit of our God"(1 Corinthians 6:9–11). I have never been comfortable in the belief that my suffering is a just retribution from God. I personally do not enjoy suffering, nor do I wish it on anyone else, but when suffering comes (and it will come to all of us some day) I cling to God's love to carry me through.

It is one of the great ironies of life that one day you could be in the deepest philosophical thought and the next day caught up in the most mundane of tasks. In between residency, moonlighting and raising a family, I had to seriously search for a real full-time job. I answered some journal ads, entertained, and then rejected the notion of starting a private practice.

One memorable interview was in Plattsburg, New York. This small city was located in upper New York State, not far from Montreal and the Canadian border. It was actually a beautiful location situated on picturesque Lake Champlain, but then one of the staff physicians described the most exciting moment as being when he sees the first blade of grass poking through the snow after five months of winter inundation. Doreen gave me that "no way on earth" look, and that ended all debate. A great offer to take a position in Fargo, North Dakota, was deep-sixed for the same reason.

Then there was the interview in Poughkeepsie, New York, that ended in disaster when my old Plymouth Duster broke down. We didn't get back home until 6:00 a.m., and at the regular hour I was back to work as usual, sleep deprived. Prospects for a good position that suited me were dwindling fast, when one day my eye caught a classified ad in a library journal. It was an employment opportunity to fill an emergency room position in Portsmouth, Virginia. Now this was a possibility that caught Doreen's eye. Virginia was a lovely state. We had both visited it before, and there was so much to see and do, including the Virginia Beach oceanfront, Colonial Williamsburg, Busch Gardens, The Blue Ridge, and it was located in the conservative Christian South. What a great place to raise our children, we thought, plus it was an easy day's ride from our families up north; so I set up an interview.

Portsmouth General Hospital was a small community hospital serving the inner city population of Portsmouth, Virginia. It was not a very busy ER, and the pay was not great, but it was a chance to get established in a nice location and perhaps one day start a private practice. They liked me, so I decided to take the job.

Meanwhile, work continued at Rutgers and at Saint Peters. One early morning, probably five , the waiting room attendant hurried into the treatment area. "There's a guy crawling across the parking lot towards the emergency entrance and he looks badly hurt!"

He actually dragged himself all the way from his motorcycle accident to the hospital parking lot. As we carefully cut away his boot what we saw shocked everyone. His tibia and fibula, the two bones that comprise the foreleg were snapped apart just above the ankle. His foot was literally hanging on by mere threads of tissue, the white jagged bone sticking out of this mass of flesh just as if it were a shank of beef hanging in a butcher shop. It was a miracle, but all the arteries and nerves to his foot were still intact. I resolved that day that I would never ride a motorcycle as long as I lived.

One other tragic case was of a young man who was killed instantly in a head-on collision. As I examined him on the stretcher, the only clue to his untimely death was a trickle of blood running down the side of his face. How sad, I thought, that someone with so much to live for should end like this. There was nothing for me to do but pull the sheet over his head and notify the coroner.

Advanced Cardiac Life Support (ACLS) and Advanced Trauma Life Support (ATLS) were two certification training programs I took towards the end of residency to round out my training. Trauma certification would be particularly helpful since I would doubtless be seeing a lot of it in Portsmouth, and having these two certifications on my resume would be a definite asset.

So having completed three energetic years of post-doctorate training, we packed up and moved to Virginia. Doreen was eager to go, but deep down harbored doubts about leaving her family. The day we left my mother cried, "I'll never see you again!" My Aunt Margie said we'd be back in a year. As for me, it was the true commencement of my medical career and I was eager to begin this new chapter in my life.

Chapter Six

Private Practice and the High Calling

"...And He shall be like a tree planted by the rivers of water,
that brings forth his fruit in His season..."

Psalms 1:3

After my Poughkeepsie disaster, I bought a new Pontiac Phoenix, a small two-door compact that was within my budget. When we left New Jersey it was packed so tight that Leah didn't have room to stretch her arms. The moving van we hired went on ahead of us. In 1983, the Norfolk-Virginia Beach area, also known as Hampton Roads, was curiously half static and rooted in the Old South and half progressive, boldly advancing into the future. At Rice & Nachman's Department Store, you could immediately be lost in the fifties, complete with the slowly turning ceiling fans and the art deco lunch counter; then proceed to downtown Norfolk where modern glass and steel skyscrapers dominated the waterfront, which was relentlessly being reclaimed for tourism.

Portsmouth lay across the spacious Hampton Roads Harbor from Norfolk and the locals often referred to it as a backwater town. Its waterfront was dominated by the stark façade of the Portsmouth Naval Hospital Tower, one of the largest military hospitals in North America. And just down the street from this imposing edifice was my first real job at diminutive Portsmouth General Hospital.

I had high hopes upon starting my work there. I had confidence in my abilities and felt I had a lot to offer, but the veteran nursing staff there was not impressed. They'd seen young hot shots come and go before, and knew all too well that the inexperience of new doctors meant more work for them. It was a struggle for me to gain their confidence, but one night after I successfully directed the care of a cardiac patient with a life-threatening arrhythmia, I crossed the threshold. The praise I received from the nurses, however, was matched by the contempt I received from the company that hired me.

The owner was a huge, imposing hulk of a man, a physician himself who hung up his stethoscope and went into the business of medicine, a consummate wheeler and dealer.

When I came to Virginia to interview for the job, I had to find my own motel room, which turned out to be a dive, and when I told him, all he did was laugh heartily about the strip club just down the street from it. I later discovered that the salary he offered me was 20 percent less than a physician who was hired just before me. I brushed off these disaffections, however, and tried to concentrate on being a good doctor.

Meanwhile, we were getting familiar with our new home. The vestiges of the Old South resonated with our Christian convictions, although as northerners we missed some things. Once I told my mother we couldn't find good Italian bread, to which she responded, "I told you, you should have stayed in the states!"

One Saturday night during a waterfront celebration, a three-year-old child wandering too close to the edge of the pier fell into the pitch black water. Her grandfather instinctively plunged his arm into the water and grasping blindly caught her and pulled her out. The poor child was terrified and hysterical, but by the kind hand of Providence, still alive. It was truly miraculous. She seemed to be unharmed. The family brought her to the Portsmouth General ER, only a mile from the waterfront, to be evaluated. She was fine, but understandably her family insisted on more tests, consultations, and hospitalization. I was finally able to assuage their concerns.

Life often seems like an unending stream of surprises and calamities. Today we all are very comfortable with the illusion that we retain total control of our destinies, but this is only an illusion. Far more is beyond our control than we realize. He who knows this and who has learned to commit his concerns and his future into the hands of a faithful God is by far the most contented and secure of all men, "Commit your way unto the Lord, trust also in Him, and He shall bring it to pass" (Psalms 37:5).

I got a lot of experience suturing in Portsmouth. There was the time a little girl was brought in by her mother with a facial laceration. Of course, we had to strap her down to do the suturing and she wasn't happy. When I finished, that little girl leaped off the stretcher and gave me such a kick in the shins. I almost buckled to the floor.

And then there was this big strapping male who warned me that he had a deep fear of needles and had passed out once before. After much reassurance about the tiny needle I would use, he reluctantly agreed to proceed. About halfway through the procedure the nurse assisting me called my attention, "Doctor...the patient." I took my eyes off the laceration to see that the patient was pale, white and clammy. His blood pressure was undetectable! "Start an IV! Put him in Trendelenberg! Start dopamine!"

It was incredible, but he had actually gone into shock over a tiny shot of Lidocaine. After that experience I learned never to discount any patient's warning. Always listen to your patient!

When I learned about the unequal pay scale (some physicians were even given paid vacation, but not me), I decided it was time to look for a new job. Of course I did have to fulfill my contract year. I must admit I did a lot of audible grumbling about it all, and my plans to leave, so one day the founder of the company made an unannounced visit to the hospital to talk with me. When I explained to him my ultimate goal of entering private practice, he challenged me with the comment, "You'll need a gimmick to succeed in private practice."

I thought about it and said, "My gimmick will be to offer superior health care with a compassionate heart," to which he simply smirked and left the hospital.

As Doreen and I became settled in Virginia I did give more serious thought to private practice. But first things first, I had to get out of Portsmouth. I ran across a local ad one day for physician opportunities to work in what was then a new kind of facility, an urgent care center, a clinic halfway between a private doctor's office and a hospital emergency room. They were an extension of Norfolk General Hospital. The job included weekends in that exceptionally busy ER. The pay was better and there was no subterfuge in the contract. Working in the urgent care centers did not require night call. In Norfolk General's emergency room, I would pull a twelve- hour shift, but at least I'd be off by midnight, and every other weekend I was free.

I interviewed for the position and was hired (I'm sure my ACLS and ATLS certifications were a vital factor in my acceptance).

So my year at Portsmouth General Hospital, my first year as a full-fledged doctor came to an end, but not without one ominous experience which, as it turned out, was a portent of things to come. On a typically busy afternoon, a father brought his teenage son into the Portsmouth General ER because he had slammed his finger in his school locker earlier that day. His finger was very swollen and barely movable. An X-ray was normal, no fractures, so I splinted it and referred him back to his family doctor for follow-up and gave no more thought about it until, a certified letter came in from an attorney threatening me with a lawsuit for medical malpractice. *Malpractice for what,* I thought? I pulled the record out from the archives. Apparently the kid never did follow-up with his family doctor, and instead returned to the ER weeks later because he couldn't move his finger. A repeat X-ray suggested torn ligaments, which was confirmed by a specialist who recommended surgery. I was flabbergasted, and didn't have a clue what to do. Someone in the ER suggested I call my employer, which I did. They asked for copies of the emergency record, the attorney's letter and any other relevant documents pertaining to the incident. Fortunately, I never heard another word about it. Presumably the lawyer realized he had no grounds worth pursuing.

That experience was a close call and had I known then what I know now I would have taken it much more seriously, but to me then, as to many physicians then and now, malpractice was just a word, a curiosity that didn't really apply to them, just something to joke about like an ambulance-chasing attorney. I did not comprehend that incident to be a wake-up call to the terrible experiences that would eventually engulf my career.

So I started working at Norfolk General Hospital and at the Secure Care urgent care centers. The improved income was very welcome and the company I was with, Emergency Physicians of Tidewater, was much more professional than my prior employer. In fact, I even got a raise after a staff meeting during which I impressed everyone with a quick discourse on the DeBaky classification system of thoracic aneurysms.

Doreen and I were getting settled in Virginia and decided it was time to put our roots down and buy a house. I also was coming around to the conviction that I would open a private practice in Virginia Beach, and began making some preliminary plans to that end. I also sought out the local chapter of the Gideon Bible Society and we began attending meetings and making friends there.

I'll never forget a young black man who came in with a deep laceration across the face. It was a sharp cut as if done by a razor. As I sutured the wound he sat there quiet and sullen. I wanted badly to say something encouraging to him. "You know, whatever happened to you, it's not worth going back to get revenge. Don't get down to their level." He made no noticeable response to my admonition, so the nurse cleaned him up and he left. (It was one of the best suturing jobs of my career, I might add.)

I was the second call doctor back then since I was new to the group and they had not tested my mettle. Most of the old timers in the group back then are gone, but at the time I forged many a solid, professional relationship.

One of the emergency physicians I worked with regularly was Phil Leavy. We had some good moments of light conversation in the midst of the general busyness. It was later one day when a nurse at Secure Care shared with me a tragic story. Phil had a toddler daughter, and one day as she was eating a brownie, she accidentally aspirated it and it lodged in her airway. In desperation, the child went off alone to try to cough it up to no avail. When Phil saw her, he immediately did what is called a cricothyrioidotomy to open her airway, but without success. The poor baby had a respiratory arrest and lingered on mechanical life support for many days before she passed away. Oh my goodness, I thought. Poor Phil!

The next day we worked together I extended my deepest sympathies for which he was very grateful. Not long after that I had my own close call. On one day off, Doreen and I were shopping when Leah, who was about three years old, was sucking on a candy lozenge when she suddenly bolted backwards in the stroller. She couldn't speak, but had this look of horror on her face. After quickly assessing the situation, I unstrapped her and laid her on her stomach across my knee and pounded her upper back sharply five times, and out of her mouth popped the lozenge and it shattered on the sidewalk. With her voice restored, she started screaming and reached up for her mother.

Recollecting that moment, especially in light of Dr. Leavy's experience, still brings a chill. To this day, Doreen and I both watch our grandson closely whenever something questionable gets even remotely close to his mouth.

So, getting back to Norfolk General, the day I sutured the young man's face, we continued non-stop busy, and about 11:00 P.M., one hour before my shift ended, rescue called that they were bringing in a trauma case, a young black male, badly hurt, with a stab wound to his chest and second degree burns to his abdomen. Upon arrival in the ER, I saw immediately that it was the very patient I had sutured earlier in the day! How evil a world it is, I thought, and how sad that this youth was both a partaker in it and a victim of it.

By August 1984 I had made serious preparations to begin private practice with a target date of January 15, 1985 to open my doors for business. I arranged my schedule so that I could devote Wednesdays and Saturday mornings to my practice while continuing my duties with Emergency Physicians of Tidewater, at least till June 30th when my contract expired.

It takes a lot of effort to start a small business. It is the riskiest venture a non-elite, middle-class individual can undertake. The amount of money you need to borrow with no guarantee of a return is staggering. Even finding a bank willing to chance loaning you the money can be a challenge, as I soon discovered. Staffing was another problem. I hadn't a clue even where to start until someone recommended me to a remarkable young woman named Susan. She too, was starting a small business management company and had much to teach me. She was a person who constantly bubbled over with enthusiasm, and it was contagious. Through Susan, and her partner Diane, I made many advantageous business connections, although one recommendation she made that flopped regarded my bank loan. I think the loan officer simply didn't like me. It was humiliating to be rejected, but on my second try at a different bank I was approved. Armed with the necessary financial muscle, I was able to find and rent a space, purchase exam tables, desks, lamps, and waiting room furniture, etc.(not computers yet, that would come later). And as a gift to start my career, Dad bought me a fine, top quality microscope. Lastly, I got a beautiful, solid wood tract holder for my waiting room. I wanted everyone who entered my office to have a chance to learn about the Savior of all mankind.

Everything was falling into place: advertising, equipment purchasing, a good location. I made up an introductory card detailing my educational training as an announcement to the medical community, but in the end it really served no practical purpose except to make my grandmother proud of me when I mailed her one. She framed it and it still hangs in my office in Virginia Beach.

The next decision was soul-searching, but ultimately turned out to be a total non-issue, and that was putting up my full, legal name on my office marquee. I guess I just wasn't sure how well a name as foreign sounding as Alessio would go in the South. Of course today in Virginia Beach unfamiliar names run the gamut from Attupuram to Zaigham, and everything in between, but in 1985 there was reasonable justification for concern. So for a short but intense period, I worried and prayed over this matter. But I decided anything less than my full name would dishonor the memory of my grandfather and my Italian heritage, so up went Alessio C. Salsano M.D. Ironically, many people took my name as Filipino or Latin American, which made me attractive to a large segment of the non-white population.

When it came to finding employees, God always seemed to turn up somebody, and in all my years of practice I never once put out a classified ad for help. I hired two women who were referred to me by quite independent sources: an LPN named Shirley Walker, and Nancy Laws. Nancy quickly became my go-to person. Shirley, a black woman, was a longtime divorced matriarch who not only supported her children but was in the process of raising her grandchildren as well. Shirley was very much the personification of the stalwart and devout Christian woman who was the bulwark for two, going on three generations of family, in the dissolute culture of the latter twentieth century.

So by January 15ᵗʰ, 1985 when I opened for business, everything was in place. Everything, that is, but the customers. Fortunately, I had six more months of steady income with the emergency group, so I hunkered down, looking hopefully to a busier future.

It was in those final months of urgent care center work that I met a most unique and gifted individual, whose path and mine would cross many times over the ensuing years, Dr. Norman Dahm. One day a nurse at the center casually asked me, "You're a born again Christian, aren't you?" I nodded.

"Well, you've got to meet Dr. Dahm. He's Mr. Christianity around here. You'd have a lot in common."

Norm rented some office space in that one particular center and one day I walked over and introduced myself. "Hi, Les!" he exclaimed with an enthusiasm which overflowed its bounds. "It's great to meet you!" We had a pleasant talk and shared our common faith. I told him of my plan to enter private practice, to which he responded, "That's great! That's great! God Bless you! I'll be praying for you."

After leaving him, I was so buoyed up I felt I could lick the world and still have some fight left over. Months later while I was struggling with my slow start-up, he helped introduce me to several doctors at the hospital.

When one physician totally deflated me by saying, "you're coming in at a tough time," Norm had calm words of reassurance. "Don't listen to it. He doesn't understand. He doesn't know the great God that we serve."

Those simple words bolstered me. Over the years, Dr. Dahm would become like a spiritual father to me.

July first finally arrived and I was a free agent. I opened my doors for full time health care, by appointment only of course (that would change). I was the master of my own destiny, if I didn't count the bank I owed money to, the insurance companies who constantly contrived reasons not to pay me, and the governments, local and federal, that imposed punitive taxes on me. Then there were hospital administrators that dictated picayune regulations on my practice of medicine and the patients, my customers, who demanded more and more of my time and energy. And where were the patients anyway?

I had been open for six months and had hardly anything to show for it, except a rising overhead. I decided to get a really long book from the library to read on the job. Surely by the time I finished it I'd have more work than I'd know what to do with. I checked out "Northwest Passage," Kenneth Roberts' sprawling epic of Colonial America. It took me almost a month to get through it.

So my first day of private practice, the zenith of achievement for a medical doctor, ended. I was excited to get home and tell Doreen about it, and on the way promptly got a speeding ticket. A fine way for Virginia Beach to welcome me into the business community, I thought.

When I finished the book a month later, I prepared myself for the deluge of activity. I walked up to the front desk to see the schedule. Nancy opened the large appointment book. "No one today, Dr. Salsano. Mrs. Campbell was on for tomorrow afternoon but she called to cancel. There's a patient on for Thursday, but he said he has no money and can't pay you till he gets a job."

It was then that the cold hard facts hit me squarely in the face. In private practice, it was not enough to be a good doctor. You had to be a good businessman, too, and that I would never be. I just did not have the entrepreneurial spirit, not then, nor to this day. I knew I needed money to survive and to properly provide for my family, but I really truly went into medicine to be a good doctor and to help people. Furthermore, in my deepest Christian conviction, I knew that the love of money was the root of all evil, and I swore I would never make wealth an idol. Once as a new Christian I prayed the Proverb, "Give me neither poverty nor riches, feed me with my necessary food" (Proverbs 30:8). When I told Doreen this, she looked at me incredulously, and since she was a believer in the power of prayer said, "Why on earth did you pray that?"

Entrepreneur or not, Christian conviction or not, I needed to start making money, and fast. My loan money was almost gone and the prospect of going deeper into debt was looming before me. I decided on two courses of action. First, I would go around and introduce myself to all the local health care practitioners and try to establish some professional bridges. I'm certain I was forgotten by most of the people I called on, but I did make some fruitful contacts and established a few long-term friendships. My second recourse was the tried and true solution for all hard-up young doctors, moonlighting. Urgent care centers like the ones I had worked in were popping up everywhere and doctors were needed to man them. The pay was good, but as always it necessitated my absence from my family, establishing a pattern that would sorely try my marriage over the next twenty-five years.

There was a third option, emergency room call. Every hospital, to be accredited, must have a doctor ready to admit patients who have no physician of their own. A university has resident doctors of course, but small community hospitals need private practitioners to be available. Since that type of work is a nuisance and unnecessary for an established doctor, volunteers for call are always needed. ER call can be frantically busy and typically you will pick-up several indigent patients who cannot pay, but enough patients have health insurance and are good customers so that you can begin to build a practice.

In the mid-1980s, the hospital with the greatest need for on call physicians was Chesapeake General in Chesapeake, Virginia. A regional medical center with a growing reputation, CGH serviced patients from all over southeast Virginia and the eastern North Carolina hinterlands. As you might imagine from this vast catch area I saw some remarkable cases.

I treated my one and only snake bite victim at Chesapeake General. A vacationing lawyer from New York was wading through some shallow water by his rental home when he felt a pinching sensation on his foot. He had been bitten by a poisonous Copperhead snake. Thinking quickly, he killed it with a stick and put it in a jar which he brought with him to the hospital. I couldn't help but think, *poor snake. He took one bite out of a big city lawyer and it killed him!* The truth, however, was that the patient had indeed suffered a significant envenomation which was extremely painful. His foot swelled to three times its normal size, and if the venom had escaped into his bloodstream his circulation would have collapsed, a life-threatening condition for which emergency anti-venom would need to be flown in. Fortunately, this didn't happen, and with conservative care (IV fluids, antibiotics, and wound care) he had a satisfactory recovery.

The downside to doing ER call is the very unpredictability of it. One night it could be completely quiet, the next time you could be up all night in critical care.

One Wednesday evening I received an admission, but had to finish in the office before going to the hospital. Wednesday being my late day (I usually saw patients till nine P.M.), it was ten o'clock before I got to see the patient. It was a pretty simple case and didn't take long, but after the long ride home it was past midnight by the time I got through the door. Then my pager went off. It was the

Chesapeake ER again. They had a young male in deep shock, on a respirator, with an adrenalin infusion running. "What happened?" I asked with a groan, knowing I would be up all night in ICU with this patient.

"We're not sure," was the answer. "He may have been bitten by a black widow spider. He was getting some things out of an old pickup truck in his back yard when he felt a pinch on his arm."

"Okay," I said with a sigh of resignation, "Give me a few minutes and I'll get back to the hospital."

Five minutes later, as I was headed out the door, the emergency room called back. "We just spoke with the family of your patient and he already has an internist, Dr. Islam, so you don't have to come in after all."

Well, hallelujah, I thought. *Thank God, I can rest tonight!* But the thought of that poor man's desperate situation saddened me. *Lord, help him through this catastrophe.* It was several weeks later when I ran into Dr. Islam at the hospital that I inquired about that young man's condition. It turned out that the day after he was admitted, the family was cleaning out his pickup truck and heard something moving under the rusted out floorboards. To their horror they saw, coiled around the chassis, a huge rattlesnake. Amazingly, the patient survived his ordeal.

Stories about rattlesnakes and black widows are great to tell the kids, but unfortunately they didn't pay the bills. Despite several months of beating the bushes, I was running out of money. My situation was getting so desperate that one day I was offered an opportunity to do some sports physicals at a Norfolk high school for a dollar per student. I dropped what I was doing and hurried over. When I got there, I discovered that I was expected to provide my own disposable gloves, so I had to check everyone for hernias barehanded! At the end of the session, the coach put all the money in a large sweat sock for me. Back at the office, I startled a slightly bemused Nancy when I presented the sweat sock and emptied it onto the counter for her to add the money up. If my situation didn't improve soon I would either have to quit, borrow more money or moonlight even more. Quitting was out of the question. I had signed a ten-year lease, and had already borrowed too much money from the bank. I could moonlight more if I wanted to kiss all sleep good bye. I was away from my family so much already that Doreen would cry when I left the house, knowing I wouldn't be back till late into the night.

So one day, sitting on the couch together, it dawned on us that we had a fourth option, and that was to pray and ask God for help. I had been so wrapped up in making things work for myself I had forgotten the gentle encouragement of old, recorded in the Bible, "Trust in the Lord with all your heart and lean not unto your own understanding. Acknowledge Him in all your ways and He shall direct your paths" (Proverbs 3:3, 4). It had been so long since I got on my knees in heartfelt prayer that I actually felt awkward doing it, but for me it was no pretense. This time I really needed God's help.

It's encouraging to hear testimonies in church of answered prayer, but until God hears and answers your prayer it all seems like empty words. That is often how I felt, but this time He would answer me in a wonderful and most unexpected way.

I had Saturday morning office hours back then and one day I got home from work, discouraged as usual. Half the patients that morning never showed up, and of the half that did, half again had no money to pay. I was sitting in the kitchen wondering if I should just pack it in when the phone rang. It was Dr. Dahm. "Hey, Les, you're not busy right now are you? (If he only knew!) I've got a patient at Bayside Hospital I need you to consult on."

Dr. Dahm was a gynecologist and his patient, a young girl, had suddenly developed a supraventricular tachycardia while in recovery after a minor surgical procedure. This condition, a very rapid abnormal heartbeat, can become life threatening if not handled properly. I had to apologize to him that I did not have consulting privileges at Bayside, but told him step by step what I would do if I were able. He thanked me profusely and hung up. "Doggone it! That would have been a great opportunity," I told Doreen. A week later I gave him a call. "Norm, how did that patient of yours make out?"

"She did fine," he said. "I did call in a cardiologist to see her and he did exactly what you had told me. Oh, by the way, I was talking with a general surgeon here named Roy Oswaks. We work together a lot at Bayside, and he agreed we need a good internist like you on staff here to consult with. Why don't you give him a call?"

Deep in my heart I sensed something positive, but didn't want to get my hopes up. I met Dr. Oswaks at his office not long after that and we got along famously, beginning what turned out to be a long and fruitful relationship. "You know, Les," he told me, "you need to get on staff here at Bayside! Norm and I both agree on that, but I also want you to meet an older G.P. (General Practitioner) in Virginia Beach named Bob Seeherman. I admit many of his patients for surgery here and often I need a good internist on consult. Here's his number."

So I met Dr. Seeherman, who curiously took an immediate liking to me, "Sure, kid, sure. Oswaks can use you, anytime. I always try to help the new guy. Glad to do it."

We talked for quite a while. I learned we were both from the Northeast. Dr. Seeherman had practiced medicine for many years in Wilmington, Delaware, before establishing himself in Virginia in the 1960s. He was an old school General Practitioner who in his early career delivered babies and performed appendectomies and tonsillectomies, something unthinkable today. He was highly respected among his peers, and although he was limiting his practice in advance of one day retiring, his word still carried clout in the local medical community. "It was nice meeting you, kid. Oh, by the way, I know of a big opportunity that could open up soon. I can't give you the details right now, but are you interested?"

"Sure," I said.

We shook hands and I departed. Something big really seemed to be happening, but I certainly did not want to presume upon God's grace. If he was answering my prayer I humbly prepared myself to receive it. And meanwhile, I continued to practice my profession.

Once I got on staff at Bayside Hospital, Dr. Oswaks was true to his word. He did call me in for consultations, and not only on Dr. Seeherman's patients. Dr. Dahm also gave me work, and things finally started to look like I might make it after all. The office was slowly getting busier too. I remember sitting down with Nancy and looking up diagnosis codes for my insurance claims. I also joined the Virginia Beach Medical Society to increase my visibility in the local medical community.

Having trained in the New York City area and encountering firsthand the evolving AIDS epidemic, I was very briefly the local authority on AIDS. Word got around and a Norfolk group invited me to speak to them about the disease one night and I accepted. My nurse at the time, Michelle, who was a medical assistant extern, accompanied me to the meeting. As I was organizing my papers, the president of the group came over to welcome me to the gathering, and to my utter amazement they were all gay. Michelle and I glanced at each other expressionless, but in retrospect I should have expected it. Now, in my mind, I faced a dilemma. How to square my oath to provide medical care (in this case imparting medical knowledge) with my Christian convictions about homosexuality? The Bible verse that immediately came to mind was Paul's wonderful words of encouragement to the Corinthian Christians, "Know ye not that the unrighteous shall not inherit the Kingdom of God? Be not deceived neither...effeminate, nor abusers of themselves with mankind...and such were some of you...but now you are sanctified in the name of the Lord Jesus" (1 Corinthians 6:9-11). Christians are sinners who by God's grace have had their eyes opened to see themselves for what they really are. There is no room for self-righteous condescension in this view. I resolved that I would perform my Hippocratic oath before this gathering and pray for wisdom to be a faithful witness. Ironically, after my talk I was able to make references to Biblical morality without being hooted out of the room. That experience was not one I cared to repeat, but I did repeat it on a more personal and intimate level back then with a remarkable young man by the name of Otis.

Otis came under my care early in my career when he chose me as his HMO doctor. On his first visit I could see he was a bit skeptical of doctors, but in time he relaxed and we forged a bond of trust that would last throughout my tenure as his internist. Otis enjoyed good health and took care of himself meticulously. He was affable and well educated. He was also gay, but not hardcore. Otis also was a Messianic Jew, a Jewish believer in Jesus. In fact, he was raised in a Christian home, his parents having accepted the Gospel long before. His was a unique amalgam of three ordinarily divergent worldviews; Judaism, Evangelical Christianity and homosexuality. Whenever he came in for an office visit we would have the most engaging conversations. In a sense we agreed to disagree with the utmost respect for each other's opinions, and after all, as his doctor I was responsible for his health care and had to retain strict objectivity in the end.

This young man, aware of his exposure to AIDS, took every precaution, except the forsaking of his high risk sexual behavior. He had earlier tested negative for HIV, but it had been several years, and because of the long latency period of the disease (typically two to five years), I recommended he be tested again. He did so, confident that his relative monogamy was a safeguard against the deadly infection. So you can only imagine the shock and dismay he felt when I called to tell him his test was positive. "Are you sure, Dr. Salsano? Are you certain it's not a false positive?" he asked.

"Yes, Otis. The western blot confirmation test was positive."

A long silence followed. I finally spoke up. "I want you to see an infection disease specialist."

Otis countered, "Okay, but I want a referral to the top AIDS authority in the country, wherever he is."

"I understand, Otis. I'll work on it. I'll also keep you in my prayers."

We had several profound conversations after that. He needed a lot of emotional support. He was truly shocked. One night by phone we talked about religion, and something told me it would be our last conversation. "I hope, Otis, I'm not overstepping my bounds here," I said.

"No, no," he said. "You have my full consent to say whatever you want me to hear."

I don't recall all I said, but I know I told him I believed his lifestyle choice was morally wrong, but that it was never too late to repent and turn from it. "You know that God loves you," I said.

"I do. You know I grew up with it."

He thanked me for my sincere concern for his welfare and we made our good-byes. I never spoke to him again nor did I see him again, except once in a discount warehouse. I thought I saw him walking into a crowd of people, but a second later he was gone. I learned years later from an intimate that he had died of AIDS. I could only hope that in the end he made his peace with God.

Many years later during an election, one of my nurses asked me how a Bible believing Christian could vote for someone who supported people (i.e. homosexuals) he hated. I answered that a true Christian doesn't hate anybody, and I remembered Otis, and my AIDS lecture, and reminded her (and myself) of Paul's declaration, "And such were some of you…But now you are sanctified in the name of the Lord Jesus."

Now it happened that I met Dr. Seeherman at one of the medical society meetings and he became more specific about the great opportunity he had spoken of. "I'm retiring."

"What?" I said.

"That's right. I don't like the direction medicine is taking, and I'm getting out. But I want to turn my patients over to someone I can trust. I have a potential buyer, but I like your style. I can tell you're a conscientious person and I'd rather sell it to you."

Oh, my goodness, I thought! Just a few weeks ago I was debating whether to quit or not. If this wasn't God's hand at work, then my ancestors came over on the Mayflower! When I later told Doreen, we agreed this was nothing less than God's answer to our earnest prayers for help. There was one hitch, however, and that was Dr. Vargas, the potential buyer Dr. Seeherman mentioned. He was a fellow G.P., who had aspirations of expanding his single doctor practice into a multi-disciplinary medical group, but he needed an M.D. to staff Dr. Seeherman's office and I was it.

Dr. Vargas and I met socially one night with our wives in attendance, and he made his proposition to me. "I'll put you on salary, and you can start seeing Bob's patients with an option to buy the practice from me down the road."

It sounded good and I might have jumped at the offer if I hadn't known from Dr. Seeherman that he'd rather sell it to me. "No, Gus, I've worked for other people before and I just can't do it again this time."

He tried to sway me, but I was adamant. Without a physician to work for him, his deal with Dr. Seeherman fell through. Not long after that, Bob Seeherman offered his practice to me. We closed on the sale the day after New Year's Day, 1986. I then proceeded to his office to see, for the first time in my career, a waiting room full of patients.

It felt good to be busy again, and Dr. Seeherman's patients were typically solid citizens with good insurance. Sure, I had to pay him, as well as the bank, but I generated more than enough income to do it. "Ask and it shall be given to you; seek and you will find; knock and it will be opened unto you" (Luke 11:9). For five years I dutifully sent him a check every month until I paid him off, likewise my bank loan. Dr. Dahm once shared with me his conviction that a Christian should be the best at whatever he does, echoing Solomon's words in Ecclesiastes, "Whatsoever you do, do it with all your might" (Ecclesiastes 9:10). And to that I added the Proverb, "a good name is to be desired above great riches" (Proverbs 22:1). To Dr. Seeherman, The Virginia National Bank and every other creditor I dealt with, I worked hard to develop a reputation for honesty and integrity.

Along with his patients, I also inherited Bob Seeherman's employees. I soon had to let the receptionist go for insubordination, but his nurse Eileen and his billing clerk, Charlotte, stayed on with me for many years. Nancy became my insurance clerk, while Charlotte became my new receptionist. It all fell into place except for Shirley. I kept Shirley on for my Wednesdays and Saturdays since I knew she needed the money (it was her second job), but when Eileen petitioned me for Shirley's hours I faced a tough decision. Some of Dr. Seeherman's patients left me because Shirley was black, and I was under great temptation to give Eileen, who was universally liked, her time. But after praying about it, I concluded it would be wrong to do it. Shirley needed the money, and besides, a true Christian must be color blind. I could not and would not cave in to popular bias. If Jesus taught us to, "Do unto others as ye would have them do unto you," then that ended all debate.

How well I recalled then, a poignant childhood memory. It was the late 1960s and the civil rights crisis was reaching its fevered climax. Once, my father had to bring my grandmother from Newark to stay with us in the suburbs when the race riots were at their height.

One evening we were all sitting at home when a booming crash sounded from outside our front door. My father's car was bouncing over the curb into our neighbor's front yard while the car that hit it slowly came to a stop, its engine demolished. Inside that car was a black man, apparently drunk. He didn't seem to be hurt and the police were called. "How typical of their kind," I heard an onlooker say.

Well, it was a week later on a Saturday morning when Dad, who usually slept late, was dressing to go somewhere. "Would you like to come with me?" he asked.

"Sure, Dad!" was my answer, as always.

Soon we were at the home of the man who hit my father's car, a cinderblock house in the black part of town. Dad said, "I need to exchange insurance information."

I felt a little insecure. I had never been in a black person's home before (I was about fourteen years old at the time). Once inside, I recognized the man who was now sobered up. His wife, a petite, sweet spoken matron smiled and offered me something to drink as Dad and he copied each other's information. The house was neat as a pin and on the walls were displayed all sorts of heirlooms and collectibles.

As we drove home, Dad, always the teacher, said to me, "You see Les, how nice that man's wife kept her home? She was no different from your own mother. She has hopes and dreams just like you and me. The color of our skin is not the important thing. It's what is in our hearts that matters."

I never forgot Dad's lesson that day. For me it is now a matter of spiritual devotion. "…for we are all His offspring" (Acts 17:28). When I gave Shirley my decision she gave me a big hug and for a while my personnel problems were settled.Which was just as well, because there were plenty of business related problems to deal with: tax problems, overhead issues, regulatory hassles and insurance mishaps. Like the time I admitted a young man with severe pneumonia. He was hospitalized for two weeks and I worked very hard to bring him back to health, yet after filing his insurance it seemed to take forever to get reimbursed. And when Nancy made inquiry, the insurance company, because of an unchecked box, sent my entire reimbursement to the patient, who promptly spent it. When Nancy figured out what happened and contacted the man for payment, he turned around and filed bankruptcy on me. A strange way to say thank you for saving his life. And unfortunately, that was not an isolated incident. In America, good health is perceived not as a privilege, but as an entitlement. It has become a basic human right, like life, liberty and the pursuit of happiness. Whether or not a doctor is fairly compensated for his efforts is completely secondary, if considered at all. So, in private practice I became the living embodiment of the saying "Feast or Famine." Here I went from practically my last dollar to being so busy I barely stopped to catch my breath. One early morning, a stomach virus hit me while getting ready for work. As I knelt on the bathroom floor, doubled over with stomach cramps, I tried to decide; should I shave first and then vomit, or should I upchuck first? (A doctor doesn't have to be a workaholic, workaholism will find him sooner or later.)

On top of being busy, private practice offers the medical doctor a crash course in dealing with human nature. If I had a dollar for every extraordinary experience I had (make that fifty cents) I would have been retired in luxury by now. Practically from the moment my name got around the community things started happening.

Once, an older woman addicted to narcotics drew me in. (Watch out for the innocent looking ones!) When she overdosed and was admitted to ICU, I called her son to explain what happened. His response to my call was short and to the point, "Man, you are f_____d (expletive) up!" upon which he had her assigned to another doctor, who sadly inherited all of this lady's insoluble issues. Being threatened, cursed at, and kicked in the shins was all in a day's work.

On another occasion I was trying to explain to a daughter her mother's condition when she just abruptly cut me off and said, "Shut-up and listen to me!" So the prestige of being a medical doctor towards the end of the twentieth century went right out the window along with income potential (as I would soon learn). Yet, even shorn of prestige and monetary reward, medicine still offered the challenge of treating disease and helping the afflicted.

I would still experience a wave of deep satisfaction when a patient would gaze at me from their sick bed and say, "Thank you, doctor, for helping me." There were to be many opportunities to help people over the ensuing years.

New experiences seemed to come on a daily basis. I once had a patient in the exam room and had to explain to her the findings on her recent heart testing which were serious. She had a badly damaged heart valve and would need open heart surgery. While I was speaking, she looked me straight in the eye, her expression went blank, and a pale bluish hue came over her face. As she slumped, I gently laid her down and checked her pulse, which was gone. She literally had a cardiac arrest right before my eyes. I called my nurse in the room and we initiated the basic life support protocol. "Nancy, call 911! Tell them we have a cardiac arrest here!" When rescue arrived, I intubated the patient and she was whisked off to the hospital, but she never made it. I reassured myself that I had done everything possible to save her, but you never want to lose a patient that way. Heart surgery would have cured her condition.

A different occasion involved a very nice elderly couple. The husband was a retired naval officer and was the personification of formal etiquette. "Yes sir," he would always say. "Thank you, Doctor. Have a wonderful day."

I thought this must be the most unflappable man on the face of the earth, but his wife was a little high strung. One Saturday afternoon I got a call from the emergency room. Apparently this very couple was having a heated argument at home and the intensity of it mounted higher and higher until the husband, literally red-faced, exploded, yelling his head off. But suddenly, according to his wife, he went pale, holding his head and staggering, as if he would pass out. She screamed and called 911. When the rescue squad got there and checked his blood pressure it was over 300! When he arrived at the emergency room, an astute physician sizing up the situation gave him a dose of Valium directly into the vein. To the amazement of all, his blood pressure stabilized, then began to drop literally back into the normal range and he was sent home. I never did uncover who started the fight, but it reminded me of the Bible verse, "It's better to dwell in the corner of a housetop than with a brawling woman in a wide house." (Proverbs 21:9).

I surprised the rescue workers with my ability to successfully intubate the patient who arrested in my office. It was a talent that came in handy, but one time it got me more than I bargained for. Since I first started private practice, it had been my habit to do my hospital rounds early. This enabled me to be able to start a full day of work in the office without the distraction of my hospital duties. In the early days of my career there was no such thing as hospitalists, that is, internists like me who spent their entire career in a hospital setting. So in the early morning hours before the day shift reported (typically seven o'clock), there was only a skeleton crew of residents and night nurses on duty.

Well, one morning I arrived on the wards when a code blue was called. Someone had sustained a sudden cardiac arrest. In the absence of a dedicated code response team, I went to the scene to help out. In the room I saw that the patient's airway was not secured. "I'll intubate," I proclaimed. Of course having trained in the pre-AIDS era, I neglected to don face mask and gloves as all the other health workers had. With blood and saliva splashing everywhere, I successfully intubated the patient just in time for his attending physician to arrive in the room and announce "Stop the code! This patient has terminal AIDS!"

What? Why didn't anyone tell me? I thought! I looked down at my hands which were dappled with bloody saliva, already contaminating several small cuts on my fingers. In a state akin to panic, I ran to the nearest sink and began scrubbing for my life with soap and disinfectant spray, bactericidal cleanser, anything I could get my hands on. "Why me?" I yelled, making a real spectacle of myself.

I remember a colleague coming up to me and saying, "I empathize with you, Les. I'd feel the same way."

The next day I saw an infectious disease specialist I knew who reassured me somewhat, but recommended I get an HIV blood test for a baseline. All well and good except for one thing. I reasoned that if my HIV test was positive on baseline, meaning that I had already had a previous exposure, my career was finished, if not my life. Who would go to a doctor with AIDS anyway? This was before political correctness made it a "protected" disease. I thanked Dr. Mooney for her advice, but decided to pass. If I contracted AIDS from this misadventure, I was resolved to leave it in God's hands, but I decided against anymore volunteering on patients unknown to me, at least not without gloves and a mask.

How ashamed I was that, unlike my less timorous forebears who braved death from tuberculosis, yellow fever and typhoid to bring comfort and healing to the sick, my overriding concern was of self-security. "Lord God, help me to extend myself to others in need and to always be mindful of the Savior's own words, 'Blessed are the merciful, for they shall obtain mercy'" (*Matthew 5:7*).

Work in the meantime had become all consuming of my time as my reputation spread and my patient population grew. It was taking away what precious little time I had with my family. Doreen, for a long time, was used to my being away on nights, weekends, holidays, but since we had no family or close friends in Virginia she found herself raising our daughter and keeping the home with no help. The stress it caused was leading to temper outbursts and recriminations, so I had to take action. First, I dropped the evening and weekend hours. Second, I made some coverage arrangements so that I was not on duty every weekend. This did help for the time being, and things settled down somewhat. We also made some friends at church and in the Gideons, which all came just in time because Doreen discovered she was pregnant.

So like a curious throwback to the 1950s, my nuclear family of four, nestled in suburban Virginia, took shape. Eventually, Leah joined the Girl Scouts and Doreen hosted vacation Bible school on our front lawn. It was all so idyllic. Little did I know the tumult and trial that were soon to engulf my life.

Year followed after year as I practiced medicine to the best of my ability. Weekends on duty I would bring my daughters to the hospital to give my wife a break and the nurses loved it. I'm not sure what they told my girls when I was in with the patients, but whatever it was, neither one even remotely considered going into nursing or medicine.

Meanwhile, in the office there was always something unexpected happening. One day a patient charged into my private office and pounded on my desk demanding her chart, until I ordered her to leave upon penalty of my calling the police. After she left, I couldn't find my nurse until Nancy told me she was hiding in the bathroom! There was Jennifer, a teenage girl who always seemed so innocent, almost the image of a "Bobbsey Twin," until she was brought in to the office for her allergy shots, by the police, in chains! It turned out that she was arrested for drug trafficking and needed her allergy shots before going to jail! As I stood there agape, I said to myself, *Oh my gosh! What if that was my daughter?* And there was Ed Worden who at eighty years of age did one-hundred push-ups a day.

By the way, in my long career I made many house calls. So if anyone tries to say that doctors are too callous or too busy to do that sort of thing you just send them to me. I began making house calls when a patient's wife called to say her husband was too sick to make it to the office. I told her I would be glad to see him in his home, and of course she was overjoyed. "Where do you live?" I asked.

"In Pungo," she replied.

Well, I thought, that should be easy to find, but unknown to me, Pungo wasn't a little crossroads a few miles from the office. It was an entire region as big as central New Jersey. After two hours of driving, I finally found their modest little home, in the middle of a vast tract of farmland nestled under a copse of trees. They were a delightful elderly black couple, and I could imagine that their home was built on a parcel of land passed down from their ancestors who were freed from slavery after the Civil War.

I learned to be more discriminating about house calls after my Pungo adventure and limited them to the City of Virginia Beach within a few miles of the office and to the elderly and seriously incapacitated. Whenever I loaded my black bag with the necessary items, grabbed the patient's chart and set off, it was to me a sort of apotheosis. I never did get much financial remuneration for my troubles, but the satisfaction of knowing I was extending myself to help the unfortunate was a great reward in itself.

Doctors, like everyone else, long to see a tangible sign of God's presence, and something like that happened in Norfolk, Virginia, back in those days. I was on duty one weekend and missed church, but Doreen went alone. She came back all excited. "The pastor gave a testimony today. One of the church members (Bennie by name) was admitted with a massive heart attack and he was not expected to make it. So the whole church began praying for him, twenty-four hours a day. One morning his doctor sent him for a heart scan to follow his progress. The young girl doing the test rubbed her eyes in disbelief. She kept looking at his chart to make sure it was the right patient. Apparently all signs of the recent heart damage were gone! Some days later when the cardiologist was sending him home he told the patient, 'Whatever church you go to, stay there!'"

Wow, I thought! I'd love to meet that man for myself, and as if by divine appointment several weeks later he came to me as a patient. The whole story up till then was glorious, but soon afterwards decline set in. His heart began to fail and he passed away. He was a very reticent man and never quite embraced his miraculous healing.

The Bible records that the children of Israel, after their miraculous delivery from Egyptian bondage, became discouraged in the wilderness and lost their faith in God's Providence, and without faith it is impossible to please God. So Paul wrote, "Now the just shall live by faith, but if any man draws back, my soul shall have no pleasure in Him" (Hebrews 10:38). Faith, and ultimately, thankfulness are so important in our brief struggle filled lives on this earth. They are the lifelines that hold us onto God's love. Bennie's incredible story taught me a powerful lesson to always be thankful, and as much as lies within me, not to doubt.

Doctors' wives may be the single most misunderstood and maligned group of people in the country. Popular culture has depicted them as gold diggers, addicted to luxury and the good life, effete upper-class wannabes. Although I'm sure some fit this mold, most that I knew personally, my wife included, more likely struggled with loneliness, as their husbands were away long hours, and expended their energies not on shopping sprees, but on raising a family and nurturing their homes. I know it was especially hard on Doreen since we had no family nearby to help. Even finding a reliable baby-sitter to have a night out was a major undertaking. I tried to give her breaks here and there by bringing the girls to the hospital with me on weekends, or by occasionally taking an afternoon off to watch them, but that didn't solve our lack of time together.

In contrast to Hollywood's warped depictions of medical doctors as men always on the prowl for an adulterous affair, I remained true to my marital vows. In my mind's eye, when I approached the church altar at my wedding, I imagined I was standing before God Himself promising my lifelong commitment. To be unfaithful to my wife was equivalent to being unfaithful to God. Nevertheless, as time went on, the demands of my career increased, and her demands at home increased, leading to frayed nerves, bickering and conflict.

As time went on, I lapsed into inactivity with the Gideons. I made excuses for myself; I was too busy and couldn't find the time, Doreen and I needed time to ourselves, or I needed a long vacation. The truth, however, was that I was backsliding, and my faith so recently bolstered by the timely offer of Dr. Seeherman's practice was being eroded by stress and by the cares of the world. Doreen felt the same way. Ironically we were both praying in secret for each other to regain his or her first love, but God answered my prayer first.

One day I came home from work and found her as excited as I had seen her in years. "Les," she said, "I was praying at the kitchen sink and I heard the Lord tell me *Get your heart ready, I'm coming back soon!*" I agreed with her that the world was a mess and that many of the biblical signs of the second coming were here, but my main reaction to her epiphany was close inner scrutiny. I needed to hear from God myself and get back my own Christian zeal.

Since before I met her, Doreen had received what once was called the Second Blessing, and in our day the baptism of the Holy Spirit revealed in the speaking in tongues, but she had let it slide into disuse. Now, she began to exhibit it with increasing enthusiasm and began to exhort me to seek God's will on it for myself. In God's economy, the man has always been the spiritual head of the home, but the woman is the spiritual heart. As we prayed each night together, I became more and more convicted that I needed a real spiritual reawakening to get back on track.

Jesus once said, "Seek and you will find, Ask and it will be given unto you" (Matthew 7:7), so it didn't take long for God to answer my plea! In a small storefront church we visited, the pastor preached about fresh oil. Just as a car, to run well, needs regular oil changes, so, he reasoned does a Christian, except in a Christian's life, the oil is the Holy Spirit of God. The world is a very tough place for the delicate seedling of faith to grow and prosper, and all true Christians must go to God to be refreshed and filled with His Spirit of power and of love and of a sound mind. And this filling of the Holy Spirit in ancient times was most often accompanied by the manifestation of speaking in tongues. In more recent times, John Wesley, the great founder of the Methodist church, was probably referring to it when he spoke of the Second Blessing, and not just a blessing for the individual Christian who receives it, but a blessing for him to share, and to overflow with God's love and bless the world around him. The next morning while in prayer, that often misunderstood, strange and wonderful gift , Glossalalia (the speaking in tongues) was given to me and has been with me ever since.

Paul the Apostle said there was nothing worse than a Christian who only cares about the material things of life and never gives a thought about eternity, "...of all men He is the most miserable" (1 Corinthians 15:19). I began to consider some things. For instance, why would God give me a thriving, successful career? It didn't seem to square with the nature of God that it was merely to make me self-satisfied and financially secure. As I prayed about it, I began to appreciate that He had strategically placed me in a situation where I could be a blessing and a help to truly hurting people, first physically with medicine, then spiritually through acts of Christian kindness and the sharing of the good news of His love. I began praying with my patients and encouraging them with the promises of God, and when I felt the time was right I shared my faith. I know some people were taken aback and some offended, but most of my patients were genuinely touched by it.

For awhile Doreen joined me when I did hospital rounds after church to pray with them. Of course treating sickness came first, but I always shared my deepest conviction that I was just a tool in God's hand. It was He who did the healing.

In the office I had many opportunities to pass on the hope that had newly been planted in my heart. A young man brooding and reticent came in one day. As we discussed his medical condition, I felt the need to say something encouraging. I didn't say anything profound or long-winded, simply saying "You know, world events seem to be following the very pattern predicted in the Bible before the second coming Christ." He raised his eyebrows, but didn't say a word. "Oh well," I said to myself, feeling a little silly for the effort, but six months later he came back for another visit, happy and excited.

"I got saved!" he said, and he meant it. We conversed a little and his enthusiasm radiated from him like sunshine. A few months after that the local newspaper actually ran an article about him. By then he was organizing a missionary outreach to some Asian nation. Just from sharing a little word of hope, I thought. Jesus was not speaking idly when he said, "The words that I speak unto you, they are spirit and they are life" (John 6:63).

Another time a young girl was made pregnant by her boyfriend. He wanted nothing to do with the pregnancy and was encouraging her to get an abortion. And to make matters worse, she had a kidney condition and her family doctor told her straight out, "If you don't abort this pregnancy, you're going to die."

The girl's mother (who was my patient) came into the office one day bawling uncontrollably. "What am I going to do, Dr. Salsano? She wants to get an abortion, but that's murder!"

I consoled the mother and said if I could see her daughter for a consult, maybe her condition was not so critical. So at her office visit, I encouraged the young mother-to-be and asked a urologist in on the case. After the exam, we spoke of spiritual things and prayed. Well, not only did she have a healthy baby, her kidneys came through the pregnancy completely unharmed. And the young man, the baby's father, actually married her, took a job and they became a family. All because a godly mother refused to cave-in to fear and despondency. It reminded me of the Lord's gentle reassurance to Jairus when he received the news that his beloved daughter was dead. "Be not afraid, only believe" (Mark 5:36).

Now the truth having been said, it's a foregone conclusion, isn't it, that when you get connected to God everything in your life works to perfection? Financial blessings fall on you like manna from heaven. Everyone suddenly treats you swell. Family problems vanish into thin air. Right? Wrong! It was from my new beginning with God that the real problems of life and career started happening. Too much preaching in the church today, including any number of contemporary Christian best-selling books, emphasize the promises of abundant life, happiness and material success that are found over and over in the Bible, yet they willfully ignore the references the Bible also makes over and over to persecution, trials, suffering and loss. Now no one, least of all me, wants to suffer, but I became a Christian because I confessed Jesus as my Savior, not because God guaranteed me an easy life. Following Christ is mentioned in the Bible as embracing the fellowship of his sufferings. Saint Peter said, "Don't think it strange of the fiery trial that will come upon you"(1 Peter 4:12). Right on the heels of my spiritual recommitment came personal and family issues, business and financial trouble, and worse. But joy comes in serving God, in doing the right thing, and in comforting others. "Pure and undefiled religion before God," Saint James said, "is this, to visit (help) the fatherless and the widow in their affliction. And to keep oneself untainted from the world" (James 1:27). I was able to shrug off my problems for the moment and was thankful for the testing. And like Job of old, I wasn't anticipating any great trial anytime soon. When and how it came I will soon relate.

Remarkable things continued to happen to me. Joan was a patient who began having arm and neck pain. All my work-up, including a cardiac stress test was negative, but still she continued to have pain so bad that she once entered the office white as a sheet in a cold sweat! Not knowing what else to do, I admitted her to the hospital. As I sat in the Radiology Department waiting for her chest X-ray to develop, I prayed for wisdom. It was then that an overwhelming impulse struck me; put her in ICU. Not having a solid medical reason, but feeling this intense conviction, I did just that. Not long after her transfer to critical care she had yet another attack, but this time the heart monitor showed she was suffering a massive heart attack, without chest pain! If this had happened on a regular hospital ward off the heart monitor it might have been missed, possibly leading to a fatal outcome. As it was, she went immediately to open heart surgery, where they found the main artery to the heart completely obstructed. Hearing God's still, small voice in response to my prayer saved Joan's life.

On another occasion I was taking call Saturday night when a young girl was brought to the ER with a severe asthma attack. The emergency physician called me saying the patient was about to have a respiratory arrest. "But that doesn't make sense," I said. "Are you sure there isn't something else going on?"

"Not that I can see," he answered.

I prayed silently, "Lord, help me to know what to do." Then it hit me, "Give her Narcan!" (Narcan is the antidote for a heroin overdose.)

"Narcan? But there's no evidence of narcotics abuse here."

Well, he gave it, somewhat reluctantly, and amazingly, the patient woke up and started breathing again. The next day when I told her how close she was to dying she recalled that earlier in the evening she had smoked a marijuana reefer which had a strange wetness to it, and it probably had been tainted. She also shared with me that her father was a pastor and that she had been running from

God. We prayed together for a fresh start in her life. There were many other such instances, too numerous to be recounted.

In yet another instance, a very sick young woman was hospitalized for three weeks with Crohn's disease (a very serious disorder of the bowels). Unbeknownst to me at the time, her father's health insurance had changed and my entire fee was rejected. When I finally contacted the correct insurance company, I was told the delay in filing would likely cause rejection of the charges, and that it would take three weeks, in any case, to process the claim. So Doreen and I prayed intensely, and three days later a check for the entire amount arrived in the mail.

It was 1991, on the eve of the first Gulf War, at the Norfolk General Hospital quarterly staff meeting where I was privileged to share my newly rediscovered faith with my colleagues. With the hospital chaplain's consent, I read aloud the one-hundred twenty-first psalm, and pronounced blessings over our soldiers and over the nation of Israel. It was for me something of a highlight in my lifelong journey through faith and medicine, and was received wholeheartedly by my colleagues, who knew my comments were from the heart.

In the midst of all this activity, a patient named Priscilla came to see me for the first time. Dr. Oswaks referred her to me because she needed a good internist. That began what would be for me a very fateful relationship. She was a very nice, outgoing older woman and we seemed to hit it off quite well as doctor and patient. We had some pleasant conversations about God as well. Meanwhile, I continued to be busy, and actually paid off all my student loans; on time I must proudly say! I also paid off Dr. Seeherman, and my bank loan, so I was completely free of debt and wanted to keep it that way. I was also able to increase my charitable giving at a modest sacrifice. For my own needs, I had always been a little tight-fisted and my family learned to get used to it, but for the Lord's work I rarely compromised. I took with utmost seriousness the Bible verse, "with food and raiment be content...for God has said I will never leave you nor forsake you" (1 Timothy 6:8; Hebrews 13:5). I resonated with Blais Pascal's famous comment that even if there were no God, to live and walk the true Christian path would still be the most rewarding life of all, So I entered mid-life on a wave of enthusiasm and spiritual fulfillment, but ripples of unrest had begun to invade my tranquil waters.

When Leah reached her teen years, she began to experience the full force of social estrangement and marginalization, as the Christian convictions she was raised with collided with the profligate lifestyle of the typical American teenager.

It didn't help that many of the young people in church were no better. She began to grow testy and obstinate.

Money was still, of course, a concern. As I reached my forties, it dawned on me that I probably wouldn't have enough money to retire on, let alone pay for college, weddings and all the other trappings we usually associate with the blissful years of maturity. I knew in my heart that God would always provide for my needs, but these concerns continued to haunt me regularly.

All these disillusionments weighed even more heavily on my wife, who endured obstinance during the day from the children, and bellyaching from me at night. We stopped praying together over the patients (although partly because the hospital did not approve of "freelance" counseling), and when we got into some trouble with our neighbors she became very wary about extending herself to strangers. To avoid such problems we moved to a large lot in the country, but that only served to encourage more isolation. The altercation with our next door neighbors was to a certain point unavoidable, but I guess I could have handled it better. Unfortunately, yet again, my smartalecking nature overruled my Christian conviction. "Devise not evil against your neighbor, seeing He dwells securely by Thee" (Proverbs 3:29). Doreen, for her part, was too sensitive to handle their vituperations, so the first chance we got we moved away.

Despite everything, I continued to be a very busy doctor and my reputation continued to grow. It was exciting at times to treat disease, to pray for your patients and especially to see them fully recover for your efforts. And for the most part people received prayers gratefully. It was about this time I consulted on a remarkable little Mexican woman who died and was revived, apparently having had an out-of-body experience.

Now medical science has yet to form a consensus on this well known but poorly understood phenomenon. I have read medical reviews on the subject that conclude it to be some sort of hypoxic hallucination and others which point out undeniable circumstances which imply that an actual extracorporeal event had occurred. Here is how her story unfolded. Jennie had entered the hospital for an elective surgery on her bladder. Post-operatively she developed a fever and shortness of breath, so her surgeon asked me to see her on consultation. The initial impression everyone had was pneumonia, but the results of the tests I ordered presented an entirely different conclusion. In fact, she was in florid kidney failure, and within forty-eight hours she was intubated, on dialysis in critical care, and tenuously holding on to life. The routine bladder surgery Jennie had done was called a Marshall-Marchetti-Krantz procedure, often referred to as a bladder lift. It was a very common surgery years ago for urinary incontinence, but was largely abandoned because of the high failure rate. This was actually her third such operation and all the scarring had blockaded her kidneys and shut them down. Which brings me to a very important side note. No one should ever lightly go into a major operation. Even in the best of hands and the most established of procedures there are risks. Of course there are times when the benefit outweighs the risk (appendectomy for example), but in many cases today, including that darling of the aging baby boomer, cosmetic surgery, the risks are just not taken seriously.

Jennie was a devout Christian, and many people including myself were praying for her, but she was going downhill fast, and one day her nurse approached Jennie's husband and told him point blank that his wife was about to die and would he consider making her an organ transplant donor. He was dumbstruck, not knowing what to say, but the truth is her heart had stopped beating and she was about to be pronounced dead. Yet, even as this conversation took place, someone came out of the room and announced, "Her heart is beating again!" From then on, her condition steadily improved, and amazingly, she left the hospital almost one month later with a normal heart and normal kidney function! In fact, the only symptom she had when it was all over was a cough, probably from the erosion of her airway cartilage from all the weeks on the artificial breathing device. It was towards the end of her hospital stay that she shared with me her strange and wonderful experience.

"I remember hearing someone yell 'her heart's stopped!'" she recalled. "And then I remember somehow being above the room looking down as doctors and nurses ran into the room shouting orders while my motionless body lay on the bed. Then, I found myself floating above a lonely abandoned road surrounded by darkness, but with a light shining way off in the distance to where the road led. I seemed to be moving very quickly along that road in the direction of the light, not under my own power. As I moved ever faster toward that distant light I thought, *Is it my time to meet God?*

"But a voice said to me, 'No, it's not your time yet.' The next thing I remember was lying on the bed with all sorts of people and activity around me."

Jennie lived for many years after that experience, and had normal kidneys until the day she died, quietly, in her sleep. She became somewhat of a spiritual conscience to me, and on her visits to the office would always have a word for me.

"Alessio, the Lord told me to tell you this…" she would begin, then give me an exhortation of one sort or another. On one visit she brought with her an old newspaper clipping. She and her husband were returning from a visit to family south of the border back in July 1984, and were returning through southern California. In the San Ysidro district of San Diego they passed a McDonald's restaurant and she asked her husband to stop there because she was hungry. When they entered the parking lot, however, as she related the story, an overwhelming apprehension came over her and she told her husband to quickly leave. Perturbed by her inexplicable change of mind he reluctantly drove off. A few blocks down the street they heard a series of popping noises. You see, that was the McDonald's where James Huberty, a troubled ex-GI and welder, perpetrated the infamous San Ysidro massacre where twenty-one people, including several children, were shot dead. Jennie was convinced that God had spoken to her heart, warning her of the impending calamity, and she kept the local newspaper clipping as a memento of her miraculous escape from death. When she did pass away years later, widowed by the recent death of her husband and burdened with family issues, it was at home in her sleep. "Precious in the eyes of the Lord is the death of His saints" (Psalms 116:15).

Jennie was one of many Christian people who sought me out as their family doctor because of my Christian beliefs, yet I made it a point of conviction to never parlay my profession of faith into a marketing gimmick, as did many of my peers. I placed discrete gospel witnesses, magazines and such in my waiting room, and always welcomed the opportunity to discuss religion (time permitting), but felt it was beneath the dignity of the Christian faith to manipulate it for money.

It was in the midst of all this spiritual revelation that God taught me a great lesson in humility. Sidney and Edith Rabinowitz were a very nice elderly couple, patients I inherited from Dr. Seeherman. Mr. Rabinowitz had taken some offense to a conservative Christian placard I put up in my office. He approached me one day with a moving personal story from his childhood. It was Christmas time and at his school classes were canceled so the children could go class to class singing Christmas carols. When Sidney told his teacher he was Jewish and could not participate she chided him, "Well go home and don't come back till you've changed your mind." When he got home in tears and related his story to his parents, his father was prepared to personally go tell the entire school board off, but his mother intervened. "Honey, don't do that, it'll only make things worse. I'll go have a talk with the teacher tomorrow. "Doc," he said, "being Jewish back then had the potential for social ostracism and worse. We can't go back to those days."

I sat there stone-faced listening to Mr. Rabinowitz's story. In my heart I knew he was right. True Christian faith is not about coercion, it's about conversion. I recalled a passage in the Book of Acts from the early church "…and the Lord added daily to their number such as were meant to be saved" (Acts 2:47). In other words, God does the calling, and He calls those who are predestined in his omniscience to believe. But this does not in any way imply partiality. Our part is to share our faith and love all men, even those who revile you and despitefully use you on account of your beliefs. God leaves no room for personal pride or self-service in this. Needless to say, I took the placard down.

This same divisive issue came up once in the doctor's lounge when a Jewish colleague, Dr. George Grayson, commented to me how as a child attending the New York City public schools in the late 1940s, he had to recite the Lord's prayer every morning at the start of classes. Of course that was mandated by ancient custom and no parent protested it, Jewish or otherwise. "But George," I said, "The Lord's prayer is the perfect Jewish prayer. After all, it was recited by an observant Jewish rabbi (Jesus) to an audience that was itself 100 percent Jewish. It's a great prayer!" I don't recall Dr. Grayson making any strong objection to that.

Since my learning experience with the Rabinowitz's, I became more discreet about sharing my faith. I never wanted to turn anybody off. I just wanted to share the love of God. Nevertheless, my reputation as a Christian physician continued to grow. Among my evangelical Christian patients were many local pastors.

One very nice young minister brought his wife to me because of severe headaches. On my initial exam I correctly diagnosed her with trigeminal neuralgia, a particularly devastating type of facial pain. Despite my starting a treatment program which helped her, her husband kept insisting on approval to see out-of-plan consultants and radical treatments which I would not grant, so he found another doctor. Months later we met at a local K-Mart and I asked about his wife and then he uttered the words that all doctors have come to dread, "I could have sued you."

Sue me? For what! I wondered. I had followed established protocols. I would have gladly referred her once a neurologist approved of it. Then he added, "but I know it's wrong to sue a brother in the Lord, so I decided not to."

"I could have sued you," the most baneful words a conscientious doctor can hear. I say conscientious because there are many people practicing medicine who have hearts of stone, who are just in it for the money or for the prestige. They live by the law of the jungle, giving as little consideration to the patient as possible and consequently little is expected of them. Ironically, they don't get sued. It's when a patient has high expectations, such as from a doctor who gains their trust, whose expectations are suddenly dashed, that the conditions are ripe for a malpractice lawsuit.

Dr. Norman Dahm, my colleague, friend and spiritual mentor, one of the most gifted and well respected surgeons in Virginia became a victim of our litigious society. He was dedicated to the physical and spiritual well-being of his patients, and they loved him for it, yet even he couldn't escape the specter of malpractice litigation. Although he and I had maintained a warm friendship, it rarely extended beyond our professional lives. So I never learned the details of his experience, but I knew it had upset him greatly. Malpractice to a doctor is almost like venereal disease or like the Scarlet Letter. It has always been, and continues to be, an object of shame. You just don't talk about it. When you admit openly that you've been sued you run the risk of being labeled as incompetent, careless or worse. All this burden, not to mention the punitive insurance rates you end up paying, as well as the unending rehashing of the event every time you apply for hospital privileges, insurance participation or medical society membership. I could see it weighed heavily on Dr. Dahm and secretly wondered, *If he could get sued, what about me?*

Chapter Seven

THE LAWSUITS AND GOING TO TRIAL

"Many bulls have compassed me. Strong bulls of Bashan have beset me round."

PSALMS 22:12

I now admit I was not mentally prepared for dealing with a major lawsuit. I had always convinced myself that my patients would never sue me because they knew I sincerely cared. Medical reviews on the subject suggested this was true, but then no one had more of a caring attitude to his patients than Dr. Dahm and look what happened to him. And even as I pondered all this in the fall of 1993, my great disillusionment came.

It began when Priscilla, whom I described earlier, underwent a difficult orthopedic surgery and was not recovering to her surgeon's satisfaction. She was anemic and fatigued with significant post-operative pain and indigestion. Although her surgery took place without my involvement, I became actively involved when she sought me out for a medical consultation afterwards. My exam was unremarkable, but it was obvious she was in some distress. When I called her surgeon he reassured me that he had everything under control. When I told Priscilla what he said she was very frank with me. "A few days ago I was praying and I asked God what could I do to help my situation and I heard, *Go see Les.* (How could she know that was my nickname?) So I made an appointment to see you." Very flattering, I thought. Maybe she did hear from God. In any case, I decided to follow along with the orthopedist and keep in touch, at least peripherally.

Then one morning I received a frantic call from her husband that Priscilla was so dizzy and weak she couldn't even rise up from bed. "Call the rescue squad and get her to the hospital!" I said. In the emergency room she was found to have a hemoglobin of 2.9 (normal is 12!). It turned out that she had a hemorrhaging ulcer in her small intestines, probably from all the pain medicine she had consumed over several months. I called in Dr. Oswaks for emergency surgery and even as he repaired the ulcer (which had actually eaten its way down to one of the main arteries in the bowel), her body slipped into profound shock. At one point during the operation her heart stopped and had to be resuscitated. In the office I got down on my knees and prayed for her fervently. Then the call came in that the surgery was successful and she would live.

I worked hard and long to bring Priscilla back to health. With the indispensible help of my consultants, after six weeks of hospitalization, she went home under her own power. Her husband was profusely grateful to me for saving her life, but swore he would sue the orthopedic surgeon who first operated on her. I felt a bit uneasy with his vitriolic attitude towards that surgeon, but since he almost lost his wife it was certainly understandable. At least, I thought, he wasn't suing me.

For the next six months, I saw Priscilla sporadically for one or another minor problem. At each office visit she gave me an update on her plans for a lawsuit. I sat expressionless as she related her husband's efforts to find the right lawyer to represent them. I tried showing concern without endorsing their actions or bad-mouthing the surgeon, the object of their vituperations. As the details of her progress unfolded I became more uncomfortable, sensing that sooner or later I might be dragged into it. Apparently my having seen her and been aware of her condition before the ulcer hemorrhaged was enough for an attorney to incriminate me. It didn't matter that the other doctor assumed the responsibility for her care. I was involved, period. Also, she was eventually counseled by a lawyer that if I was not brought into the lawsuit the surgeon could absolve himself in court by laying the blame on me. After all, diagnosing and treating ulcers was not the surgeon's job, it was the internist's job, and I was the internist. Practically simultaneous to my realization of this, Priscilla stopped seeing me and soon transferred her records to another doctor. No action had been filed against me, and I tried to forget it all and get on with my career, hoping and praying that nothing would come of it. Life goes on, piano lessons, help with homework, taking out the garbage, and work. Sickness doesn't punch a time clock. One thing I learned in my years of doctoring was that you can't fall apart over a setback, because the next person who will need you is just around the corner and you must have a clear mind to approach their medical problems with confidence.

Even as this transpired I continued to be busy, adding new patients to my practice almost daily. To become more available to my patients I broadened my insurance participation, signing on with various HMOs, PPOs and keeping an open enrollment with Medicare. I need to make this clear, I didn't do it for financial reasons, but it was typical for employers to switch health plans on their employees, and patients in such a situation would beg me to join their new health plan. All flattery aside, I felt it was important to be available to my patients, so I joined. Similarly, with Medicare I continued, unlike many of my peers, to accept new patients. I reasoned; why did I even become a doctor if I'm not going to make myself accessible to the very people who need my services the most?

There was another patient about this time who, as events unfolded, also was destined to impact my life greatly. Lisa was a delightful sixty-one year old woman referred to me for the evaluation of vaginal bleeding by her daughter Joanne who had also been my patient. Lisa lived in North Carolina but was unhappy with the care she received there, so her daughter recommended her to me. The type of bleeding she was suffering, well after menopause, is never normal. Although the cause often is benign, it could be something serious such as cancer, and needs to be investigated.

I first saw Lisa in December 1992, and my exam revealed a large pelvic mass and rather significant hemorrhage from her uterus, so I admitted her that very day to expedite the diagnosis. A CAT scan confirmed a mass in her right ovary, so I asked Dr. Dahm in on consultation. Lisa was a very nice Christian lady and we prayed together for God to bring her healing and swift resolution. She underwent surgery the next month and what at first had seemed to be a deadly cancer actually turned out to be a large abscess that had engulfed her entire right ovary and fallopian tube, and once it was removed all her symptoms went away. She returned to North Carolina cured and ready to resume her life.

Lisa had recently been widowed and was in a very meaningful, "second time around" relationship moving towards marriage. Her story had all the trappings of a fairy tale ending, almost. About seven months after her operation, she began having some vague abdominal discomfort, bloating and right-sided pain, different from her earlier illness. I saw her again in October and repeated a CAT scan of her abdomen which revealed the shocking truth; she had cancer of the colon with massive involvement of the liver. In other words, she was terminal. But how could that be, I thought? I pulled out the original scan and sat with the radiologist personally to review it. "Do you see any sign of cancer in the original scan, Lamarr?" I asked.

We compared the two scans. "No, there was no sign of it in the December scan, Les," he told me. So in ten months this patient went from no sign of malignancy to full blown terminal cancer. When I explained that to her daughter she was devastated.

I could see the look on her face, "Surely someone must have made a mistake." I empathized with her greatly and tried consoling her with encouraging words from the Bible, but to no avail. The poignancy of all this was more keenly felt because it rudely cut short her mother's cherished dream of a new life. Lisa passed away shortly after I made the diagnosis of cancer. I sat with Joanne one last time in my office, reviewing again all the findings and trying to reassure her that what happened was not a result of someone's mistake, but was an unforeseen and unavoidable situation. She left unconvinced, and we never spoke directly to each other again. As with Priscilla, I had a very uncomfortable feeling that this would not be the end of it.

Again putting this aside I went on with my life and career. An opportunity arose back then to move my office to a better location with a much lower rent. So almost ten years to the day I moved to my new office, without a major mishap. With a much reduced overhead, a busy career and a tranquil home life, I truly seemed to be at the zenith of my accomplishment, and then came my denouement.

It was a Monday in mid-January, literally the first day in the new office, when a package arrived by registered mail. It seemed to be a quite large bundle of documents. I signed for it and anxiously opened it. It was from a Richmond attorney representing Priscilla Granger. It was a legal document called a motion in judgment, officially charging me with negligence which led to the personal injury suffered by his client, and naming me (along with the orthopedic surgeon) in a medical malpractice lawsuit.

Even though I knew this day would come, when it arrived the shock I felt was something like being suddenly hit in the head by a flying brick. Negligence? Her husband thanked me for saving her life! For a few minutes I sat paralyzed at my desk staring into space. What should I do? What will this mean for my future? My career? Am I finished, bankrupt? Do I ignore it, deny it, or fight it? And then came the spiritual recrimination. Why did God allow this to happen? I asked forgiveness for any unrepented sins I had committed. Then I started to analyze the situation. I remembered reading journal articles about this, what to do and what not to do if you're served with a lawsuit. One thing all experts agreed on, never personally call the plaintiff. She is bound to tell her attorney everything, and such a call makes a clear impression of guilt if you ever go before a jury.

Once I regained my composure, I realized my first step was to notify my malpractice insurance carrier. After giving the agent a quick synopsis, I was reassured that an attorney hired by the company would be contacting me. Hearing that brought some hope back to my soul and color back to my face. After ending the call I took a few deep breaths, made a silent prayer, put on my white coat and prepared to start the work day. By then there was a waiting room full to overflowing with patients. My staff gave me a slightly distressed look as I entered the first exam room to begin what would be one of the longest days of my life.

When I got home that evening I broke the news to Doreen and it was almost like the last straw. "I don't want to hear it!" she yelled.

"But I…let me tell you…," I sputtered.

But she repeated, "I said I don't want to hear it! That's your problem, you deal with it."

I realized it was too much for her to bear. It was all too clear that God would have me walk this crisis alone, trusting in Him alone. "Yea, though I walk through the valley of the shadow of death I will fear no evil: for Thou art with me" (Psalms 23:4).

I felt sorry for myself, and I felt sorry for my wife, too. I knew that a doctor's wife often has to endure in silence, but that was more about long hours of separation and loneliness. No wife, doctor's or otherwise, should have to endure the strain of her husband being exposed to unwarranted malignment, public trial and potential financial ruin.

The day arrived for my meeting with the appointed attorney from the firm of Wright, Robinson, Osthimer & Tatum. His name was Dan Filetti. We met at my office and after a brief and friendly introduction I related my story. He listened very intently, frequently taking notes. When I finished he scribbled a few more notes and put his pen down. "Dr. Salsano," he said. "I am convinced of your innocence. I believe that the patient could not find a local attorney to represent her because of the dubious case against you, which explains their having to retain a Richmond attorney. You'll need to fill out some paperwork and I will file a brief. I'm going to speak with their counsel and recommend that you be non-suited."

This all sounded so positive to me that I was ready to write-off the whole experience right then and there. In my ignorance of the legal system, I couldn't appreciate that all this was just the opening scene in what was to be a long and convoluted ordeal.

Just as Mr. Filetti promised me, I had to fill out paperwork, and more paperwork, and more paperwork. I couldn't imagine, if my case was typical of the American legal system, how there could be any trees left on earth in twenty years. I then entered on a crash course in what Mr. Filetti called the language of 'Legalese.' Interrogatories, voir dire, motion in limine. Were these real words or did someone just make them up to confuse people? I also was told to prepare for a deposition. This would be done at my lawyer's office and would involve my giving legal testimony with the opposing lawyer present and a court stenographer to record all proceedings. The prosecuting party (i.e. Priscilla) could be present if so desired, but it was not mandatory.

When the day came, I was coached by my attorney not to be nervous, and to speak confidently about my medical expertise. Apparently, if the opposing lawyer sensed some diffidence on my part he would exploit it to his maximum benefit and my maximum detriment. As I waited sheepishly to enter the deposition room, Priscilla's husband Colin was sitting there, and with a big grin, wide enough to swallow a camel, he simply said, "Hello, doctor."

So I was called in to the deposition. As I entered the room I thought, who was this prosecutor anyway? This monster, this aberration of humanity, callously seeking to destroy my career, my family tranquility and my future out of pure undiluted greed!

He was a slightly overweight, balding, mild-mannered middle-aged man who kept politely calling me "sir" and "Doctor Salsano," and he kept thanking me for every answer I gave even when it detracted from his case. It was like being interrogated by Mr. Rogers. Was it possible that such a nice guy would want to do me in?

When I finished the deposition, Dan congratulated me on an excellent presentation. Maybe, I hoped, the case against me would be dropped after all. Priscilla actually did show up and sat in on the deposition. As I gave testimony, I could see her out of the corner of my eye studying me, occasional conferring with someone in the back of the room. As I left the lawyer's office her image haunted me. I could see that she was obviously not well and walked with a cane. I felt so bad about the whole thing, and found myself wishing that we never met. I imagined her praying to God for a favorable outcome even as I prayed for one myself. Only human arrogance, I supposed, could conclude that God was on my side alone, so I prayed for His will to be done and asked humbly for his favor in my cause.

Frankly, for me, I could only conceive of all this legal activity as an unnecessary burden in my life. As if I didn't have enough to do, paperwork, depositions, phone conferences, etc. And with all this going on I still had to get up early put my pants on (one leg at a time), and go take care of the sick, run a business, and see to the needs of my own family. After her emphatic refusal to hear about the lawsuit, I spared Doreen with the blow by blow updates, and I resolved not to tell my broader family. This was partly the doctor's stereotypical "I'm ashamed" response, but also I didn't want to use my family as a sounding board to gripe against. I wanted to leave it squarely in God's hands. I found that reading the Psalms brought great comfort to me. Many of these inspired poems of King David spoke of his being plagued by troubles, victimized by merciless enemies and humiliated by perfidious friends. I found some verses in particular that profoundly resonated with my soul. "Let them be ashamed and brought to confusion, who seek to destroy my life" (Psalms 40:14). "...Even my own familiar friend in whom I trusted, who ate my bread, has lifted up his heel against me" (Psalms 41:9). "For it was not an enemy who reproached me; then I could bear it. Nor was it one who hates me..., then I could hide from him. But it was you, a man my equal, my companion and my acquaintance" (Psalms 55:12, 13). There were many others. All this I could now deeply and personally relate to. Mr. Filetti said he would push to have me non-suited (dropped from the lawsuit) or at least for my case to go before a medical review panel for an early out-of-court decision favorable to my cause. Of course, this would all take time. Meanwhile, it was back to work.

I tried to put the whole lawsuit thing out of mind, but it was not easy. It bore heavily on my mind as I went through my daily routine. In retrospect I admit I was becoming testier with my staff. The new office was up and running and I became even busier as new patients arrived on a regular basis. Nancy, who was with me from the beginning, and Charlotte, whom I inherited from Dr. Seeherman, began showing signs of strain. As they acted out their frustrations, my response was more threatening than understanding.

Around that tumultuous time, a new patient named Ursula came to me. She endeared herself to my office. Ursula was a morbidly obese German lady, about sixty years old when I first encountered her. She was extremely withdrawn and timid in the beginning and I suspected she had been treated badly by previous health professionals, probably because of her weight, but the unfeigned courtesy she received in my office endeared me to her for life. She was always baking desserts for the staff and buying us all Christmas gifts. She was very sweet with what seemed to be a happy, serene disposition, but which in truth masked an undercurrent of depression. She had grown up in post-war Germany, living a hardscrabble existence in an abusive marriage which ended in divorce, when a kindly GI, a black man, fell in love with her and they married. Such a mixed marriage was still a taboo in the sixties, and I suspect that neither extended family ever really accepted it. Obesity perhaps has never been culturally acceptable, and the end result of all this negativity made Ursula a very insecure person. She clung to anyone who would show her kindness, and would pour out kindness in return.

Now Ursula had a heart condition (also diabetes, hypertension, gout and arthritis), and one day I brought up the weight issue. We discussed options and I recommended bariatric surgery, commonly known as stomach stapling or gastric bypass to help her lose weight. "Without it, Ursula, your life expectancy may not be long," I said.

Well, she was all for it, and after the usual insurance hurdles and pre-operative medical clearances she underwent successful surgery and began a dramatic weight loss, which gave her a new lease on life. For this, her gratitude was unending and my esteem in her eyes was elevated beyond reproach (and as it turned out, I would soon need an esteem boost badly).

Busy, busy, busy, always busy. As I said before, one of the first things you learn as a doctor is that illness doesn't punch a time clock or take a vacation, and the added burden of dealing with the lawsuit meant less time with my wife and family than ever. It was from then on that Doreen began her often repeated suggestion, "You need to find another job! All this one is doing is draining you. Your job has become a monster!"

Deep inside I began to wonder if she was right; and there was more to come.

It was mid-summer 1994 when I received a phone call from Norm Dahm and my personal (not malpractice) attorney. First to speak was Dr. Dahm. "Les, I just got served a notice. Lisa Hansen's daughter is suing both of us for her mother's wrongful death."

"Oh no!" I said. I knew this was coming, but had always hoped it wouldn't.

My lawyer also called. "Les, we got served papers too, just for documentation. I'm sorry you have to go through this. Good luck. I'll be praying for you."

So now I had two lawsuits! Lord God, why? I searched my heart, asked forgiveness for any unconfessed sins as before. I remembered when Jesus came upon a blind man in Jerusalem. His disciples asked him if the blindness was there as a punishment for the man's sins or possibly the sins of his ancestors. The Lord's answer was both unexpected and astounding, "This man was born blind not for his own sins or the sins of his parents, but that the works of God should be made manifest in Him" (John 9:3). So maybe God was allowing all this to happen to me for some unforeseen, greater good He was planning for my life. The same Providence that gave me the practice was now leading me through my present calamity. I felt like Job of old "…What? Shall we receive good at the hand of God, and shall we not receive evil? In all this did not Job sin with his lips" (Job 2:10). Yet I also felt sick inside, knowing what I would be in for, and was still going through in the Priscilla Granger case. Then, it suddenly hit me, *My God, what is this going to do to my malpractice insurance rate?*

Wright, Robinson, etc. Law Firm was retained again and I found myself sitting in the office with Attorney Filetti yet a second time. "I really am a good doctor, Dan. I don't know why this is happening to me."

He gave me a slightly puzzled look. "Don't get discouraged, Les. This is the nature of the business. That's why I'm here to help." As before, I gave him my story, he took down some notes and the whole litigation process got under way, again. I tried not to be discouraged, and I prayed earnestly every day for God's help. Jesus said to pray for them that despitefully use you (Matthew 5:44). I did this, but too often my prayers were against my adversaries, not for them. I was on the beginning slope of a very steep learning curve in humility.

I continued to pray for my patients, and with them, but somewhat more discreetly. In the case of both Priscilla and Lisa, I had come on strong with prayer and spiritual encouragement, even calling upon the Lord for immediate healing, and look where it got me! I have become convinced, looking back on all this, that when you, as a physician, open up to a patient on such a deep and intimate level as religious belief you make yourself a lightning rod for disappointment. If you pray for healing and it doesn't come, someone will become the target of resentment and redress, and since God cannot be sued (if He could, some lawyer would have done it by now), it has to be you.

This again brought me back to an earlier observation that people tend to expect more from a caring and compassionate physician than from someone who is merely a medical businessman. I must admit that it was becoming harder to be compassionate, at least not on the intense level I had been. Up until the two lawsuits, when a patient came to see me my first thought was, *how can I help them?* Afterwards, my first thought became *how can I avoid them suing me?* It was the difference between a new soldier marching happily off to war for the first time, and a hardened veteran, blood spattered, knee deep in fouled water in a trench with bombs raining down on him from all directions. I no longer saw any glory in it. When my nephew back then asked my advice about going into a medical career, I had to choke back the cynicism. I simply told him, if you love the science of treating disease, of if you have a strong conviction to help people and relieve their suffering, then become a doctor, but if your primary goals are to make a lot of money or gain a lot of prestige, then you're just going to be disappointed, trust me. He decided not to become a doctor.

So the time arrived for my deposition in the Lisa Hansen case, and I got to meet my adversary. Priscilla Granger's lawyer was disarmingly benign appearing. This new attorney was just the opposite. He was large and intimidating. He carried himself with an air of utter confidence in himself. As I sat there totally dejected, waiting for the deposition to set up, he commented to me, "Don't take it so badly, doctor. It's not you, we're just doing business."

Just doing business, I thought. And what about the toll on my health, my marriage, and my relationship to my patients? And what about the pernicious effect this "business" was having on the health care industry as my experience multiplied into the thousands all across the nation? His comment was symptomatic of an attitude very prevalent in this country; that of, I can "get rich quick." A lawyer who had dedicated his career to defending doctors in malpractice cases referred to it once as the "litigation lottery." Apparently it no longer matters in America if something is right or wrong. If you can make a lot of money off of it, it's right. It's bad enough in health care where lawyers and extended family turn grieving into greediness, but now the very same attitude has affected our youth. They no longer want to be teachers or doctors (I can't blame them there) or homemakers. Now it's models, actors, or professional athletes. Meanwhile, state lotteries and the gambling emporia are overflowing with activity. The whole society has seemed to gone mad over this. For heaven's sake, I wondered, where is it all going to end?

For Dr. Dahm it ended not long after that deposition. After a long and distinguished career in which he dedicated himself to the care of his patients, Dr. Norman Dahm called it quits. Long hours, falling insurance reimbursements and lawsuits all took their toll. The first casualty was his marriage and then his profession. It is an indictment on the enemies of health care in this country that such an outstanding and compassionate physician would be driven into retirement, but Dr. Dahm did what he had to do to salvage what was left of his life. I felt deep empathy for my colleague and pondered soberly his debacle in the light of my own ordeal. It was from then on that I began to regret ever having chosen a medical career.

Another patient I will scarcely forget, John Nugent, was a hard drinking, angry loner. His family endured his rancor as best they could. In time, the alcohol addiction eroded his health, first with bleeding ulcers, then pancreatitis (an extremely painful inflammation of the abdomen), and finally with cancer of the throat which ultimately took his life. John was by nature a fighter, but now he was in a fight he couldn't possibly win. As his body wasted away, he went into a deep depression. John had to be hospitalized frequently back then, and on one particularly long hospitalization I asked a psychiatrist to see him. The psychiatrist's findings were very revealing. Much to my amazement, all of his anger, frustration and bitterness came down to a single experience, when as a youth some valued possession was taken away from him, an incident he recalled with tears even in old age. With my mouth agape I marveled at this, but recalled an incredible warning in the Bible, "...Let no root of bitterness spring up from within you and thereby defile many" (Hebrews 12:15). Bitterness starts very small in our lives, like a seed. And if that seed is allowed to germinate and grow into a mighty tree, it not only takes over and defines our very life, but spreading its branches far and wide it affects everything in its immediate vicinity, namely family, friends, coworkers, etc. "Please Lord," I prayed then and ever since, "Please Lord, whatever happens, don't let me get bitter."

Of course, his childhood experience wasn't the only disappointment John suffered in life. It was just the core that became buried under one layer of misfortune after another, like the layers of an onion. By the time he was seventy years old the inner core was virtually unreachable, but not to God. I prayed hard for some chance to inject some Christian hope into this poor man's life as he neared the end, but he seemed to be unapproachable. One day I bought a tract at the Christian book store with the simplest message. All it really showed was a big red heart with the words "God Loves You." On the inside in large print and very tersely stated was the old Gospel story with a place to sign your name if you accepted Jesus as your Savior. On morning rounds the next day I entered his room. As usual, John was wide awake staring blankly at the ceiling. I asked him how he felt, and if he had any pain. His answers were short and emotionless. After examining him I summoned up the nerve and handed him the tract. I said, "Here's something for you, John. I hope it encourages you." He thanked me curtly, took it, and returned to his expressionless vigil. I left the room, not sure if I had accomplished anything.

I was off duty that weekend, and when I came back to his room on Monday, the tract was thumb tacked to the message board and he had signed it. As we spoke, I could tell that a change had come over him. His demeanor was more pleasant and relaxed. After he went home over the next few weeks his medical condition deteriorated, and he was clearly terminal, yet paradoxically, his attitude kept improving. In fact, his family, which had been so estranged all the years I knew them, were drawn together with him and reconciled in a most wonderful way. My last impression of John Nugent came when I made a house call to see him (as it turned out the last house call). He was near death, but had a wonderful look of peace on his face, and his family, in attendance at his bedside, were saddened, but full of hope, that his death would not be the end. Once again, even in the clamor of my personal and business crises, I was a partaker of God's high calling in my dual walk of faith and medicine.

Anyone who has dealt with or perhaps has been a victim of the American legal system discovers very *quickly* how *slowly* things move. Two years had gone by since I was put on notice by the Granger's attorney and the whole matter was still in process. You learn to put it in the back of your mind because if you stress over it from day to day you'll become a basket case. Yet like the sword of Damocles, it's forever hanging over your head and any moment the string holding it up could break.

Well, by the summer of 1995 my string was about ready to go. First of all, I lost my representing attorney. It turned out that the firm Robinson, Wright, Osthimer & Tatum had broken up and Dan Filetti was off the case. In his place was John Easter from Richmond. Dan was always upbeat and positive, but John was totally pragmatic. In our first meeting he came right out and told me, "You're going to have to settle with Priscilla Granger. If you go to trial you're going to lose."

That statement went through me like an electric shock. "What do you mean? I was told I had a strong case."

I couldn't believe I lost Dan for this! He went on. "Mrs. Granger's attorney deposed an expert witness, and his testimony was extremely damaging to your case." He went on to point out that I had not done the proper medical evaluation when she first came to me after surgery, and it would not hold up that I was absolved of any responsibility because the surgeon claimed to be managing things. After all, I was the internist. Upon hearing this I was stunned and speechless.

Apparently my entire cause had been demolished by what in medicine has been derisively called the "hired gun," that is the expert witness.

If you ever saw the classic western, *Shane,* the character played by Jack Palance, the professional assassin retained by the rancher to cause terror among the homesteaders, was a hired gun. And in the practice of medicine, a hired gun is a medical doctor who hires out his testimony to an attorney for the purpose of demolishing his colleague's career. Such a doctor might solace himself with the notion that he's some sort of watchdog for the health care industry, but the truth is that he's in it for the money. And the money to be had, I'm told, is very good. Now in my opinion such an individual has jettisoned his conscience long ago, and in his own way, by analogy to the gunslinger in *Shane* is quite ready to shoot down his opponents in cold blood.

"Well, what do I do now?" I asked in sullen resignation.

"Nothing. At this point we'll negotiate a settlement with them. I think we can bring their monetary demand down. You just need to sign a release agreeing to settle out of court."

I signed because I didn't know what else to do. If Mr. Easter was right and I went to court and lost, it would cost me far more. I laughed scornfully to myself. So much for her husband thanking me for saving Priscilla's life. After that quick but brutal reality check I was almost afraid to ask my next question, "So what about the Lisa Hansen case?"

"Now that case looks very positive," he said. "We're going to take that one to court."

When we parted I could see he was looking out for my best interests. I had to keep telling myself God was in control. "He will keep thee in perfect peace whose mind is staid upon Him" (Isaiah 26:3).

At our next meeting, Mr. Easter brought a young female attorney with him. "Les, I'd like you to meet Kate McCauley. She and I will be representing you in court."

She was a very pleasant young lady, but I couldn't imagine putting my future career in her hands. My first impression of her was that of the Markie Post character on *Night Court,* but I was soon to learn how wrong that impression was. We reviewed some pertinent issues, including the setting of a trial date. She said, "You'll need to close your office for a week, and cases like this typically last all day." She could see I wasn't happy about the whole thing. "Doctor, just think of it as having some time off," she said.

"Yeah. Kind of like a perverse vacation."

"That's right," she countered, with a smile.

"Oh yes," John added. "We just heard that they non-suited Doctor Dahm."

"What does that mean?" I asked.

"Basically it means they think they've got a very good case against you, so they're going after you one-hundred percent."

How nice, I thought, to be considered so important to someone!

By the time my trial date arrived I had become thoroughly cynical about medicine, questioning my decision to become a doctor, and wondering if it was all a mistake and not the high-calling of God after all. But then I called to mind patients like Ursula and John Nugent and regained some confidence that I was where I belonged.

And then came my trial.

How can I relate how it feels to defend yourself against unfair allegations before a group of strangers who have the power to pass judgment on you with untold consequences? It's as if your life, your personal integrity, and your mental soundness are all put on display and called into question. Nothing is sacred in a jury trial. I heard things said of me that my worst enemy wouldn't whisper behind my back.

Now I've taken plenty of tests in my lifetime and studying is in my blood, but how do you study for a test in which your own life is the subject? The only thing I felt I could do was pray and ask God for strength. Ironically, as it turned out, before the Grangers and I settled, a court date had been chosen, and following Kate McCauley's advice I took that whole week off, too. Now it was only a couple of months before the Lisa Hansen trial, so rather than return to work I decided to use the time wisely and I devoted it to prayer, devotions and fasting. In fact, I fasted for three straight days, making it a week of serious spiritual undertaking. Oh yes, and I also cleaned out the garage.

By that time I had virtually conceded negligence by settling with Priscilla Granger, and I was facing a courtroom battle with Lisa Hansen's daughters with possibly further humiliation. Up until then I had followed King David's example in the Old Testament, praying the Psalms, asking God for deliverance from and for vengeance upon my enemies. Well, I wasn't delivered and there was no vengeance. I really needed a fresh word from God in the matter. I was innocent. Why weren't my prayers answered? After praying and fasting God did answer me, not from the Old but from the New Testament. A thousand years had passed from the time of David until the time of Jesus. By then the Jewish people had lost their kingdom and their independence and were chafing under a brutal subjugation by the Roman Empire. They were desperately asking God the same question two thousand years ago as I was. Why?

In the Sermon on the Mount Jesus spoke directly to this spiritual paradox. Why do the true children of God suffer abuse while their persecutors get off scot free? I'm sure Jesus' listeners then were as dumbfounded at what he said as I was, here and now. I marveled at the words of the holy one of God, for never a man spake like this man. "Blessed are you when man shall revile you and persecute you and shall say all manner of evil against you falsely, for my sake…For great is your reward in heaven" (Matthew 5:11). "But if someone smites you on the right cheek turn to him the other, and if any man sues you in the court of law and takes your coat, give him your cloak also" (Matthew 5:39-40).

Our lives on earth are short, almost like a puff of smoke, in light of eternity. God is far more concerned with our immortal souls than our temporal ease, and if He allows false rumors, smiting and yes, even lawsuits to embattle us, it is to wean us from our desire for worldly things and give us his perspective, an eternal perspective. Trials and temptations will always drive off the cardboard, counterfeit Christian, but to the true believer they are the refining fire that turns his heart from a lump of coal into a glittering diamond. The Lord taught me more. Jesus said, "Agree with your adversary, quickly, while you are in the way with Him, lest at any time he delivers you to the judge and the judge delivers you to the officer, and you be cast into prison" (Matthew 5:25). We live in a corrupted world that has fallen into a pit of sin and decay. Conflicts will always happen between individuals, whether it's medical malpractice or simply a misunderstanding of two minds. Someone has to be a peacemaker. Agree with your adversary. I thought about what happened to Priscilla. She was alive, but was seriously incapacitated for life (she died only a few years after the event). It seems, I thought, that we all fight hard for our convictions, yet it's possible our convictions are all wrong. The time to find that out is not when we're standing before the judge, because if it turns out we were wrong all along then we will pay the uttermost penalty. I could clearly see God was dealing with my pride. In humbling me in the short run, he was drawing me to Himself in the long run where it counts. "God resists the proud, but gives grace to the humble" (James 4:6). There is no doubt that humiliation hurts, but the eternal fruit it brings in the life of the believer has no earthly measure, "…for great is your reward in heaven" (Matthew 5:12).

My week of soul-searching and garage cleaning was in September 1997, and on February 17, 1998 the Lisa Hansen trial began. I canceled all office hours that week as advised, but I did continue to see my hospital patients. I arrived at the Virginia Beach municipal courthouse, my lion's den, early that morning. It's a massive brick edifice, almost foreboding. Outside the courtroom I exchanged greetings with John and Kate while across the hallway I saw Lisa Hansen's daughters sitting together. We carefully avoided eye contact.

"A" court officially, perfunctorily opened its doors, and we all entered quietly. I took my seat at a large solid wood table to the left of the judge's bema seat. In ancient Jewish custom the bema was the podium from which the theocratic authority over Israel issued its judgments (In today's modern synagogue the lectern situated beneath the Torah scroll is still so-called). In Christian theology it is the symbol of the final irrevocable judgment of God. "So this is where I am to be judged," I thought with a smirk. Well, at least I have a chance to defend myself before my accusers. Even in our country, rifled with corruption and moral ambiguity as it is, this great fruit of democracy still flourished. It was more than I could expect to receive from a lot of places. Kate leaned over and whispered, "John and I have done some research on the judge presiding over your trial and he has a reputation for ruling in favor of the defendant in malpractice cases. That's good news for you." That was good news for me, but what if he had been of the opposing bias? I guess the preservation of democracy will always be a fight.

The bailiff entered the courtroom. "All rise. This circuit court of Virginia Beach, the honorable Judge Stockwell presiding, is now in session. All yea, all yea, all yea, those persons having business with this court will now draw near and give their attention. God save the commonwealth…You may be seated."

The preliminary functions were boring but critical. My lawyers and the opposing lawyers were given the opportunity to reject a juror as possibly having a bias deleterious to their client's case. I remember a registered nurse who was rejected by the prosecution because of a perceived sympathy for the doctor. This was necessary, it seems, to prevent an orderly trial from deteriorating into a salacious brawl.

As Miss McCauley kept walking up to the judge's bench to present various papers, I realized I was right (at least partially). She walked back and forth just like Markie Post in "Night Court," or rather Markie Post walked just like her. In any case, John and she seemed to be on top of the matter of my defense. I could clearly see and appreciate their expertise, exerted on my behalf. It instilled in me some much needed confidence to my sorely battered ego. Thus ended the first day of my trial.

Back at the office, everyone asked me, "How'd it go?" After giving them a quick summary, I proceeded to take care of office business; callbacks, mail, etc. When I got home I gave Doreen the blow by blow account. We agreed to keep it in intense prayer. The next morning the actual trial began.

The prosecuting attorney gave his introduction first. I'll never forget it. Dramatically, he addressed the jury. "You have been called here to carefully consider what you are about to hear. How an innocent individual only seeking the help of a professional person had her life tragically cut short through that person's negligence and carelessness. To her grieving children there must be a redress of this terrible injustice. Nothing you do can bring their mother back, but through your consideration and diligence, as you learn of the details of this case, you will conclude that compensation is due Lisa Hansen's family for the intense suffering and loss they have endured."

Oh my goodness, I thought! *Was I responsible for all that?* If my own career wasn't on the line, I would have probably lobbied for my own guilty verdict. But there was a subtle thread of prevarication in this opening statement. It implied a callous disregard for the patient on my part which could not have been further from the truth. I deeply cared about all my patients, including Mrs. Hansen. I did my best on her behalf, and I knew I had not breeched any standard of care. As much as my heartfelt sympathy went out to her daughters, I couldn't sacrifice my professional integrity if I were to be true to myself.

After giving the jury a lengthy, detailed (though biased) account of Mrs. Hansen's illness, he brought forth his expert witness, that black-hatted professional gunslinger of modern medicine. Dr. Frankel was a medical oncologist (cancer specialist) from a prestigious university in the Washington, D.C. area. His resume was so long it made mine look like a footnote. He was erudite and confident as he gave his testimony. He went into intimate detail over the diagnosis and staging of colon cancer, and most importantly, in reference to my involvement, on its prevention and screening.

Indeed, since time immemorial, a doctor's training has always involved taking a patient's complaints, doing an exam, running appropriate tests and making a diagnosis. So until the 1980s doctors were quite capable of making diagnoses, but all too often, especially in the case of cancer, it was too late to alter the course of the disease. Then, a sea change in the approach to disease occurred. Now much of what I do is to advise people on screening tests for early detection: mammograms, prostate antigen levels and colonoscopies, to name a few. By screening for disease and by early detection, many forms of cancer can be treated and cured or prevented altogether.

It is amazing how much medical training we all underwent once in what was called the systemic signs of malignancy. In other words, we learned to diagnose cancer by the subtle indirect physical signs it caused in the patient, but the irony of it was that the cancer was usually too advanced by that point to be stopped. It was all academic, as the patient was terminal.

But what did all this have to do with Lisa Hansen? Mrs. Hansen died of colon cancer. Early detection by a colonoscopy could possibly have saved her life. Everyone agreed on this. In fact on her first visit to me I had even made a note that she had a family history of colon cancer. The critical point was that the Plaintiff's attorney was making the allegation that I was responsible for the patient not having a colonoscopy when it could have made a difference. Was I responsible for that nice lady losing her life? Even as I sat there pondering my defense I couldn't help but accede to the attitude so prevalent in our modern American culture, that when tragedy happens, it's someone's fault, and someone should have to pay.

After Dr. Frankel finished, I glanced over to the jury and imagined seeing them preparing a hangman's noose. There was no question that his testimony did a pretty good job at making me appear if not willfully negligent then at least incompetent, but the issue upon which the entire trial hinged was whether or not I was responsible for Lisa Hansen not getting a timely colonoscopy. Before we went to trial on our last meeting, Lisa's daughter raised her concern that certain findings on her mother's initial testing which suggested colon cancer were ignored, but it was clear upon reevaluation that the cancer which took her mother's life was undetectable when she first presented to me. The care I rendered to Lisa Hansen for her acute illness was exactly appropriate. My innocence would stand or fall on what would be decided about the issue of the colonoscopy.

After Dr. Frankel, the prosecution brought forth the daughters for their testimony with the obvious intention of generating emotional sympathy from the jury. They each told their story, often pausing to choke back their tears, and I found myself welling up in tears over their loss as I relived the sad events. I could only guess at what impact it was having on the jury, my peers. They appeared to be sitting inflexible without the slightest show of emotion. After this, the court recessed for lunch. In the cafeteria, John and Kate could see that I was in a deep gloom. "Their testimony was pretty compelling, wasn't it?" Kate asked me.

"Oh yeah," I said. "They even had me in tears."

"Well, their attorney was bound to use them for sympathy, but we get our turn this afternoon. Don't worry."

I smiled timidly and braced myself for the next session.

I was not involved in the decision making that led to the three witnesses chosen on my behalf, but looking back I applaud the sagacity that brought them to my defense. The first witness was Dr. Dahm. Since he was dropped from the suit, he could now be a witness for my defense. His easy going demeanor and undisguised honesty resonated deeply with the jury. The second witness, Dr. Robert Shank, was a local oncologist known to me who discussed the medical details of the cancer itself, and finally, the third was completely unknown to me, a public health care expert from none other than that Bastion of Northeast Liberalism, Massachusetts.

But before all these testified, I took the stand. The questions at first were easy, "State your name, your specialty, how many years have you been in practice?"

Questions then came about my involvement with Mrs. Hansen, all rather routine and objective, in quick succession. Then the bombshell. "Why didn't you follow-up on the abnormalities that raised a suspicion of colon cancer?"

My answer was firm. "At the time of her first presentation to me, all of Mrs. Hansen's symptoms and test results were accounted for by her tubo-ovarian abscess. That's T-U-B-O-dash-O-V-A-R-I-A-N (I always had a habit while under oath to spell out difficult medical terms for the stenographer. It was probably unnecessary, but looking back I believe it cast me in a positive light to the jury). When she returned to North Carolina she was completely well. I guess the cancer was probably there, but none of her recent symptoms and signs were related to it."

The plaintiff's attorney countered, "Why didn't you order a colonoscopy then?"

Again my answer was firm, "The patient had come to me for an acute problem, and once it was resolved I assumed she would return to her family doctor in North Carolina for her routine health needs."

"No further questions, your honor," was the response.

The prosecution rested and I heaved a deep sigh. Kate and John welcomed me back to our table with handshakes and nods of approval. I felt like a prize fighter returning to his corner of the ring at the end of a round.

Dr. Dahm was called next to testify and his main witness on my behalf was to recount the actual surgery he performed on Mrs. Hansen and to state very clearly that there was no evidence of colon cancer that was clinically evident. The plaintiff's attorney pressed the issue hard, but Norm was adamant. "After removing the abscess, I examined the entire peritoneal cavity, intestines, liver, everything looked normal."

Then the lawyer tried to catch him on a technicality. "Dr. Dahm, in your deposition you stated that when you released the patient from your care, you warned her to keep close follow-up with her family doctor to make sure nothing unforeseen would be missed."

He answered, "That was boiler plate. Every patient is told that to ensure they make proper follow-up." (Lord, thank you for Norm Dahm's friendship.) My mind traveled back to the first day we met and shared our common faith. It had been a tortuous journey since those days.

Dr. Shank, my oncology expert, next took the stand. John Easter definitely did his homework in choosing him for my defense. He was believable, erudite, but able to communicate to the jury in layman's terms, unlike the plaintiff's expert who tended to talk over their heads. After reviewing the case in summary, he went on to give a brilliant discourse on the natural history of colon cancer. "This patient had a most unfortunate situation. Her cancer had arisen in the caecum (the dead end sac) of the colon. This is the one area of the colon where early detection of cancer has not been universally successful. This is because it tends to metastasize early, and not by the lymphatics which slow the spread of the tumor, but into the bloodstream where it travels directly to the liver, becoming incurable. At the time of her presentation to Dr. Salsano, this spread had almost certainly occurred already, even though it was invisible by exam. It is a sad thing to contemplate, but Mrs. Hansen was destined to die of this disease, and there was nothing anyone could have done to change that outcome."

A hush fell over the courtroom, and Joanne's attorney was speechless. At that point I knew my innocence was proven, but I could still lose the case on a sympathy vote.

My final witness, as I already mentioned, was a public health and epidemiology expert from Massachusetts. Now, having been raised in the Northeast in an immigrant inner city working class family, I was heir to a tradition of liberal democratic convictions, but as I grew in my evangelical Christianity I swung in the opposite direction and became a moral conservative and overwhelmingly Republican. So naturally I was inclined to distrust anything from the Leftist Northeast, including this expert now committed to testify on my behalf. I thought to myself, what could this person possibly say that would help my case? As it turned out, a whole lot! His testimony addressed very directly the entire issue of colonoscopy and preventive screening, the issue upon which the opposing side had staked their entire case. "Dr. Salsano," he affirmed, "did nothing to breach the standard of care in this patient. Colonoscopy to be sure is an important preventative procedure, but it would have been absolutely inappropriate for him to have ordered one on this patient while she was under his care. To begin with, on her initial presentation she was suffering from an acute gynecologic illness, uterine hemorrhage, and evidence of a deep abdominal infection. A colonoscopy done under such conditions could have been catastrophic, causing perhaps a perforated bowel. And even upon her last visit to him before returning home she was still healing from her recent abdominal surgery. Dr. Salsano's care was entirely appropriate and were the outcome different the care he rendered would have been considered life-saving."

Wow, I thought! I resolved then and there never (well, almost never) to speak badly about someone just because they hailed from the liberal heartland.

I was definitely in a more buoyant spirit by the end of the second day. There was no question that the defense witnesses overwhelmingly carried the day for me, yet the sympathy factor is well known to be stacked against the doctor. Juries routinely award the plaintiff a large settlement if for no other reason but to help alleviate their grief and loss. And the impression that Lisa Hansen's daughters made on the witness stand weeping for their mother was very powerful. On the third day of the trial, both sides would make their summaries and concluding remarks, followed by the jury's deliberation. I still had a lot of nail biting ahead of me.

I was always impressed by how thorough my attorneys were in preparing for this case, but on the third day my appreciation took an exponential leap. It began when John Easter stepped forward to make his summation. He had an easel set up for the jury upon which he set a series of charts. His command of the statistics and of the pathophysiology of colon cancer was incredible. In the brief time that he researched for my defense, he literally learned more about colon cancer than I did in four years of medical school. Now, I have no doubt that after the trial much of his knowledge would be lost through non-usage, but in that he would be able to repeat such a crash learning course on any variety of subjects as the need arose was frankly astounding to me. As I sat there watching him make his presentation, I could see that the jury was equally impressed. His conclusion brought all the strands of thought of the previous testimonies together to make a resounding case for my innocence.

Next, it was the plaintiff attorney's turn. As before and throughout the entire trial his appeal was to base emotionalism. "A person died," he thundered, "and someone should have to pay!"

At one point the judge, who I suspect by now was getting tired of it all, even said, "Okay, Mr. Travis. Just take a few breaths and calm down."

By noon time it was all over. Judge Stockwell gave the jury some stern instructions on making a fair and just decision. "The plaintiff has the burden of proving by the greater weight of the evidence that Dr. Salsano breached the standard of care and that his breach proximately caused the injuries to the plaintiff."

We broke for lunch before the jury returned to deliberate on the case. In the cafeteria my confidence was returning and unlike the first day I began to unwind and start joking. I found out that Kate McCauley was half Italian, which brought on a whole bevy of funny remembrances, like the Italian mother's obsession with keeping the furniture in its plastic casing to keep it pristine. I shared how my wife's grandfather had to read the newspaper after work in the basement because her grandmother didn't want him smoking on the encased furniture. "Did you ever notice how Italian mothers say such weird things?" I asked.

"Oh definitely," she answered. "There was the time we first moved to Virginia, and I called my mother one day and happened to tell her we could not find good Italian bread, and her response was *See, I told you to stay in the states.*"

Kate laughed heartily. In all this, I remembered reading once how Abraham Lincoln would unwind from the terrible strains of the Civil War by sharing funny stories. In the Proverbs it's written, "A merry heart does good like a medicine" (Proverbs 17:22). And so it is.

But before we returned to the courtroom the conversation turned more serious. "It's still hard for me to believe I was sued at all, let alone twice," I replied.

"Well, doctor," Kate told me, "by current statistics a physician in this country will on the average be involved in a malpractice suit every seven years."

"Well," I answered, "I guess that means I'll be safe for the next fourteen years.

Besides, I learned one thing from the Priscilla Granger case. I will never take another doctor's word that he is managing something if I'm in any way involved in the patient's care."

"Then you've learned something from all this," she said confidently. "It wasn't in vain."

We returned to the courtroom to see the jury formally sent off to make their fateful decision. "What do we do now?" I asked Kate.

"Nothing. We just wait. You're free to leave the courtroom, but stay nearby. The bailiff will make an announcement when we reconvene."

It was probably just a couple of hours, but it seemed like the whole afternoon as the jury considered their verdict. Now the joking was over. I walked off to a quiet unused corner of the building to pray and to ponder my past and my future.

Ever since the motion in judgment from Priscilla Granger, and culminating in the Lisa Hansen trial, I had grown cynical about medicine, but not irreparably. If, however, I lost this trial, I would have to brace myself for the repercussions. I recalled reading a physician's account of how his malpractice carrier had supported him through the vicissitudes of a lawsuit only to abruptly drop him afterwards even though he won the case. And trying to obtain malpractice coverage under such circumstances is like trying to buy life insurance after you've been diagnosed with leukemia. And without malpractice insurance you can't admit to any hospitals or participate in any health insurance plans. So I had a lot more to lose in this situation than my self-esteem. I rehearsed all this in my mind as I sat by the window looking out over the placid courthouse lawn. "Dear Lord," I prayed, "Give me the strength. Deliver me from evil. Help me to overcome these circumstances." David prayed in the Psalms, "Oh that I had wings like a dove. Then would I fly away and be at rest" (Psalms 55:6). I echoed his plea.

After a while I returned to the courtroom where my two attorneys were already seated awaiting the jury's return.

The jury had by then returned to their box, and then the bailiff entered the room. "All rise…"

The judge took his seat. "Ladies and gentleman of the jury, have you reached your verdict?"

The foreperson arose, "Yes, your honor. We the jury find in favor of the defendant, Dr. Salsano." Suddenly, there was an ear-piercing scream from one of Lisa Hansen's daughters who almost fainted at hearing this, followed by intense sobbing. How strange, I thought. Was she crying because the whole trial reopened the wound of losing her mother, or was it because she had her heart set on a big financial settlement?

Perhaps it was a little bit of both. Judge Stockwell then spoke, "Upon motion of defendant, judgment is hereby ordered adjudged and decreed that this matter be dismissed with full prejudice and stricken from the docket of the court."

"Congratulations, Dr. Salsano," John Easter said, shaking my hand vigorously with Kate McCauley's equally vigorous affirmation.

"So is there anything I need to do now?" I asked.

"Nope," he said. "Just go home. You're finished here."

I did go straight home and related everything to Doreen. We both thanked God for His grace and mercy, and then it occurred to me; both Lisa Hansen's daughters who were professing Christians had certainly been praying to God for their own cause which was antithetical to mine. It was as Abraham Lincoln once said of the North versus the South, "both prayed to the same God, but the Lord had His way in the matter." Nonetheless, I felt as if a heavy burden had been lifted off me, but I knew I wouldn't get off completely unhurt. My malpractice insurance rate would almost certainly jump significantly, but at least it was unlikely that I would be dropped (though not impossible). Now I felt I could have a nice talk with my father about the whole experience.

As I wrote earlier, I decided not to talk up the whole malpractice thing with my family, but keep it squarely in God's hands (though I admit now it was partly shame that kept me silent). When I divulged the whole thing to Dad, now having been brought to closure, I was surprised that he was actually irate. "Why didn't you say something? I can't believe you didn't tell me!" He was not impressed by my explanation. Dad was a problem solver his whole adult life, and I guess that my problem was one that, the solution of which, he would have wanted to be a part of. Maybe too, he was a little hurt that I hadn't confided in him. In any case, he listened intently as I related the whole story to him. It had been a three and a half year nightmare.

I came out of the Lisa Hansen trial intact, but humbled and, I am sorry to say, very cynical. Gone was my wide-eyed love of medicine. I still was pledged to the care and welfare of my patients both physically and spiritually, but a very subtle shift of outlook had occurred in my professional life. Since the two lawsuits, I had become much more circumspect about offering spiritual encouragement and prayer. Of the two patients to whom I was so devoted, they were the very ones who went after me with all aggressive intent for punitive damages. Jesus was not speaking lightly when he warned his followers not to cast their spiritual pearls so casually to those who had no appreciation for their true intent. It was a hard lesson to learn but learn it I did. I continued to pray with my patients, but with greater discrimination.

Another attitude shift involved my practice of medicine in general. I now began ordering tests, and more tests. I did not do so totally unnecessarily, but often just to cover myself. Even If I knew a patient's chest pain was not coming from his heart, I would run a gamut of cardiac testing anyway. Whereas my thoughts towards a new patient once were, *How can I help this person*, now my first thought was, *is this person a potential lawsuit*? If it's a stretch to call the practice of medicine fun, I was at least able to call it rewarding or fulfilling. But for me it was becoming more and more of a tedium, with long hours, sacrifice of family time, and the loss of sleep now having no counterbalancing benefits, not even monetary ones. I briefly toyed with the idea of leaving health care altogether, but there was nothing else I could do. I was a highly trained professional with a very narrow portfolio. I had in essence become trapped in a velvet prison!

But all these ponderings, deep as they were, meant nothing when I started work on Monday morning following my courtroom experience. The high calling of medicine, for better or for worse, was my lot in life and to its banner I rallied.

Chapter Eight

CONFIDENCE LOST AND REGAINED

"Many are the afflictions of the righteous but the Lord delivers him from them all."

PSALMS 34:19

It did not take me long to find fellow physicians who had shared in the ordeal of malpractice litigation.

I've known and worked with Dr. Mitchell Roberts for over twenty years. He was (and still is) a preeminent intestinal and liver specialist in Eastern Virginia, yet even he had become, by 1998, a victim of a personal injury lawsuit. Mitch's story was all too familiar to me. He did everything right, but something unexpected happened.

Now it happened that a patient of mine named Sharon came to the emergency room one Saturday night with abdominal pain, vomiting, and blood in the stool. I came in to see her and admitted her to the intensive care unit. Intestinal bleeding like this is a true medical emergency, and it was critical to uncover the source of bleeding and stop it to save the patient's life. I immediately called Dr. Roberts for a consultation, who dutifully came in to see the patient. After his evaluation, we met at the nurse's station. "Well Mitch, what do you think?"

"Les," he said, "it's going to be difficult to say."

It turned out that this woman had undergone a surgical procedure known as a gastric bypass many years ago to lose weight, and although I knew this and also knew that it increased her risk for stomach ulcers and hemorrhage, Mitch had to enlighten me about her present dilemma. "You see, Les, the very reason the bypass is done is to have food pass around the main body of the stomach to give an immediate full sensation when eating. And it's that very bypass that prevents me from getting my scope into the main portion of the stomach to diagnose the problem. She could be bleeding to death from a part of her intestines I can do nothing about."

We never could get her stabilized enough to undergo any aggressive intervention, and as she lapsed into a coma her husband made clear her wish not to be put on artificial life support. Once end of life measures were in place there was nothing left to do but go home, yet neither of us did, despite the lateness of the hour! And I knew why. We began to share our common litigation experiences, and he also shared with me his frustration, angst and bitter disappointment. "And you can't depend on anyone to cover for you," he told me. "You've got to check everything yourself!" (Boy, did I find that out the hard way with Priscilla Granger!) Nevertheless, I could hear in Mitch's retelling the Lord's still small voice exhorting me to put away bitterness.

I began by forgiving the people who sued me. All the consequences of my recent lawsuits; rising malpractice premiums, hospital and health insurance participation issues, bearing the potential label of incompetency among my peers, all paled in comparison to my not allowing unforgiveness and bitterness to take root in my soul. "After all," I said to myself, "the Bible says it is the glory of a man to forgive an offense" (Proverbs 19:11). And the first test of my resolve was near at hand, for even as Sharon was on the verge of death, her husband William asked me to speak to his son, who was barely ten years old. "Dear Lord," I prayed. "Help me to say the right thing to this precious little boy who is about to lose his mother."

We all walked together, William, his son and I, to the hospital chapel and sat down. I struggled to find the words to say. "Your mother is very sick," I said calling him by his name. "She fought real hard to live, but she isn't going to make it. I know your mother and she's a good Christian woman. I know that she'll be with God forever. Heaven is a wonderful place and Jesus said he would go and prepare a place for us."

His tears started to flow and my words became more halting as I felt my own tears welling up. "God wants us all to trust Him, even when bad things happen. He knows you're hurt and He feels everything you feel but He really cares about you and He loves you, now more than ever."

We held hands and prayed, and returned to the ICU waiting room. "William, I'll keep you posted," I said, and left.

Not long after that, Sharon passed away. Her husband has continued as my patient to this day, but I never met his son again. The whole incident was a reminder to me that if I was going to continue to be a caring physician to my patients, then unforgiveness and cynicism had to go. The spirit of bitterness is completely incompatible with the true spirit of Christianity.

So private practice went on for me, and my reputation grew, seemingly unperturbed by the malpractice incidents. New patients were coming to me practically on a daily basis, and my colleagues interacted with me with ever deepening respect. Because of conditions in the health care field, Doreen became more withdrawn and more discontent with my work situation. "You should never have gone into private practice," was her constant refrain, and I was coming around to agreeing with her. The girls were fully into their teens, and the constant struggle to shield them from pernicious influences (mainly teenage boys) and find positive social outlets was a fulltime job.

Leah graduated from high school in 1998 and was on her way to Bob Jones University in South Carolina. It was a day in August when I planned to drive her there, but Hurricane Bonney hit the Hampton Roads area the day before our trip. My goodness! If a category one hurricane could do all this, I thought, what would happen if we encountered a category five storm? I briefly pondered the option of canceling the trip, but Leah had to get to school so I went on with my original plan. How fragile is our existence in this life. Like Job, the rewards of a lifetime of hard work can be swept away in an instant. Natural disaster, financial collapse, devastating illness, (malpractice lawsuits) can suddenly appear and sweep away our tranquility and security and perhaps even our very lives. Job 14:1 speaks of man coming forth like a flower only to be cut down. But I found comfort in the words of Moses written some three and a half millennia ago, "So teach us to number our days, that we may apply our hearts to wisdom" (Psalms 90:12). This natural disaster arriving on the heels of my medical-legal ones added a sobering touch of irony to my newly reconstructed view of life. But despite all this, as the new millennium approached, I was beginning to regain my earlier optimism and was prepared to consign my malpractice experiences to the dustbin of history, but then, Michael happened.

Michael was a very pleasant, outgoing black male, and he had everything to live for. A rising executive in a local corporation, he had youth, energy and what appeared to be excellent interpersonal skills. Michael was a diabetic on insulin, but he hardly ever came in for check-ups.

One of the last things Kate McCauley told me was to learn from my mistakes, and a big one was not to trust another doctor's say so on a mutual patient (this was my undoing with Priscilla Granger).

Now when Michael first came to me, he came with a history of deep vein thrombosis (a blood clot) in his leg. That illness had occurred years before he came under my care and was attributed (according to his doctors at the time) to diabetes out of control and dehydration (it was at that time that he was started on insulin). In hind sight I should have been more suspicious of the original assessment and treatment plan, especially as things turned out, but yet again, the pressure to move quickly and generate income led me not to pursue any supplemental work-up (although it did cross my mind). The patient was stable and healthy, so I moved on to the next patient. One red flag was the absence of any obvious triggers to his blood clot and the fact that he was on no blood thinners except for one aspirin a day.

After many years under my care, Michael came in one day complaining of pain in his leg. Just as before, he had no triggers for a blood clot such as trauma, recent surgery or recent prolonged bed rest. He had no underlying heart or lung disease or any circulatory disorder, but because of his past history I made a detailed exam of his legs which was completely unremarkable. Upon further questioning, I did learn that he had taken a recent plane trip and studies have shown that even healthy individuals develop incipient blood clots in their leg veins which quickly dissolve without incident. So I decided to play it safe, and despite the dubious history and normal exam, I ordered a Doppler ultrasound to look for clots.

Now, ordinarily I order such a test to be done ASAP to confirm the diagnosis and start effective treatment, but unknown to me Michael had a very important business meeting coming up, so he scheduled his test for one week later. He never made it. Two days after that fateful visit, I was having a busier than usual schedule when my nurse knocked on the exam room door. "Dr. Salsano, it's the emergency room. Michael Davis was brought in by rescue squad in full cardiac arrest and they just pronounced him dead."

Oh no! I thought. *This can't be true! This can't be happening!* The ER physician got on the phone. "According to the family, the patient was leaving for work when he stopped on the sidewalk in front of his house, clutched his chest, and fell to the ground. He went into a convulsion, then stopped breathing. We never were able to get a pulse. He was essentially D.O.A. (Dead On Arrival)."

"Were there any objective findings to indicate a heart attack?" I asked.

"No. He was in asystole (flat line) the whole time we worked on him. Sorry Les." Deep down I knew what happened, but did not want to believe it, and that was that his leg pain really was from a blood clot which had broken off and traveled to his lung. A massive pulmonary embolism, it's called, and it stopped his heart, causing instant death. "I sent this patient for a Doppler of his leg to rule out a DVT. Do you have a report in the system?" I asked.

He checked the computer. "No, I don't see one. Are you sure it wasn't at another hospital?"

I started to feel the same apprehension as I did with both Priscilla Granger and Lisa Hansen. I'll have to speak with his family, I thought. It's better to be up front with them. Besides, it could have been something other than an embolism. I know, I thought. I'll press for an autopsy. Michael's family reluctantly agreed to the autopsy, which confirmed that he indeed had suffered a massive pulmonary embolism. The blood clot which had formed in his leg had broken off and floated up to his heart where it was then pumped at high force directly into his lungs. The clot, however, being fragile shattered into literally thousands of smaller pieces which showered into his lungs causing a complete shutdown of blood flow, cardiac arrest and death. It was during this time that I discovered the patient had postponed his Doppler test, but that was a moot point. To the family and perhaps ultimately to a jury, I would be perceived as having missed the opportunity to diagnose a deep vein thrombosis and prevent his untimely death.

Now, in truth, pulmonary embolism is a common disorder and often occurs with little or no symptoms and so passes unnoticed. Furthermore, these events are known to occur in patients even while taking blood-thinning medication, so a medical doctor often is faced with a real dilemma. How can you ever be sure that you won't miss making the diagnosis? Mr. Davis' exam was normal, and he had no established precipitating factors. As I sat there going through these mental exercises, Kate McCauley's warning, "…learn from your mistakes" echoed in my mind. It might have been that his bloodstream had an intrinsic tendency to clot (and without warning). Such conditions are rare but not unheard of. Often there is a lack of some protein, or too much of another, and the result is to throw the clotting mechanism out of balance. Such conditions are usually, but not always, genetically determined. In retrospect, the patient would likely have been put on blood thinners the rest of his life. Even if I had started them within twenty-four hours of his office visit, the growing clot in his leg might have embolized anyway. So again I was the victim of having assumed that another physician had rendered the proper care, and in my deepest heart I knew it would cost me.

Michael's sister was saddened but pleasant as I explained to her the facts leading to her brother's death. Then again, so was Colin Granger, and so was Lisa Hansen's daughter in the beginning.

Mere words are not sufficient to express the ambivalent feelings a doctor has when he loses a patient in this way. First there is remorse; could I have prevented it, did I not do something that could have made a difference? Then anger, first with yourself; why did I trust the previous doctor's care, why didn't I run the necessary tests? Finally, fear; what will the family do? Drooling personal injury lawyers post TV ad come-ons day and night, 24/7.

At home, even the doctor's family cannot quite sympathize, "Why did you ever become a doctor?" is the often repeated refrain. No wonder medical doctors have a high suicide rate!

Michael's sisters wasted no time. Hardly three months had passed and a lawyer's motion in judgment was on my desk. I sat there transfixed as twice before, rehashing in my mind what happened and wondering how I would handle it. I felt that I had a good case. After all, my exam was normal, and I did order the appropriate test. If the patient postponed it, was I to blame? I was hopeful, but not certain that my case would be vindicated if it went to court. Yet, win or lose, I knew in my spirit that this was my third strike, and as far as my malpractice underwriters were concerned, I would be out.

I was hoping for Dan Filetti again or John Easter, but they had all gone their separate ways. Instead, I was assigned an attorney from a highly esteemed Norfolk law firm. This company had a well established reputation for defense in personal injury cases, and was known to be doctor-friendly.

I met attorney Jarvis Hastings at my office and immediately launched into my version of the story. Gone was my wide-eyed innocence and ardent desire to clear my name. Now all I wanted was to get those people out of my life and to minimize my financial reverses.

"Well," he said, "the first thing you'll need to do is complete some…"

"Interrogatories," I interjected.

"That's right," he said quizzically, not expecting my response. "And I'll work on getting some vascular surgeons to review the whole thing once I get all the records. It sounds like you did everything right." (Boy, had I heard that before!)

"I think you have a good case Les," Mr. Hastings told me, "but the firm Mr. Davis' family retained has deep pockets, and they're not reluctant to use them. By the way, they're asking for two million dollars."

Two million! I thought. *Well, I'm finished.*

Some time later we met again. "I sat in on the sisters' depositions. They make a good impression. They come across as caring and polite. They dressed very conservatively and made lots of Christian references in their testimonies."

So here we go again. I'm being sued by Christians, my fellow believers. Money obviously was more important than brotherhood. I recalled the apostle Paul's scathing indictment against the Corinthian believers for doing the same thing in the first century (1 Corinthians 6:11). "Jarvis," I asked, "I checked with my staff about the scheduling of the venous Doppler test. Mr. Davis put off his test because of work considerations. Can't I claim that his failure to follow my instructions caused his death?"

"Les," he answered, "you cannot use a deceased man's testimony against him in court since he no longer is able to defend himself by presenting his version of the story. Your testimony on what Michael Davis did or said is inadmissible in his absence. This is known as the dead man's statute."

"But that's not fair!" I exclaimed.

Jarvis simply shrugged. "We have plenty of other evidence to support your cause. We need to concentrate on that."

"Jarvis, where will the trial take place?" I asked.

"Norfolk," was his answer. I couldn't help but conclude that my defense in Norfolk, presented before a largely minority populace, against such a close knit minority family would be suicidal. Better, I thought, to settle, but not for two million! My only hope was to make a good deposition.

The deposition was held in the Bank of America tower overlooking the picturesque Norfolk waterfront. Gazing through the window I could see the spot where I sat with my family, watching the fireworks on our first Independence Day in Virginia. As I stood pondering those early days, I heard a voice say, "Doctor, we'll be starting momentarily."

I sullenly took my seat. Someone swore me in and the court stenographer began busily clicking away as I answered the attorney's questions.

After the usual demographic questions came the probing for weakness, errors in judgment, willful negligence becoming the real question.

"Yes," I retorted. "My exam was normal, but in light of the patient's past history I decided to order the Doppler anyway. Ordinarily, there are other risk factors involved, trauma, surgery, prolonged bed rest, which was not the case in this instance."

I could see in the opposing lawyer's face great earnestness, could almost see the words forming in his mind, ready to catch me up in a contradiction. "Let me add," I said, anticipating his next reference, "I was aware that Mr. Davis had recently taken a plane trip and that recent studies have shown incipient clot formation in plane traveler's legs. But these proto-clots quickly dissolve and there is no proof that prolonged air travel of itself is a cause of venous thrombosis. It seems that trauma, surgery, underlying heart or lung disease are necessary precursors because they set up the pathophysiology that promotes clot formation."

"Why did you wait to run the tests?" he asked.

"I told my staff to schedule him, but because of the negative exam and lack of co-morbid factors, I conceded to the patient a delay in scheduling to allow for his work demands."

Some minor bantering followed and the deposition ended. I wasn't sure if I had accomplished anything until Mr. Hastings called me excitedly. "Congratulations! Your testimony was so compelling they've dropped their asking amount from two million to under a million. I think we can work them down to two-hundred thousand. If we go to court I believe you can win this case!"

I thanked Jarvis for his encouraging words, but put the whole thing squarely into God's hands. After my experience with Priscilla Granger, I came to understand it was wrong to pray against people, no matter what they say about me or do to me. History records that even in the early church there were some who put personal gain and security ahead of faithfulness to God's calling. But Paul made the better way very clear, "Render to no man evil for evil. Provide things honest in the sight of all. If it be possible, as much as lies within you live at peace with all men" (Romans 12:17, 18).

Leaving to go to work in those days, I felt like a soldier going to battle, and my enemies were many, not just disease, although that would be enough. In addition I had to contend with recalcitrant third party payers, intrusive medical review committees, hostile lawyers and deadbeat patients, just to name a few. And on top of all this, being conscientious, I strove to be a supportive husband and father.

Now in all this I never doubted God's faithfulness. I knew in my heart what Saint Paul declared was true, "That all things work together for good, to them that love God" (Romans 8:28). I asked then, even as now, for God to help me love Him more, to walk obedient to His calling. I knew that life was just a vapor, here one day and then gone. Once life was over all our accomplishments, desires and hopes, perish. Only what we do in the spirit has eternal consequences. As Blaise Pascal put it, even if there was no God, a life well-lived, doing good, helping the poor, visiting the fatherless and the widows in their afflictions and keeping yourself untainted from the world is the better way.

Though at times I was tempted to doubt God's veracity, I held firm. "What times I am afraid I will trust in you" (Psalms 56:3). Yet it was at that very time in my life that events would happen which would give us all, as Americans, reason to doubt God's veracity.

It started for me as a typical Tuesday morning, actually quieter than usual. I arrived at the office from hospital rounds a little earlier and the morning was not too busy. It was the day after my birthday and I was still enjoying the fading echoes of birthday frivolities when Doreen called the office. "I was listening to the news and there was some sort of accident in New York City. A plane flew into the World Trade Center." It was September 11, 2001.

In the office we turned on the radio to hear the announcer say, "A second plane had just flown into the south tower and exploded in a fireball. Authorities now are certain these were not accidents, but premeditated terrorist attacks on our country." 9/11 had arrived and nothing would ever be the same. My personal agonies were now enveloped into and eclipsed by our greater national agony. "This is the end of the world!" I shouted out loud with all earnestness.

More tragedy followed: the downing of flight 93, the Pentagon, and then the anthrax scare. As an internist, this last crisis resonated with me. Eastern Virginia Medical School even sponsored a series of lectures in Norfolk on bioterrorism. As a nation it was as if we had been turned on our head and shaken out. At the height of the scare, a suspicious brown paper package arrived for me that fit all the criteria for a terrorist mailing. I almost disposed of it, but mustered the courage to open it, and found that it was an old Cary Grant movie that I had purchased from a mom and pop outlet in Canada. (Boy, did I feel silly.) As recovery set in, like most Americans I was left haunted, especially by the images of well dressed young executives leaping to their deaths from the doomed trade center towers.

Thinking back, I recalled the one time I visited the top of the World Trade Center, back in the 1970s. On a day trip to Manhattan, Doreen and I took the elevator to the very top of the skyscraper, recently opened to the public. And when the elevator doors opened there was no elegant "Windows on the World" restaurant, but a vast unfinished space an acre in size. Looking down the windows to the pavement was a dizzying experience. Remembering that day, it's hard for me to comprehend having to jump from such a height or to imagine being the tortured individual who had to choose between burning to death or being crushed after a 1,500 foot fall. 9/11 was truly our generation's Pearl Harbor. I especially could empathize with the nation's tragedy because of my own. I even solaced myself with the hope that the national calamity would somehow preempt my own, that business as usual would come to an end. Of course it didn't. True to his promise in scripture, God did not take away my trial, but in his great Providence, went through it with me.

So as my third lawsuit moved quickly to a resolution, what I really questioned was my own decision to become a doctor. Maybe, I supposed, everything went wrong because I stepped out of God's will. I recalled how upon my conversion experience I felt a strong notion to go into the ministry, but fear overruled my taking that step, including fear of not being able to pay back my student loans and fear of displeasing my father, lying in a hospital bed recovering from a major heart attack. So what, I thought, if I accomplished many good works as a doctor. It's obedience that God is after. "If you love me, you will keep my commandments" (John 14:15). Many times my wife, being an exceptionally intense exhorter, would say to me, "Les, you don't love God like you should." Maybe I was experiencing the sorry fruit of disobedience.

I remembered a true story about a dedicated Christian surgeon who once said to his wife, "Our marriage and family, and our Christian faith mean more to me than my medical career. So I'm going to work as hard as I can while I have my youth and strength. By age forty I should have made enough money so that we could be financially secure, and I'll retire from medicine to serve the Lord with you the rest of my life." His wife, presumably speechless, simply nodded her head in agreement, and so he began his career. True to his word, he worked practically 24/7. His wife hardly ever saw him, And when his goal of financial independence by forty years of age was in reach, he announced to her, "I'm ready to retire and we're going to start our new life together by taking a world cruise, first class all the way."

Needless to say, she was amazed, and began preparing for their trip, but before they booked their passage, he suffered a massive heart attack and died. Now up to this point, even the most discriminating moralist could see the lessons embodied in this tragic story, but the final chapter presented the most incredible lesson of all, for while his widow sat in mourning at the funeral, several women came forward and admitted to her that they had all had affairs with her deceased husband. So I learned that the best intentioned plans, even those with a Godly motive, when done outside of God's will, must certainly end in disaster.

It was soon after that my attorney called me to say my insurance company wanted me to settle rather than go to trial. "What do you think, Jarvis?" I asked. "Well Les, I still feel you should take it to trial." When I asked my insurance agent if by settling the company would drop me, he emphatically said, "No, the amount of the settlement was not considered a significant figure, it had dropped to $205,000."

Well, that sounded encouraging. I just was not up to another courtroom experience, so I agreed to settle, against my attorney's advice. And to demonstrate to the insurance company that I was a good client, I paid to participate in a malpractice seminar they themselves were sponsoring. I had read about doctors being advised by their malpractice carriers to settle, only to be summarily dropped as clients, but surely, I reasoned, that wouldn't happen to me. I was a good doctor. I had been with them for fifteen years. I had a good reputation. All my lawsuits had questionable merit. They couldn't drop me, they shouldn't drop me, yet drop me is exactly what they did!

About two months after the settlement was made, I received a certified letter announcing the termination of my policy, effective on January 1, 2003. The only problem was that the letter came at the end of November. I had just thirty days to find new coverage, which given the fact I had just paid out on a malpractice lawsuit would be virtually impossible. And to compound the vindictiveness of the corporate decision-makers to drop me at the eleventh hour, they flatly refused to grant me retroactive coverage, which for a client of fifteen years was practically an industry standard. If I couldn't get malpractice coverage by New Year's Day, I would not be able to practice at the hospital, participate in health insurance plans or in Medicare! In effect, my career would be over. I cannot express to you the consternation and helplessness I felt, or the frenzied searching for insurance I engaged in during that final month of 2002. Yet on Christmas Eve, by the Lord's providential grace, I was accepted by an insurance company, and although the premium was triple what I was paying before, and I had to pay out $35,000 (the retroactive coverage), at least on January second I was able to open my doors for business. I was still in practice, but I was cashed out. I was still on my feet, but essentially broke.

God, however, was with me. Since Doreen and I were obviously not in a holiday mood, we planned on a simple, quiet Christmas, and much to my amazement, because of an accounting glitch the caterer I hired for the holiday gave us the dinner free of charge. I knew it was a token of God's faithfulness that even opposite the tens of thousands of dollars I had lost, he would take care of me. It was just like he told Israel in the Old Testament during a time of grave national peril, "I am the Lord and I change not, therefore you sons of Jacob are not consumed" (Malachi 3:6). The Jewish people, the apple of God's eye, can never be destroyed (consider Adolph Hitler) because of God's faithfulness. And neither can anyone else who truly calls upon the name of the Lord.

God had rescued me, but more trials lay ahead. "Though I walk in the midst of trouble, you will revive me" (Psalms 138:7). It turned out that I was received by the new malpractice company in a provisional status because of my prior claims history. In practical terms that meant my annual premiums would automatically escalate yearly (even without any further mishaps) to a maximum of about $65,000 by 2008. Even in 2005, my premium was $36,000, four times the standard rate in Southeast Virginia for my specialty. In the light of such ruinous costs, my future in health care looked bleak, and as if to top it off, my billing company of several years went through some sort of internal crisis which caused an acute drop in income, necessitating a switch to a new company and an even more protracted downturn. I personally calculated the loss of close to $40,000 dollars for professional services that was practically irretrievable. It was almost six months before my cash-flow recovered.

In the light of all this, at least outwardly, I was unflustered, but inwardly I had had it with being a doctor. I continued to be busy as ever, new patients registering every day, but to me it no longer was a profession. It had become a job. If the Lord miraculously gave it to me, then it had to be my own intransigence that ruined it, or maybe I was just a bit too naïve about my career. It slowly dawned on me that a person had to be pragmatic and worldly wise to succeed in business.

"You should have listened to Mr. Bell," I thought. Mr. Bell was my high school guidance counselor who didn't think I had the potential to become a doctor. "Alessio, you should consider becoming a biology book illustrator." "But Mr. Bell," I said, "I want to be a doctor." Like many others throughout my past, he just shrugged his shoulders. As I sat at my desk pondering all the setbacks I yelled, "Mr. Bell, you were right!"

One day while sitting in my office, I was reviewing medical journals and noticed a category in the classified ads; medical practices for sale. "That's it!" I exclaimed. "I'll sell my practice…yeah, and do what?" Also in the classified section were ads for something called Locum Tenens. Locum Tenens is the temporary placement of a physician in a practice somewhere, usually to take the place of a doctor who has retired or relocated or who was out sick for an extended period of time. Locum Tenens pays the malpractice insurance. However, you could be placed literally anywhere in the country where the need arises. The thought of leaving my family to practice medicine on the other side of the country was not appealing, but I could see how the good might outweigh the bad. First, my malpractice would be paid. This was critical, before my insurance rate escalated to over $60,000 a year, pretty much ending my medical career permanently. Second, I would be able to concentrate on practicing medicine again, being unencumbered with the burden of running a business. All the headaches of collecting money, fighting with insurance companies, and dealing with disgruntled employees would be over. If it was too late to be a biology book illustrator, I could at least go back to what I was trained to do, which was to take care of sick people. No, Locum Tenens was sounding better and better, but first I had to sell my practice. That should be easy, I thought. It's busy, thriving, and in a good location. Who wouldn't want to make the investment? Scanning the classifieds, I came across an ad for a medical practice sales consultant. "Okay, here's where I start."

I contacted the consultant, Jerry, and told him my situation. He listened closely while peppering me with some very focused questions.

I answered as best I could, and then we got down to brass tacks. "I'll fax you a list of documents I will need to properly assess the worth and salability of your practice," he said. "I do require a $1,000 deposit up front. Of course, that will be deducted from my final fee once I sell your business."

"What is your fee?" I asked.

"Ten percent of the sale price."

"Okay," I said with a shrug. "I agree to your terms." I can't possibly convey to you how intense my conviction was at the time to leave private practice.

Jerry was a very knowledgeable and savvy broker. He was an ex-hospital administrator who knew the business of medical business, yet two years later it was my fate that my practice was still unsold. If I said fate, I misspoke, for in truth it was God. I received that practice as a specific, direct answer to prayer. It was a gift from my Heavenly Father when I really needed it, and the Bible says "The gifts and the calling of God are without repentance" (Romans 11:29). That is to say, when God does something, he never changes his mind or modifies his plans to meet changing circumstances. "…my counsel shall stand, and I will do all my pleasure" (Isaiah 46:10). The fact is, He creates the circumstances! The problem was with me. I had lost my confidence in myself, and forgive me, though I never admitted it, in God! I just could not accept the inevitability of my present situation. When I spoke in this vein to Jerry, who was a self-professed agnostic, and asked him why I couldn't sell my practice, he floored me with his answer (especially when I knew him to be the last person to make excuses for himself). "Well, Les. All I could figure is that a higher power is involved here." Meanwhile, the practice of medicine continued to roll on.

How ironic that at the very time I was trying to divest myself of private practice, my case load was busier than ever. And the medical conditions were getting more complex. This may have been in part because fewer internists were accepting Medicare patients, so the elderly, with typically more difficult problems, were finding their way to me.

And then there was Ursula.

After her gastric bypass surgery, her weight loss stabilized and she began to have complications from the many years of morbid obesity, especially low back pain from severe arthritis. One time I went to the office in a blizzard (one of the few Virginia Beach has had) to meet her son with a written prescription for pain relievers. On another occasion, Ursula was hospitalized with a hip fracture. When I discharged her, I had forgotten to give her a B-12 shot (a common need following stomach surgery). So when she called about it, I filled the syringe at the office and went to her house to administer it myself. Ursula was a person you didn't mind extending yourself for, and in her gratitude she paid me back double with Christmas gifts for my children and staff, and with home baked pastries (German of course) that she brought to the office constantly. She had particularly endeared herself to my workers, so when she passed away quietly in her sleep we all grieved her loss. I made a point of attending her funeral and perhaps did my last service to her by attending one of her relatives who passed out right in the middle of the eulogy. I am convinced that every physician needs at least a few patients like Ursula to stay focused on the true meaning of why they became a doctor in the first place. I will always miss Ursula, and Ronnie her husband, who followed her in death one year later.

It was also around that time that my nurse casually mentioned to me that she saw Colin Granger's obituary in the newspaper. (Priscilla had preceded him some years before.) And as much as I railed against lawsuits and personal injury lawyers, I had to feel sorry for the Grangers. Even though our paths crossed in adversity, we were fellow travelers in this life, and they were now gathered to their eternal destinies. How brief is our life, I thought, and how true the word of God when it says, "All our days are passed away in wrath and we finish our days with a sigh…so teach us to number our days, that we may apply our hearts to wisdom" (Psalms 90:9, 12).

"There is nothing new under the sun. That which has been is what will be, and that which is done is what will be done" (Ecclesiastes 1:9). All those things which seemed so important to me, and all my adversities, were simply history repeating itself. Job said, "Man is born unto trouble…" (Job 5:7) and it has been that way since Adam's fall from grace. So at fifty years of age, I braced myself for whatever challenges lay ahead of me, and well I should have since I was about to experience "L'annee Terrible," the worst year of my life.

Although it didn't happen first, the death of my father punctuated the entire year. In fact, Dad died in his sleep on Christmas morning. When he was more than his usual couple of hours late to the family dinner in New Jersey, my sister drove to his apartment where the police were needed to break through the door. They found him seated in his sofa chair in his pajamas with the TV on. Although no autopsy was done, it was typical of a heart related event for the individual to develop symptoms in the early morning hours and have to sit up to preserve breathing as the failing heart caused the lungs to fill with fluid. But try as I may to detach myself emotionally from the event and medically analyze his final days, it was my father and I cried. And it was the more poignant to me because I always felt I would have time to be at his bedside praying for him, holding his hand and rejoicing in his salvation, but in God's Providence it was not to be so. When I flew up to New Jersey to attend to his personal belongings, however, I found a card with a prayer among his pocketed items! The prayer read:

"Blessed is the man that trusts in the Lord, and whose hope the Lord is. For he shall be as a tree planted by the waters, and…neither shall cease from yielding fruit" (Jeremiah 17:7, 8).

So the Lord left me with a glint of hope that Dad had made his peace with Him, and I heard His still small voice whisper, "Trust me. I'll make all things right." Nevertheless I was haunted for many months by the thought that I never had a chance to say good-bye to my father. In our last conversation together, over the phone, all I did was complain about the malpractice dilemma (my rate by then had risen to a ruinous $36,000), and his answer to me was totally unexpected. "Les," he told me, "I'm sorry I encouraged you to become a doctor."

I was ashamed of myself for extracting such a confession out of him. Ashamed for flouting the fulfillment of his promise to his own father. Apart from that I was proud of his memory, and truly humbled by the outpouring of respect at his wake. The funeral home was packed with people. Here was a man whose life had obviously touched many lives for good, regardless of any personal failings.

One particular family consisting of a mother and her two adult daughters were all literally sobbing. I had never seen them before, and when I inquired, the story went like this: The mother, a Hispanic immigrant, had come under my father's tutelage as a social worker in Newark, New Jersey. She was penniless and homeless with two little toddler girls she couldn't even afford to feed. Just when she was about to give them up as wards of the state, Dad stepped in. He first got her approved for welfare support, and he did more. He gave her support out of his own pocket and found a job for her, too. As her situation improved, she got off welfare and raised her daughters, who by the time of Dad's death, were college graduates embarking on professional careers themselves. I may have seen them through rose-colored glasses that night, but there was something clean about them, something bright and replete with promise. It was through my father's kind intervention that they were set on the right path, certainly a road quite different from the one expected of two homeless immigrant girls growing up in an inner city ghetto.

This was my father's legacy. I wondered if at my funeral there would be a similar scene, with people whose lives were touched by me. Of course, in the final analysis, it is what we do for God that matters most. If you help others out of a Godly motive then you won't lose your reward. Jesus himself said this, "Whoever gives one of these little ones (the poorest and most humble among us) a cup of cold water in the name of a prophet (that is, the person I've sent) I tell you he shall by no means lose his reward" (Matthew 10:42). The Bible is very clear in its pronouncement, "True religion and undefiled before God is to help the fatherless and the widow in their afflictions (Dad helped both), and to keep oneself untainted from the world" (James 1:27).

Dad's funeral was followed quickly by a new revelation when my sister called to tell me, "Mom is over $60,000 dollars in debt from credit cards. We're going to have to declare bankruptcy!" And that rude awakening was the prelude to yet one more when we discovered that our older daughter Leah had eloped with and married a young navy man we hardly knew! It was almost too much to all take in, and as if to give the knife in my side one more twist, I suffered a kidney stone attack. I had two extreme bouts of painful colic, but after a week I passed the stone painlessly in the middle of the night, and as I looked at myself in the mirror I mumbled, "Private practice is killing you. You've got to get out of it."

And then, as if to say good-bye, one by one of my longtime patients began to pass away. The bond that a family doctor makes with his patients after twenty years of service is almost as strong as that of a family member. Often when these patients came to the office they were greeted with hugs from my staff. One does not easily get over the loss of such a person. These were often men and women who belonged to the great generation, heroes of World War II and of the Great Depression, those who did their part, suffering in silence.

There was Alvin Thomas, ex-marine and WWII veteran, and Frank Garth who fought the Japanese in hand-to-hand combat, whose story was featured on the History Channel. Both were heavy smokers and both died of lung cancer. There was Wayne Vance, Pearl Harbor survivor, who died in his sleep, and John Grenville who patrolled the streets of Norfolk for civil defense in the bleak months that followed the Pearl Harbor attack. And there were the unsung heroines of the home front, who without fanfare raised their children and kept their homes in quiet dignity, in a meek and gentle spirit which as the apostle said, "Is in the eyes of God, of great price"(1 Peter 3:4). I remember Kathryn Moore, a delightful Christian woman whose daughter and husband still come to me, and Anna Mueller who lived just past 100 years. I closed my office one afternoon for her so my staff could throw her a surprise birthday party. There was Ruth Mintz, a very sweet elderly lady. She will always hold a special place in my heart, so with your permission I will share her story in detail.

Ruth was already in her eighties when she first came to me. By then I was the family doctor to her daughter and son-in-law and to her granddaughters and their families. She was a diminutive matriarch (barely over four feet tall), and quite drove her granddaughters crazy with errand requests and emotional support, but she had a good heart and their devotion to her was accordingly unconditional. Ruth was Jewish and she was orthodox. I remember her granddaughter once telling me how her grandmother, literally on her hands and knees, scoured every nook and corner of her house looking for leaven, fulfilling to the letter the Passover commandment in Exodus, "Seven days shall you eat unleavened bread, even the first day you shall dispose of all leaven out of your houses" (Exodus 12:15). Mrs. Mintz took her religious faith seriously, but unlike so many strict practitioners in all religions, she didn't do so dourly, wearing her religion on her sleeve. She rather did it devotedly, because it was what God commanded, and because her mother did it, and her grandmother before her, and all her ancestors from time immemorial. Her orthodoxy was not fanatical, but was tempered with kindness.

Ruth's amazingly good health began to decline as she entered her nineties, requiring frequent hospitalizations. It was always a pleasure for me to sit at her bedside holding her hand in prayer. It was from my encounters with Ruth that I learned the "Shema," Moses' great anthem of the Jewish faith, "Sh'ma Israel, Adonai Elohinu, Adonai Ehud." "Hear O Israel, the Lord our God, the Lord is one" (Deuteronomy 6:4). Ruth suffered her whole life from asthma and as such she was prone to lung infections. These became more frequent and more severe with advancing age, leading to many hospitalizations and high doses of antibiotics which led to other complications.

I prayed often with Ruth, but my prayers were very generic. We prayed the Sh'ma together and asked for God's grace and healing touch, but I always knew something was missing. I had grown very fond of Ruth. In many ways she harkened me back to my own grandmother, who died of breast cancer at too young an age. Deep within my soul I knew, felt overwhelmingly convicted, that I had to share the gospel with her, give her a chance to believe in Jesus (Y'shua, as His name is in Hebrew). One day in the hospital I sat at her bedside as before, and held her hand as before, but this time I said to her, "Ruth, I really care about you."

She nodded. "I want you to know that "Ha Shem" (a title for Almighty God used by the orthodox with deep respect) sent his son Y'shua to die for your sins and my sins, and He loves you too much for you not to hear and to believe." In many such words I presented the gospel to her, and when I asked her if she wished to pray to God and ask Y'shua to be her Savior she said yes, so we prayed the salvation prayer. I had many opportunities to pray with others in this way over the years, but I admit this time it was special. Afterwards, I kept wondering if it was real. Did she just pray with me to placate me? Only she knew, and only God knows, for not long after that she was called home, gathered unto her fathers, as it says in the Bible. I decided not to broadcast our special prayer together to her family. I didn't want to raise a controversy during their time of grieving, but it was and still is my sincerest joy that Ruth is in heaven. And when I see her again I will give a big hug to that little lady!

Something went out of me when Ruth Mintz died that I was never able to recover. I prayed less and less with my patients, concerning myself only with the tedium of medical care. It was as if the high calling, the priesthood Dr. Ream invited me to embrace long ago, was slipping through my hands like gossamer. And not long after these adjustments another longtime patient, Clarke Stengel, an irascible merchant marine sailor, who was with me from the very beginning of private practice, passed.

Clarke was every bit as cantankerous as Ruth was placid, but deep inside he had a good heart (very deep inside). Clarke often needed to be hospitalized, typically for chest pain, sometimes for abdominal distress, sometimes for bronchitis. I could write his admitting orders blindfolded I did them so often, and the most remarkable order of all was for carbonated soft drinks. Yes, Mr. Stengel was a Coke addict, Coca-Cola that is. He would not go in the hospital unless he was guaranteed to have a case of Classic Coca-Cola delivered to the room. I often wondered how he came into such a habit. My best guess was that in the wake of ulcer surgery that he had in the past, as often happened, his natural acid production was terminated, and bile, which is alkaline, backed up into his stomach causing an inflammation of its own which the acid in the soda neutralized. I never asked Mr. Stengel how he acquired his fetish, so he took his answer to the grave.

Clarke Stengel died alone in his home of many years, and his daughter found him by having the police break-in, much like what happened with my own father. But unlike Dad, Mr. Stengel had alienated most of the people in his life, so when I attended his funeral there were only a few people present, just the opposite of Dad's. As I stood there watching his interment I thought, *here he lies nameless and abandoned, soon to be forgotten by all men, but not by God.*

If Clarke was a Christian, then whatever happened to him in this life mattered nothing. As the Lord himself said, "What does it profit a man if he gains the whole world but loses his soul?"- (Matthew 16:26). Thus, one after another of my long time and most devoted patients preceded me into eternity.

Meanwhile, at home, tenuous income and escalating expenses conspired with issues over raising teenage daughters to generate an atmosphere of tension and strife. Doreen and I were either praying or arguing with no in-between. Jesus warned that a house divided against itself cannot stand, and I knew we could not go on like this indefinitely. I pinned my one hope on the selling of my practice, which had become for me an albatross, and my quest to sell it like the quest to find the Holy Grail, but just like that fabled search, my hope was not to be realized.

Yet, one does not easily divest himself of covenant with God. I almost felt like

Jonah of the Old Testament days, who being called of God decided he wanted out, but the Lord hunted him down and held him to his course even over his protests. A second sales agent was no more successful than Jerry. One prospect appeared, made a half-hearted offer, then lost interest. Well, I thought, Jonah balked at first, but in the end conceded the wisdom of God over his life. Maybe, I told myself, this was all for the best. I kept reminding myself that the Lord had something better for me. "Dear God," I prayed. "Give me the patience and endurance to wait on you, to seek your perfect will for my life."

I found I was not alone in my feelings. There was Randy Gould for one. Dr. Gould is one of Virginia's finest surgeons and a personal friend. One Saturday afternoon Randy was jogging as was his custom when he suddenly passed out. Upon awakening, he found he was being prepped for emergency heart surgery. Dr. Gould underwent successful coronary artery bypass and was soon back on the job, but not at the blistering intensity he had formerly indulged in. Randy's story could be multiplied into the thousands in my profession. The rubber band stretched thin simply breaks. After his recovery, I remember a brief conversation I had with Dr. Gould. I could sense the same angst and frustration in his comments that I felt from Dr. Roberts, and in myself, the revelation that you've sacrificed your emotional and physical well-being and at times your financial and professional integrity for a health care system which in the end overwhelms you. Yet as in most of life, sweeping generalizations are hard to justify.

The outpouring of sympathy to Dr. Gould from his patients and colleagues was immense. First of all, he was a man of faith and had a reputation for being a compassionate physician, which reinforced my conviction that the ancient shibboleth was true, that trial and temptation typically befalls those who are sincerely trying to live for God.

Another incredible story involved a surgeon, Dr. Wilkes Hubbard. Dr. Hubbard, a dedicated Christian physician, developed a mysterious illness that sidelined him from work for an entire year. It turned out to be Lyme's disease, which was extremely rare in Virginia back then. "Les," he told me, "it all began after I tempted God in Bible study by bragging about how well my life was going." As he choked back the tears he said in earnest, "I'll never do that again."

Such were only two of the many personal stories I could share that made for powerful lessons about life. They also made me realize in myself that it was far too easy to focus on the negative. But Saint Paul said it best when he gave some simple words of advice to the Christian (and by extension to everyone who will accept it), "Be thankful in all things…"(1 Thessalonians 5:18). Yes, even in the bad things, be thankful. We have to take the long view (which is God's view). And we need to have the attitude of Joseph, the Old Testament hero, who was unde-servedly cast into a filthy dungeon and suffered years of privation without becom-ing bitter, and later rose to the heights of Glory as Pharaoh's prime minister. It was Joseph who boldly declared to his own brothers who sold him into slavery, "You meant it for evil, but God intended it for good…"(Genesis 50:20). So it was by small increments that I began to see more clearly my rocky, turbulent road to spiritual victory, but more vicissitudes awaited me.

Four years of trying had passed and I had yet to sell my business and get out of private practice, and what made it doubly discouraging, as I said before, was to know that in that period at least four other medical businesses practically sold themselves. I began to explore alternative strategies, but everything I considered had a fatal drawback, and in the end I was more despondent than ever.

Then, like a ray of sunshine penetrating into my desperate situation, came a phone call from an old friend. "Hello, Les? This is Norm, how are ya doing?" It was Dr. Dahm!

"Norm," I answered with a pause, "how are you doing? Are you still living in North Carolina?"

Yes, Norman Dahm after his premature departure from medicine, had moved with his wife Lee to a small country town along the way to the outer banks of North Carolina. I remembered once asking Roy Oswaks if he ever heard from Norm and he told me, "Oh yeah, he's content to just drive his pickup truck down those old country roads running errands for his neighbors. I don't think he has much money, but he's happy."

No money, I thought, but a lot of happiness. "Norm," I asked, "what are you doing these days? Are you still retired?"

"Yes, but you'll be amazed how the Lord has been working. I had thought about opening a small general practice down here, but I didn't have much money to get started with. Then, out of nowhere, I was offered a building already fur-nished for a fraction of the usual rent. I'm doing family practice, not gynecology particularly. Of course, because I don't carry malpractice insurance (oh my good-ness I thought, he's practicing bare), I can't participate with any health insurance outside of Medicare so my patients mainly pay me cash, but I can keep my fees low because I have so little overhead."

I was totally amazed. "Norm, when we last spoke you were pretty downcast, and your faith was at a low point." (Like mine now, I thought.)

"Well, Les, I really was backslidden, but I thank God because he got me through all that. Now Lee and I pray together and have fellowship with other Christians down here. All the rat race is behind me, and I'm serving the Lord again."

Wow, I thought, serving the Lord again. I found myself envying his new found peace of mind. How wonderful. It reminded me of Paul's encouraging words to the Ephesian Christians, "I beseech you that you walk worthy of the calling wherewith you are called" (Ephesians 4:1). At that moment it hit me like a cold splash that I had lost my spiritual momentum, my first love. Yet if God could get Norm back on track, he surely could do the same for me. "Norm, is there anything I can do for you? You've always been a good friend to me. Remember when I was just starting out and everyone was getting me discouraged? Only you had words of hope and encouragement for me."

"I remember those days well, Les. Wasn't it great? But I did want to ask you, if I ever run into a non-gyn problem in my practice, can I call you for some advice?"

"Sure, Norm," I said. "Absolutely. Say, Norm, maybe you could come up to Virginia Beach some time, and we can get together."

"Sure, Les, let's set up a time right now. Maybe we can go to lunch or something."

We exchanged a few more pleasant words then said good-bye. I was so uplifted by our conversation. Maybe, I thought, the Lord will use Norm again to lift me out of my gloom and get me back on track, materially and spiritually.

When we did actually meet, it turned out he was as much in need of prayer as I was. I could hardly believe as we sat and talked that this man, once tops in his field and successful beyond all imagination had to now pinch pennies and eke out a living. Yet he offered no regrets about his decision. Such is the confidence one gets when he is truly walking with the Lord. In Proverbs it says that, "The wicked flee when no man is pursuing them, but the righteous are bold as a lion" (Proverbs 28:1). Martin Luther, the great reformer, when he was a hunted fugitive with all of the power of the Holy Roman Empire and the medieval church arrayed against him, for encouragement would often quote Psalm 46, "God is our refuge and strength, a very present help in trouble. Therefore will not we fear, though the earth be removed and though the mountains be carried into the midst of the sea"(Psalms 46:1, 2). I wanted that confidence back again.

One answer to prayer came in 2007. Because I maintained a clean malpractice record for five years, my rate finally dropped to the industry standard for the area. Hopefully, I thought, quadrupled insurance rates were behind me, still it was poor compensation for the more than $100,000 extra I paid out over the past five years because of my three lawsuits. I complained about this one day to a colleague and his answer was, "Well, that's a lot of money, but then again in the long run it's not."

Not a lot of money! Though indignant at first, I had to concede the logic of his statement. And besides, if God owns the cattle on a thousand hills (Psalms 50:10), surely He could handle my money issues. The state of my finances in the end were in fact not as important as the state of my heart. Years of wrestling with lawyers, billing companies, health insurance providers and creditors in the flesh had played havoc with my spiritual walk, but not completely. If I could just grab hold of the "hem of His garment" I knew I would be alright.

Now the truth is, I wasn't alone in my struggles. Christians in Tidewater, Virginia, and across the country, Christians of all denominations, were meeting spontaneously in small groups to pray for each other and for the country, and to seek God's face. The pressures of existence were bringing about a true grass roots revival movement. Doreen began attending just such a local prayer group and soon I joined her, and it was high time that the church got serious about seeking God. Over the twenty-five years since we moved to Virginia, scandal, celebrity, prosperity and spiritual complacency had sapped the church of its strength. When my daughters were growing up, they were snubbed and marginalized by the "church kids" because they were branded as outsiders. Self-righteous teenagers echoing what they learned at home could not bring themselves to show unconditional love to their fellow Christians unless they stood to gain from it. Outwardly they paraded before the church leadership with bright haloes in place, but inwardly, as my daughters never tired of reminding me, all they really cared about was wealth, popularity and sexual conquest. It was hard to keep a balanced attitude towards church people in all this, and if our girls were ambivalent about their own Christian walk it was the church that was largely to blame.

This was the Church by the twenty-first century, self-centered and proud, rich materially, but poor spiritually, lukewarm, blind and naked. Yet Samson, after he was blinded and chained to a millstone, repented and cried out to God who heard him and restored his strength for one final act of glory. Now I could truly relate to Samson, at least to the part about being chained against your will to a millstone, especially when I considered the ungrateful people who pounced on me as soon as the opportunity for gain presented itself. Not just patients, but insurance adjusters, peer reviewers, unethical contractors, all of the above. But then I remembered the good people, the hugs and the tears, the unsolicited thankfulness and the loyalty. It was with those recollections that sharp pangs of guilt swept over me as I contemplated leaving private practice. It was uncanny how patients not knowing my plans would ask me, "Doc, you're not retiring anytime soon are you? You can't retire. We need you."

Maybe they sensed something or then again, maybe it was the gray hair.

So I thought long and hard, and prayed for wisdom in what I was to do. Maybe God wanted me right where I was, or maybe He was perfecting my patience waiting for the right time to reveal His will. Wouldn't it be nice, I thought, if I could sell my practice to someone and continue to see all my patients as before except now as an employee, not as a business owner.

The Lord, I instinctively knew, had something better for me. And yet, the early Christians who were largely slaves and underprivileged, doing their master's wills, trapped in the lower rungs of society, in constant drudgery, turned the world upside down. "Lord," I prayed, "if you have a better way for me, give me the wisdom to find it or the grace to endure where I am and to regain my confidence in you."

"For the Lord preserves the faithful and plentifully rewards the proud (confident) doer" (Psalms 31:23). Once Dr. Dahm told me, "Les, we serve an awesome God," and despite his trials and his fall from the pinnacle of worldly success, he was as confirmed in that conviction as ever.

Bennie Hinn, the great evangelist, once told a story of how while traveling in India he chanced to have a chauffeur who was a Hindu. As they discussed religion, the evangelist prayed for a word of exhortation with the young man. When it came to him, he simply asked the driver, "Does your god love you?"

After thinking for a minute the young Hindu answered frankly, "No, I don't think so." But the truth is that the God of the Bible, the true and the living God, does love me and He loves you. "For God so loved the world that He sent His only begotten son, that whosoever believes in Him should not perish but have everlasting life" (John 3:16). I had forgotten that one simple yet profoundest of all statements, "God loves you." Those three simple words changed John Nugent's life on his deathbed and untold millions of others throughout history. They changed my life, and I needed to always remember that and cling to it.

About that time, a patient of mine was diagnosed with recurrent stomach cancer. Mariann had just buried her mother one year earlier. Prior to that, she had undergone surgery in what was hoped to be a curative procedure, but the cancer returned, and this time it was terminal. Mariann knew what was coming, but when I sat by her bedside in the hospital and gave her the prognosis, she broke down in tears. She had every reason to cry about a lot of things, but what she did say brought tears to my eyes. "Oh, Dr. Salsano, I'm not afraid to die, but what will happen to my grandchildren? I'll never see them again!"

What poignancy, I thought! Those words and tears had welled up from the innermost depths of her soul. I held her hand and patted it gently. "Mariann, God will look after them. He wants to give you His peace now. You believe in Jesus?"

She nodded. "God loves you. He sees your tears and He feels every pain you feel. The Lord promised us he would prepare a home for us in heaven. *Let not your heart be troubled.*"

We prayed together and she fell back on her pillow and rested. Mariann did not live much beyond that meeting, but I still choke back the tears when I call to mind that last cry of her heart.

It was while sitting at Mariann's bedside that I realized I could not afford to become bitter. Not for my patient's sake and not for my own sake. It's easy to see the effects of bitterness in a person's life, good intentions gone awry, multiplied disappointments, loss of faith and finally cynical resignation. I think this was the downward spiral Charles Dickens personified in his character Ebenezer Scrooge. Yes, bitterness is easy to spot in someone else's life, but how about in my own? Solomon declared, "The spirit of a man is the candle of the Lord, searching all the inward parts" (Proverbs 20:27). The stakes are too high to let your candle be extinguished by bitterness and rancor.

I recalled a patient, Fred by name, who was an object lesson in this to me. Fred was a Christian. He was a freelance painter by profession, and a very good one (I hired him more than once to paint my office and my house). Unfortunately for him he was not an astute businessman and in the dog eat dog world of general contracting he often got shafted, and sad to say, too often by his fellow Christians. Eventually Fred reached a point where he couldn't let the trespasses go and often at his office visits he would lend free expression to his disappointments, railing non-stop against the swindlers and rip-off artists he had to deal with. Now deep in my heart I know God forgives us for such things, but Jesus said, "Judge not that you be judged…forgive and you shall be forgiven" (Matthew

7:1, 6:14), and when we retain bitterness and unforgiveness in our hearts, we literally push God out of our lives and forfeit his blessing.

Fred's pride and joy was his Christmas tree collection. He invited my family over to see it one holiday season and it was truly amazing. Every room in his house had an artificial tree with its own special theme. One room was toys, another angels, etc. He easily could have been registered a landmark and charged admission! Well, it came about one day that my office received a frantic call from Fred's wife that he needed a strong tranquilizer. It turned out that a fire broke out in one of his Christmas tree rooms and his house literally burned to the ground. Then, sometime later while painting a flagpole, he slipped and fell to the ground, injuring his painting arm beyond repair. He never worked again. My last recollection of Fred was as a broken, chastened man. He left Virginia Beach shortly after and I never heard from him again. "Dear Lord," I prayed as I pondered all this, "help me to forgive and to forego bitterness. Please don't let me end up like that poor man."

So in my life and in my career I walked a very wavery path between faith and cynicism. I knew that the Lord was directing my life, and I knew he had good thoughts for me, but in the daily grind of work, family, paying bills, tending to the sick, and running a business it was hard to keep those sublime thoughts in focus. For awhile I attended the weekly Gideon prayer breakfast in Chesapeake, and it felt good to unite with other believers in prayer, but again, the needs of work and family called me away. Leah had eloped and Doreen and I knew the young man she married was not right for her and this upset her mother greatly (After she heard about it she didn't eat for three days). In fact later, when Leah was pregnant, her husband walked out on her, literally one month before she delivered a beautiful baby boy she named Kevin (which means handsome). With helping at home on top of the demands of work, I had no energy left to make it out to the Saturday morning prayer meeting.

Cynicism was my downfall and despite the object lesson of Fred and the clear warnings against it in the word of God, I continued to cultivate it. And this was especially true at work with employees and patients, the very people to whom I had always hoped to be a good Christian witness. It was very hard for people to listen to me talk of the things of God after they heard me rail against lawyers, inconsiderate patients and my disgust with medicine in general.

The drug reps were particularly good foils for my sarcasm. Every so often one would ask me, "Doctor, you're always so busy. Will you be taking a vacation soon?"

And my answer would always be, "I don't take vacations. You see, I'm a firm believer in the motto *Arbeit Macht Frei*. Work brings freedom." That comment would usually generate a chuckle and a nod, until I clarified for them that it was the proclamation spelled out in wrought iron that stood over the main entrance to the Auschwitz death camp.

So I continued to practice my profession, the high calling of medicine as it had been put to me long ago. Outwardly I probably exuded supreme self-confidence to my patients and perhaps my peers, but inwardly all my concerns and insecurities continued to churn. One night while getting ready for bed a strange discomfort came over me. Partly a queasy feeling in my stomach, it quickly escalated to a sensation of flushing and faintness. As I lay in bed squirming I cried out, "Please Lord, take this away from me. Forgive me my sins, I trust in you!"

Shortly after that prayer, whatever it was left me. I thanked God for his merciful healing grace and drifted off to sleep. The next day at work I tested my urine which was positive for blood, confirming my suspicion; I was having another kidney stone attack. A CT scan confirmed the diagnosis, but also revealed that the stone was too large to pass on its own. So I went to see a urologist, my friend and colleague Dr. Dennis Lester. "So what do you think of my kidney stone, Dennis?" I asked.

"That's not a kidney stone, Les. It's the rock of Gibraltar!" was his reply.

"We're going to have to do a lithotripsy." This was a procedure where you're sedated, put in a tank of water, and your kidney is bombarded with sound waves so intense that they crush the kidney stone into powder. Of course the kidney absorbs some of the shock as well. I never knew a person could be in so much pain. Only ten milligrams of intravenous morphine would relieve it. Three days later, I was still in pain, passing bloody urine and visibly weakened, but I made it to work anyway. In between patients I had to lie down in the lounge to avoid passing out and to recover some strength. "You can't keep going on like this," I told myself.

Once in the locker room at the health club I attended, a conversation broke out about work; what was good, what was bad, who had the worst boss. I chimed in with a casual comment, "Well, I work for the worst slave driver on earth." That got everyone's attention. "Who do you work for?" they asked in one accord.

"Myself," was the answer, and everyone went silent.

But this time even I conceded that until my kidney healed, a full work day was out of the question for me. In fact, most of December in 2007 I worked half-days and then was closed for the holidays. I continued to do my hospital rounds, but the reduced schedule caused a not insignificant drop in my cash flow. Still, it was nothing I couldn't handle, until, that is, my new billing company dropped an unexpected bomb on me; although looking back I saw it coming but ignored the warning signs. Earlier that year the business changed hands and many of the original staff left, including those most knowledgeable about my account. My insurance billing, that all too critical function of any medical practice, was handed over to one inexperienced hiree after another. That coupled with the new owner's conversion to a whole new computer system caused my income to crash precipitously. "No no! This can't be happening to me again," I groaned.

For practically the next ten months I was again on a nail-biting rollercoaster ride of finances. "This is the last straw! I've got to get out of this mess," was my oath to myself, but how? I had tried everything, putting my business up for sale, hiring one consultant after another, merging into a larger physician group, and when I approached a large hospital corporation all they wanted was to take everything I spent my entire career working for while offering me nothing in return but office space. It all seemed quite hopeless. As I sat at my desk despondently staring into space, I silently uttered a prayer, "Dear Lord, please give me the grace to find a way out of this dilemma. Forgive me for despising the gift of this practice you gave me years ago. Help me to support my family." In my heart I heard the Lord repeat to me His promise in scripture, "Behold…I will even make a way in the wilderness and rivers in the desert" (Isaiah 43:19). His answer to that prayer was not long in coming.

Dr. Lester had a beautiful office in a new medical building not far from my own office. Once we were talking about it, and I asked him about the medical corporation that put up the building, Bon Secours. "Oh, they're a great organization, Les, and they're trying to establish a presence here in Virginia Beach."

"Are they recruiting primary care physicians?" I casually asked.

"You know, I think they are," was his answer. So I inquired, and to my amazement, after years of dead end leads, they were genuinely interested.

Bon Secours is a health care organization that has its roots in Roman Catholicism, and even has as a part of the application process a statement of acknowledgement of the right to life and the dignity of the dying patient. These were both beliefs that were close to my heart, and needed no apologies on their part. I gladly signed the statement. So just as in the case of Dr. Seeherman's retirement, I could see the fruit of God's faithfulness unfolding before my eyes. Every perceived obstacle to employment with the company seemed to melt away. But more importantly, the Lord made it clear to me that my security and hope were to be found in Him alone. So when I handed my practice over to Bon Secours for a fraction of its true worth, I did so without too much rancor. It was not the time for second-guessing the Almighty.

Yet I still needed reassurance and prayed for God to send me some sort of confirmation, and one day while discussing a patient with Dr. Lester, I asked his opinion on my decision to join Bon Secours and he answered emphatically, "Les, do it! Trust me. If you get the opportunity, take it! You can't practice solo anymore. All I do is work to keep up with my overhead. I would do it if they asked me to join. You have nothing to lose and everything to gain."

Well, I thought, *I guess I can take that as a confirmation.* All that was left was to sign the contract and seal the decision.

It was on a Monday evening when I met Stephanie and Janie, my two Bon Secours contacts, to sign the contract papers. My lawyer had already reviewed them for me for a fee of $467, representing barely two hours of work. (I should have been a lawyer!) As I took pen in hand I felt a strange hesitation, as if my hand had acquired a consciousness of its own. "Are you sure you're doing the right thing? Is this really the answer to your prayers?"

I pondered this riposte for a moment, then moved past it and signed. Alessio C. Salsano M.D., P.C., solo internist and family physician, my great adventure in private practice, after twenty-five years had come to an end.

Now, as it turned out, there was about a two month interval between my signing the contract and my commencement as a Bon Secours physician. Two months filled with non-stop activity as I transitioned from business owner to employee. Patient care, of course, continued unabated as it had always been.

My very last patient before leaving solo practice was one of the granddaughters of Ruth Mintz, mentioned earlier. Lynne was critically ill with a rare bleeding disorder, acquired factor 8 deficiency. It was truly a close struggle between life and death in the hospital intensive care unit, but despite the expert care given her by my consultants and the hospital staff, Lynne did not make it. Her final words to me as I left her room were, "Please don't leave." I reassured her I would be back, but two hours later she was dead. It was as if she had blown out like a candle. I took the news starkly, and sat down at my desk dumbstruck. "God forgive me for not staying at her bedside to offer her prayers of hope and eternal consolation." This was not the way I envisaged ending private practice, but such was the way of Providence. Moses, the man of God, had it right when he penned the words, "You have set our iniquities before you, our secret sins in the light of your countenance…we bring our years to an end as a sigh…teach us to number our days that we may apply our hearts to wisdom" (Psalms 90:8-9, 12).

In a final observation, I couldn't help but take note that Lynne's death occurred within a year of her husband's. So many times over twenty-five years of practice I saw this phenomenon, where a longtime spouse dies within one year of their partner. Ironically, it didn't seem to matter whether their relationship was good or bad, just that it was long-lived, permanent. As if the ancient pronouncement to Adam and Eve that they should be one flesh was being fulfilled in their lives together. How can a living being exist when half of it is taken away? So I pondered my final spiritual lesson as I closed the book on my solitary experiment in patient care, my high calling from God.

EPILOGUE

"In all these things we are more than conquerors, through Him that loved us."

ROMANS 8:37

Health care has gone through a sea change since I first strolled the atrium of Rutgers Medical School in 1971. The move towards specialization and away from the traditional "cradle to grave" family doctor has continued unabated. Despite this, the American public seems wedded more than ever to the ideal of the "Marcus Welby" do-it-all family doctor. Yet, as of this writing, Congress is debating the most sweeping health care overhaul in history under President Obama's mandate. Such government intrusion into the practice of medicine will almost certainly be the "midnight call" for Marcus Welby, and as I look back over my career I can honestly say I came as close as anyone I've known to that ideal. I finally quit because health care outgrew me, and if Marcus Welby practiced medicine today they'd be carrying him out in a straight jacket too. In the final analysis, I did it not because I planned to, but because it was instilled in my nature. From my father's nurturing my childhood interest in science, to my Christian epiphany, to the realization of Dr. Ream's high calling, and Dr. Reitman's pearls of wisdom, I know the hand of God was guiding me through all the ups and downs, the heartbreaks and the triumphs. These will forever be etched in my mind, memories both good and bad. The good, such as Nancy, my first employee meeting, falling in love with, and ultimately marrying Daniel, one of my first patients, their wedding ceremony actually being performed by our office mailman (who was also an ordained minister). And the bad, such as the day Lucy Pardue called the office in anguish to tell us that her husband, Andrew, one of my very first patients and a fellow Gideon had, without any forewarning of trouble, committed suicide by shooting himself in the head.

My fondest memories though, will be the times I held a suffering patient's hand, offering words of spiritual comfort, or held hands with family at the bedside praying for God's healing embrace, always in the name of the great Savior of mankind. As time progressed, such intimacies became harder to engage in, especially in the overcharged, litigious climate of medical practice today. In the end,

I suppose I didn't leave private practice as much as private practice left me. It is now the domain of the entrepreneur businessman, and the extreme medical specialist. But the Lord who opened the door mightily for me to enter in, just as He led the children of Israel into Egypt, also opened the door mightily for me to exit, just as through Moses He led them out again in the Exodus. I can't lie and say that the tough times were not very tough (the scars they left on my family are still not healed), but I can say happily as Saint Paul did, "The Lord stood with me and strengthened me…"(2 Timothy 4:17). So as I turn one more corner in my brief sojourn of this life, I am prepared to boast of one thing only, that the Lord is with me. I earnestly look forward to my new position with Bon Secours, and hope that more of my faithfulness to God shows through and less of my cynicism, and with it a healthy portion of good-natured laughter which God himself told us does us well like a medicine (Proverbs 17:22).

And with this my story ends, or actually begins, but in the transition one thing will not change; my pager will go off and I will answer it. Someone will need my services and I will respond to that need just as I swore by an oath many years ago. And I'll place my stethoscope not in a jar, but upon the breast of someone in distress and by doing so will establish a bond of trust, the ultimate expression of the high calling.

I don't think it's a coincidence that the Caduceus, that ancient Greek symbol of the healing arts, snakes entwined about a pole, has a striking equivalent in the Old Testament. In the book of Numbers, Moses erected a brass serpent on a pole for the children of Israel to embrace and be healed when poisonous snakes had invaded their encampment in the Sinai. And centuries later in the New Testament, Christ, trying to explain His mission to an inquiring religious leader, applied that very symbol to himself, "…and as Moses lifted up the serpent in the wilderness even so must the son of man be lifted up that whoever believes in Him should not perish but have eternal life" (John 3:14, 15).

The war against sickness and death is never-ending, at least now in our present age, but God's promise is that one day He will restore all things to their original perfect state. Until then however, there will be doctors, like me, to whom the suffering will often turn. "Lord, grant me always to be a healing tool in your hands that you may get the glory in what you do through me, in Jesus' name, Amen."